HOW TO READ THE CONSTITUTION—AND WHY

HOW TO READ THE

Constitution

AND WHY

KIM WEHLE

HARPER

An Imprint of HarperCollinsPublishers

HarperCollins books may be purchased for educational, business, or sales promotional use. For information, please email the Special Markets Department at SPsales@harpercollins.com.

FIRST EDITION

Designed by Jen Overstreet

Library of Congress Cataloging-in-Publication Data has been applied for.

ISBN 978-0-06-291436-1 (library ed.)
ISBN 978-0-06-289630-8 (pbk.)

19 20 21 22 23 LSC 10 9 8 7 6 5 4 3 2 1

This book is dedicated to Isabel, Caroline, Chloe, and India—
my beautiful children.

Contents

HOW TO READ THE CONSTITUTION—AND WHY

Introduction

This is a book about the Constitution. It is not a comprehensive guide to every provision of the Constitution. It is designed to give you a better understanding of the headline news and analysis that deals with the Constitution. But if you are looking for something that will confirm your side of things politically, you might be wasting your time. This book does not have all the answers. It doesn't summarize Supreme Court cases or even provide a comprehensive explanation of any one constitutional topic. The objective of the book is to begin to teach you how to approach constitutional text, to point out the inevitable gray areas in what has become a very black-and-white political conversation, and to note how these gray areas arise in the headlines as well as in everyday life.

First, what *is* a constitution? The US Constitution is a document that puts certain things beyond popular vote by making those things clear in writing. It was designed as a machine that lasts forever. For that reason, it is *very* hard to change. Hate Trump? Hate Obama? Guess what, the Constitution was designed for both of them. When it was written, in Philadelphia in 1787, it did not contain a bill of rights. The people who drafted the Constitution did not think one was necessary. They thought that the structure of government was enough to protect individuals' rights. The Bill of Rights was added later.

The question for generations, therefore, has been whether the framers of the Constitution got it right. In order to begin to answer that question, every generation needs a basic working knowledge of what the Constitution does (it sets up a structure of government and lists individual rights) and what it doesn't do (it does not crown a king). This book helps build that knowledge and also answers questions such as:

What are the powers of government?
What are the limits on those powers?
And what does it mean for individuals to have rights under the
    Constitution?

Before getting further into what the Constitution says about the government, let's ask another basic question: What is the government in the first place? An easy way to answer that question might be to compile a list. The government includes the president, Congress, and various clusters of people in Washington, DC, who make and implement lots of rules. It includes state governors, state legislators, and judges too. Then we have police officers, public school teachers, boards of election and education, mayors, district attorneys, and city council members.

But what does this list say about the definition of *government*? Looking at the list, we might notice that it includes many people whose paychecks come from taxpayer dollars. Many of them are elected. Others—like the US attorney general and federal judges—are appointed. Some of them have powers that private people do not. Police officers have the power to throw people in jail if they don't comply with the government's rules. The CIA has the authority to gather highly secret and sensitive information that regular people cannot access.

Generally speaking, the government gets to tell people what they can and cannot do, and if people don't comply, the government can impose consequences—usually financial, but sometimes the government can take away an individual's liberty too—or in the extreme case, it can deprive a citizen of the ability to live on this earth a single moment longer. The government has powers that regular people do not. If a regular person poisons someone else to death deliberately, execution-style, she will go to jail. The government, in fact, will see to that.

The government's ability to take actions that regular people cannot makes some of us angry. The notion that the government might force a person to get its permission before he can own a gun, or that it might put a woman in jail for terminating her own pregnancy, or that it can make a young man pay a penalty if he chooses not to spend his paycheck on private health insurance can seem outrageously overbearing in a country that was founded on the notion that the government cannot infringe too much on an individual's rights. Why don't those rights include "the right" not to make a wedding cake for a gay couple? Or "the right" not to have one's taxpayer dollars spent on people who live in the United States illegally? Or "the right" not to have one's tax money spent on nuclear bombs?

We put up with all this because the government also does things that make our lives work. Although we don't like everything the government does, we all like at least a few things (whether or not we realize it). We like that the government paves roads and builds bridges so we can get to where we want to go. And that it makes and enforces rules that keep known toxins out of our food and prevents passenger airplanes from routinely crashing into each other midair. The government creates traffic rules and puts up stop signs and red lights so that simply driving your kid to school is not a life-threatening, chaotic mess. The government makes sure that doctors have the proper training before they cut people open on an operating table, and it takes away that prerogative if doctors hurt or kill their patients. It makes sure that violent criminals face consequences for their actions and takes steps to protect the public from those people. The government talks to our international neighbors and foes around the world—kind of like a schoolyard monitor on a global scale—to protect our national community from invasion. It also makes sure that the money in our pockets has actual value so we can buy food, clothing, and shelter—and maybe engage in pleasurable things from time to time—even though complicated economic forces could have the very opposite effect. We could go on and on with examples of how the government is both bad and good.

Of course, by accepting government, we do not accept every part of it. Government is more like a buffet. There are appealing items for everyone, as well as things to avoid. When we see the government's menu items as good, we are happy and go about our business. We don't worry much about it or what it's doing, except to the extent that we cast our votes for people who will maintain the status quo. When the government is bad, we get upset. We make some noise and cast votes for people who will change the status quo.

But these days, the American system of government seems off. The simple levers of democracy aren't working the way we've always assumed they must. We are not the shining light of freedom for the rest of the world anymore. Lots of things are going on that undermine the government envisioned by the framers of the Constitution. The framers didn't foresee, for example, a national political process awash in money flowing from superrich people and big corporations—and the resulting need for politicians to incessantly hunt for reelection dollars in lieu of actual governing. They did not foresee that electoral districts would be drawn in such a way that incumbents can become shoo-ins for reelection. They didn't anticipate the explosion of big-data technology and how it would forever morph the very concept of individual privacy. Nor did they expect that technology would open our electoral system to hostile influence by foreign governments (read: Russia in the 2016 presidential election).

Yet, perhaps most ironically, the framers *did* anticipate that deep ideological factions could rip the country apart and leave space for the kind of autocracy that they denounced in the form of the British monarchy. As a result, they wrote the Constitution to avoid a government that could devolve into a purely "tribal" political system under which certain points of view become more important than fostering the interests of the public as a whole. Today, we find ourselves mired in just that kind of political death spiral. What on earth is going on?

The cracks we see in our constitutional system of government derive in part from a largely unspoken but counterintuitive reality: that the very concept of government is a mirage. Under the US Constitution, the federal government is composed of three branches—the legislative (Congress), the executive (the president), and the judicial (lower court federal judges and the Supreme Court). Of course, this is all in addition to the state governments, each of which has its own legislative, executive, and judicial systems. The Constitution spells out how the people within each of the three federal branches get their jobs and, for the most part, how they can lose their jobs. But the Constitution *does not* say that the people who obtain their jobs in the manner described by the Constitution are *the only ones* who get to do those jobs. Of course, only the president is the president—he is elected under the terms of the Constitution. Only members of Congress get to be members of Congress. But what about the job of investigating, prosecuting, and otherwise enforcing laws? The president is not the one who actually does that. Lots of people in his chain of command do it though. Lots of people who aren't even in the government as we defined it—who are not paid through taxpayer dollars or hired through the electoral process—enforce laws as well.

The same goes for making laws. Congress does it, but so do people outside the legislative branch. People in the private sector—lobbyists and consulting firms—make laws too, meaning that they propose what rules should bind private conduct (for example, who should be able to get guns easily) and pass them on for legislators to enact without much knowledge or intervention from the public. If we account for the people outside the Constitution's structure who actually perform the various functions of government, it becomes strangely evident that government does not really exist as we may assume it does. It is inextricably enmeshed with the private sector in ways the pages of this book cannot fully account for.

Does it matter that government is not an easily quantifiable entity? The answer is yes. It matters because people who work in the private sector—corporations and think tanks and lobbying and consulting firms—have different incentives than government employees do. Their job is primarily to make money. The rules of the Constitution mostly don't apply to them. And they don't care if they get reelected, because they weren't elected in the first place. The voters' needs are irrelevant if they don't align with profit margins.

The financial needs of private firms, by contrast, *are* entirely relevant to what the government does. Private corporations want rules that help their bottom lines and make them more money. By supporting lawmakers in election campaigns, private entities effectively step into the shoes of individual voters. Lawmakers react by making governmental decisions that help their donors amass more money. Importantly, the same holds true for foreign governments. If foreign governments are poised to make decisions for or to exert influence on elected officials, we can be certain that their motives are not fully aligned with the interests of the American public.

Let's be clear about one thing, for starters: the Constitution is not a bulwark. By this I mean it does not erect an impenetrable wall around the citizens of the United States to defend them against tyranny and abuses. It is porous. It needs shoring up from time to time.

The people of the United States must carefully identify emerging holes and plug them as quickly and effectively as possible. That task is easier than it sounds. Why? Because the most important thing to understand about answering questions under the Constitution is that *it all depends*. It depends on what the Constitution says, to be sure, but more important, it depends on whether there are systematic consequences for violating its rules, both expressed and implied ones.

Now let me say a few opening words about implied rules. Some social contracts are memorialized in writing. Others function along unspoken terms that ultimately derive from baseline norms or values that may differ from one person to another. If there's enough money and tenacity to get a contract dispute before a judge, for example, the judicial process works only if the losing party is willing to abide by the judge's order. If that party violates the order, the judge must impose consequences for that too; otherwise, the judge's order—like a contract that goes unenforced—becomes basically meaningless.

The Constitution works in much the same way. It is a relatively terse document that leaves much of its necessary terms and meaning unwritten. The Constitution is held up by conventions and norms that developed over centuries of American history—the expectation, for example, that presidential candidates will make public their personal finances; that presidents will enable timely and exhaustive vetting of officers and employees who will have access to classified information; that the leadership within the executive branch will be staffed by experienced people with meaningful expertise; that the loser of a presidential election will concede to the victor in order to facilitate the peaceful transfer of power; and that the president will conduct himself in public with decorum and dignity. Likewise, what people consider core American values—such as the opportunity for financial success and upward social mobility, rewards for hard work, cultural diversity, and unrestricted individualism—may not be expressed anywhere in the Constitution. These and many other "American values" are part of an unwritten social contract. If they are taken for granted or not socially enforced, these values will cease to reign in America.

To be sure, as a society of individuals, we also subscribe to a more hard-line concept of the rule of law. The rule of law is shorthand for the legal rules and standards that we collectively believe are worth having. The ultimate boss in this regard is the Constitution. Below the Constitution in the hierarchy of laws are statutes passed by legislatures, then rules and regulations issued by administrative agencies, and then decisions by courts of law. The collective assumption and agreement among we the people is that we all follow the rule of law—or else. Consider the rule against killing other people. Political affiliations aside, we all probably agree that, in order to live freely, a person needs to be able to leave home without worrying about being shot by an angry neighbor on the front lawn. Thus, we have laws banning murder.

But the laws themselves only go so far. A prohibition on murder is meaningless if there are no police officers or prosecutors to enforce it or if a judge's order sending a convicted criminal to prison can be ignored for the right price. Likewise, a routine contract has effect only if the parties are willing to adhere to it in good faith and, barring that, to go to court to enforce it through the judicial system.

So, too, if a federal judge determines that the president—or any other elected leader or government employee—has run afoul of the Constitution, the document itself cannot enforce the court's order. If the head of the executive branch violates it, a consequence *must* follow.

Otherwise, the rule of law becomes meaningless. There is no "Constitution cop" lurking on our democratic street corners who is tasked with enforcing the Constitution. Accordingly, if a provision of the Constitution is *not* enforced, it becomes worthless. It's kind of like jaywalking—we all do it because there are virtually no consequences for violating laws banning the practice of crossing a street anywhere but at a designated crosswalk. But imagine that, one day, hidden cameras are installed on certain street corners. The cameras capture jaywalkers red-handed, so people start to follow anti-jaywalking rules on the streets that have cameras—but only on those streets, because no consequences for jaywalking lie elsewhere.

Today, the Constitution is at risk of becoming a sort of anti-jaywalking law—something that can be ignored or violated with no consequences. Its vitality is eroding under our noses, but few people realize it. A big reason for this is that most people do not really know what the Constitution says and does. And even if they've taken the time to read the document, it's impossible for anyone to understand how the Constitution actually works without some sort of additional explanation—a guidebook that fills in the blanks left by broadly worded language written more than two centuries ago. The Supreme Court fills in those blanks all the time—which is why nobody can get a grip on the Constitution today without knowing about lots of Supreme Court cases, as well as other stealthy changes to the document that occur by virtue of the passage of time.

This book provides that explanatory guide. It outlines the basics of constitutional structure, theory, and individual rights for lay readers. It explains the sources and limits of power that each branch possesses, and perhaps most important, it describes how individuals within each branch can—and should—use their respective powers to hold the other branches accountable.

In teaching readers how to think about the Constitution, this book also walks through many of the what-ifs that are weighing on Americans' minds right now: What if a president fires a special prosecutor charged with investigating possible criminal wrongdoing by his top advisers, and even the president himself? Most of us know that President Richard Nixon resigned under threat of impeachment in the wake of just such a maneuver, so why are we still talking about whether it is constitutional to do it? What if instead of being impeached the president is criminally indicted? Would the Constitution allow that? Although President Bill Clinton struck a deal with prosecutors to avoid a criminal subpoena, he was impeached nonetheless. When does the Constitution call for impeachment, and how does the impeachment process differ from what a special prosecutor does? In the Trump administration, there's been a lot of friction between the Department of Justice (DOJ) and the FBI on the one hand and the president on the other. If DOJ lawyers work for Trump under the Constitution's structure, how is it possible that they can become so polarized against their boss?

I teach law school courses that lay the groundwork for answering these questions. My classes often begin with the following hypothetical. Imagine a presidential election in which the winning candidate promises sweeping reforms. The public wants change: immigration, the environment, jobs, small business, abortion, health care, taxes. The president-elect vows to fix all of these by employing skills gleaned from a lifetime of success in business. He promises to "drain the swamp" in Washington—a code for upending the federal bureaucracy with the pull of a plug. Now that he is president, can he actually do it?

The answer to this question, on the surface, seems relatively simple. Article II of the Constitution gives the president his powers. Like a cookbook, one need only turn to the chapter on the executive branch and read the recipe. A decade of studying separation-of-powers theory has taught me, however, that the Constitution is not a cookbook; it is infinitely more complicated and nuanced. But just like a chef needs to understand foundational cooking concepts—such as the difference between braising and roasting and how to thicken a sauce—there are a number of critical, commonsense concepts that undergird constitutional theory.

By theory, I mean the philosophy behind the law—the abstract goals and rationales for American law as a whole or for specific provisions of the Constitution in particular. The content of legal theory can be a mixture of philosophy, sociology, psychology, political science, and a number of other disciplines. It is different from what is known as legal *doctrine*, which comprises the basic rules that come out of disputes before courts. Theory is also more abstract than *policy*, which is about the ostensible reasons and justifications for a law; basic policy does not delve into the intersections between the cultural and power relationships in society and how they influence the legal system.

First. **Having a cop on the block matters.** It is important to grasp something about human nature that drives legal systems: a law is mean-ingful only to the extent that it is enforceable. In other words, if people who drive over the speed limit don't get tickets, laws mandating that people drive at or under the speed limit are not, as the saying goes, worth the paper they're written on. Hide a speed camera on a half-mile stretch of a busy road, and in short order the traffic will slow down for that half mile but pick up again when there is no longer a consequence for speeding (i.e., the dreaded ticket in the mail with a blurred photo of your car's rear license plate). Likewise, any experienced parent knows that rules must be enforced with kids or they cease to be rules. If you tell a child that no television is allowed in the mornings before school but you need to make a critical phone call one day so you allow your five-year-old twenty minutes of TV "just this once," the child instantly learns to tune out the no-TV rule completely. It becomes ad hoc and optional.

Constitutional doctrine and theory is no different. It is only mean-ingful to the extent that there are active levers that can be pulled or pushed to enforce its provisions.

Second. There is a big difference between policy and politics. I walked into my first-year civil procedure class prepared to teach litiga-tion discovery rules on November 9, 2016, the day after Donald Trump won the Electoral College vote, and was met by a palpable sense of col-lective fear. Many students knew only an Obama presidency and were just beginning to feel a sense of social agency beyond their immediate family and friends. I instinctively knew that I had to bring sanity to the chaos without alienating those whose candidate had won. In seconds, my brain constructed a different class.

"What is the difference," I asked, "between policy and politics?"

Hands shot up. "Policy is the rationale behind a rule; the reasons behind a statute or regulation that governs private conduct."

Good.

"What does policy mean in a presidential election?"

Silence, then hands again, timid this time. "Candidates have policy views about how to regulate the environment, what to do about health care, immigration, things like that."

Again, good.

Next question: "In this election, how much of the media coverage and debate—both public and private—was about policy?"

Several people blurted out, with confidence, "None." Nervous fidgeting followed.

"Imagine you are a policymaker. What kind of information would you want to take into account in formulating policy?" I asked. This one evoked a nearly instinctive response. We had drilled down on the policy rationales for civil litigation rules all semester long: efficiency, fairness, accuracy. Policy should be formulated in a way that minimizes waste and bureaucracy, is as fair as possible to everyone implicated, and produces accurate results based on empirical evidence. Thoughtful policymakers may debate how best to balance these objectives, which are not exclusive, but they cannot reject them altogether.

To understand in simple terms how a policy is made, consider the 65 mph speed limit on the I-95 corridor between New York City and Washington, DC. The 65 mph rule is efficient because it establishes a bright line that can be tested with technology that stakeholders agree is generally accurate. Adjudication of a violation is relatively easy—a speedometer either clocks a car moving above 65 mph or it does not. The rule is fair because it applies equally to all drivers on the road. But a 65 mph rule does not always produce accurate results. In a severe snowstorm, 65 mph may be too fast to avoid accidents.

An alternative rule could be to simply drive safely. A drive-safely standard would account for snowy weather, requiring drivers to slow down in a storm, but it would be much harder to administer. Judges would inevitably have to hold evidentiary hearings with witnesses and consider real-time weather data to determine whether an individual driver was in violation of the rule given the road conditions on a particular day. In order to be at a legal speed limit, a grandpa with cataracts would need to drive at a slower speed than a professional NASCAR driver.

There would thus need to be an inquiry into the grandpa's eyesight, whether he mistakenly took medication that made him drowsy, and his driving record, among other questions. The speed limit rule would become highly fact specific and individualized. A drive-safely rule would give judges a lot of discretion to make decisions that wind up being inconsistent and even unfair, leaving the public in the dark about how to comply with the law. Thus, all things considered, Maryland state lawmakers presumably decided in favor of 65 mph over a more pliant, subjective standard.

How, then, does policy differ from politics? Politics can be confused with policy to the extent that the term *political* is associated with the activities of government. Our federal system comprises three branches— legislative, judicial, and executive—each of which makes decisions based on policy rationales and empirical evidence, as well as normative goals and values. But *political* has another meaning that has eclipsed the other in recent months and years: to politicize an issue is to associate it with an ideological bias or viewpoint that may be fiercely guarded by certain clusters of people. When an issue is politicized, ideological bias drives policy, regardless of the merits and the facts.

Take climate change. The scientific consensus is that the earth is warming, and that there is a 95 percent or higher probability that the warming is predominantly caused by humans. Responsible lawmakers on both ends of the political spectrum may debate whether halting this trend is—as a policy matter—important enough to justify the impacts of environmental regulation, such as increased cost of compliance for industry, which may be passed along as higher prices for consumer goods and services. Various lawmakers duly balancing considerations like efficiency, fairness, and accuracy might arrive at very different responses to climate change as a policy matter—without evading established empirical facts regarding the causes of a warming planet.

What does this have to do with understanding the constitutional issues arising from the current presidency? There are many things in life that impact us greatly but that we cannot individually control. The election of an American president is one of them. What we *can* control is how we engage around divisive issues. These days, most law students arrive on campus highly skilled at identifying what they need to know and regurgitating it back to the professor. What I tell students is that this skill will get them a C in my class. People don't pay lawyers if Google has the answers to their legal questions. To get an A in law school, they need to garner the facts and the law on both sides of an issue, reconcile competing policy objectives, and produce a thorough analysis of rival claims. On a law school exam, the conclusion is often irrelevant.

For policymakers and judges interpreting the Constitution, as well, what matters most is *how* they arrived at the conclusion: Did they attempt to reconcile competing arguments? Did they account for all the facts? And did they consider the policy implications for each party or constituent group involved? These steps make up a "best practice" for solving any hard problem. What I tell my students is that they are learning a skill that they can utilize, model, and teach so that maybe the next election can go differently for a few more people. This distinction—between policy on the one hand and politics on the other—is also of critical importance to understanding how the constitutional structure of the government does—or should—work.

Third. **Once something gets in the government's "toolbox," it can be picked up for use at any time.** When I was a young lawyer, a few years out of law school, one of my first jobs was as an associate independent counsel on the Whitewater investigation under Independent Counsel Kenneth W. Starr. I was recruited by a career prosecutor who was on detail from the DOJ to work on the investigation of events that took place in the White House's travel office. What has come to be known as the Starr Investigation started in the early 1990s as a probe into failed real estate investments by Bill and Hillary Rodham Clinton. It mushroomed into numerous ethics and criminal investigations relating to the Clinton administration, including one that looked into the firing of seven employees of the White House travel office in 1993 and, ultimately, the Monica Lewinsky sex scandal. At some point during my tenure there, the question came up as to whether the attorney-client privilege protected the communications between then First Lady Hillary Clinton and the White House lawyers from being disclosed.

The attorney-client privilege is a judge-made doctrine or rule that keeps communications between a lawyer and client confidential if they are made for the purpose of obtaining legal advice. The policy rationale for it is that if people thought that conversations with their lawyers could be obtained by an opponent and used against them, they wouldn't talk to lawyers in the first place. The theory behind the attorney-client privilege is something like: society benefits if people talk to attorneys when their legal rights and obligations are at stake.

The First Lady is not a government employee; that is, she is not paid for her service with taxpayer dollars. Prosecutors within the independent counsel's office argued that the attorney-client privilege did not apply to Mrs. Clinton because she was not a government "client." An appeals court later found that the privilege did *not* protect Mrs. Clinton's conversations with White House lawyers, and the US Supreme Court refused to hear the case, so the lower court decision stands.[1]

I share this anecdote because it was the first time I grasped the importance and longevity of decisions about the powers of the government. What it means today, for example, is that conversations between President Trump's government-paid lawyers and his daughter and adviser Ivanka can likely be subpoenaed in a civil lawsuit or criminal investigation without contending with the attorney-client privilege. The debate within the ranks of the independent counsel's office revolved around questions of precedent: "We want this for purposes of this investigation, sure, but if we get what we want, what does it mean for future White Houses—maybe Republican-led ones?" Once the subpoena power was construed to include the ability to obtain this kind of information from a sitting president's spouse, it went in the next prosecutor's toolbox, where it remains.

A more haunting example of the toolbox phenomenon has to do with the so-called war on terror under President George W. Bush. Famously, then deputy assistant attorney general John Yoo drafted a set of memoranda that defined torture as severe pain associated with "death, organ failure, or serious impairment of body functions," accompanied by "prolonged mental harm" over a duration of months or years. With such a high bar to a torture ban, the memorandum gave the president a green light to conduct interrogations in ways that most people would find abhorrent and abusive. The torture memos made possible the notorious Abu Ghraib scandal of 2003 involving human rights atrocities by US Army and Central Intelligence Agency personnel in an Iraqi prison. Around the same time as the torture memos, now professor Yoo authored another memo asserting that presidents have plenary power during a time of war to monitor the communications of US citizens on American soil without first obtaining a warrant. In effect, the memo suggested that the Fourth Amendment's ban on unreasonable searches and seizures—and the Constitution in general—does not apply to the president when the country is at war.[2]

The correctness of Professor Yoo's conclusions as a matter of constitutional law was—and remains—hotly debated. The torture memos were immediately withdrawn by Jack Goldsmith, who succeeded Assistant Attorney General Jay S. Bybee as head of the Office of Legal Counsel (and became Yoo's boss) under the same Republican president.[3] However, once ideas of unfettered authority to torture or to spy on US citizens without a warrant were put into action, they became part of the lexicon of presidential power. Although Congress has since placed some limits on torture, that presidential power is now in the toolbox, so to speak, to pull out later if a president with a "Yoo view" of executive power sees fit. As a result, politicians and judges of all political stripes must be very careful about how they exercise power when they have it, because they are setting precedents for those who will hold power in the future.

***Fourth.* "Strict reading of the Constitution" is a myth.** I want to unravel the idea that some judges "strictly read" the Constitution and others do not.

Think, for example, about Article II of the Constitution, which gives the president his powers. It includes language stating that "the executive Power *shall* be vested in a President of the United States of America" (emphasis mine). Some conservative thinkers argue that this constitutional language is not subject to interpretation—that it must be implemented precisely as written, because it is the intent of the (long-dead) drafters of the language that matters even today.

So how does one go about imposing the "plain" meaning of this language on current-day disputes? For one, the word *shall* itself seems mandatory. The president gets the executive power, full stop. But that's not the end of the story. The next logical question is, what does *executive* power mean? The Constitution does not define it. In searching for an answer, one might use common sense, or historical practice, or a dictionary, or the writings of the framers around the time that this language was ratified in 1787. But how to pick among these sources? Does it matter that presidents today have TV, the Internet, and a much larger government to run? What about the fact that the federal government in 2019 serves upward of 325 million people versus the 3.9 million in 1787? And that we live in a global economy that the framers could not have envisioned?

Article II goes on to state that the president "*shall* take Care that the Laws be faithfully executed" (emphasis mine). Does this additional mandate suggest that there are limits on what the president can and cannot do? Can he ignore laws passed by Congress on the theory that execution of the laws necessarily includes the power *not* to execute laws? You can see where I am going with this. There is no such thing as a plain reading of the Constitution. Yet the false dichotomy between "strict" and "liberal" readers of the Constitution is tossed around among the pundits the minute someone is nominated for the Supreme Court. It is misleading.

Many people take as a given that liberal or progressive judges subjectively interpret the Constitution as a living, breathing document that adapts to modern-day social norms, values, and challenges. Judges who consider modern-day, pragmatic glosses on the constitutional text are sometimes decried as activists. The critique is that judges who interpret the meaning of constitutional or statutory text are no longer judging; they are amending the Constitution or legislating from the bench, which they cannot lawfully do under the Constitution because it defines the judicial power much more narrowly. The conservative debate is thus framed as one aimed at keeping judges in their constitutional sandbox and leaving it for Congress to make laws.

The problem with the strict-reading-of-the-Constitution mantra is that words often have different meanings, either standing alone or in the context of other words. Consider the Fourth Amendment's familiar ban on unreasonable searches and seizures. We can probably all agree that *unreasonable* is a highly subjective term. Honking your horn when the car in front of you hasn't moved through a green light for ten seconds might be reasonable to some people and unreasonable to others. In New York City, *not* honking could be unreasonable in crushing traffic. In Bottineau, North Dakota (population 2,300), it might be unreasonable to honk under circumstances that do not put public safety at risk.

Likewise, the word *search* can have different meanings. In 1791, when the Fourth Amendment was ratified, a search likely referred to men in uniform banging down front doors and rifling through drawers and closets without a warrant. But did the Constitution's framers really consider whether taking thermal images of a person's home to find marijuana growing inside constituted a search?[4] What about tracking a Jeep with a GPS device during a drug investigation?[5] Of course not. Yet in both these cases, two centuries and massive technological advances after the amendment's ratification, Justice Antonin Scalia—a notorious conservative—concluded that the Fourth Amendment was violated, i.e., *that these were searches*, and that they were unreasonable ones. Surely, no framer of the Bill of Rights (which, as a reminder, comprises the first ten amendments to the Constitution) had GPS devices in mind when the Fourth Amendment was drafted. So were these decisions by Justice Scalia those of a strict reader of the Constitution's text, or something else?

The bald reality is that words have meanings that are not always clear. The meaning of other foundational documents, like the Bible, the Torah, and the Koran, have been debated for centuries. Why would the Constitution be any different? Its inevitable vagueness is why we have split decisions among the highly skilled, respected, and educated members of the Supreme Court, with some justices reading words of the Constitution or legislation one way and others reading them another way. Conservative judges may apply the "plain" meaning without revealing their true biases. Liberal judges might admit that language is ambiguous and argue that it's better to look to the goals of, say, the Fourth Amendment and the reasons why we have it, and to then construe the language in a way that serves those goals, than it is to simply pick a meaning that makes sense to the particular judge reading the language on a given day. We might end up at the very same place under both approaches, but on the liberal side we might have on the table a candid rationale for why one meaning was chosen over another.

The truth is that any good judge—and certainly anyone sufficiently credentialed for the Supreme Court—begins analysis of constitutional or statutory language with the actual text. (Some constitutional scholars debate this commonsense notion, which illustrates why this book leans away from high-minded theory.) But oftentimes, a document's plain language raises more questions than it answers. Which branch of government gets to pick between two competing readings? And if it's the judiciary, how should judges decide which reading is the better one? These are deeply complex and theoretical questions that law professors and judges have grappled with for decades. An intellectually honest foray into this debate is head-spinning.

So when I hear pundits blithely pile conservatives in a happy plain-meaning camp and liberals in a comparatively suspect progressive-reading camp under the guise of honest constitutional theory, I cringe. Good judging—like good governance—requires transparency, reasoned decision-making, and sound judgment. To expect judges not to make judgments is illogical. To pretend that those cloaked with the strict-reading mantra are somehow not judging—but merely translating English into English—is folly. In the world of separation-of-powers theory, which branch of government gets to resolve such ambiguity—and how—is a central question that the Constitution does not answer.

Fifth. American values are not laid out in the Constitution. The idea that American values are not in the Constitution is one that piggybacks on the debunking of strict reading of the Constitution, and it is extremely important. As mentioned previously, when we think about what it means to be American, many values spring to mind. They might include concepts like honor, humility, transparency, openness, ambition, hard work, innovation, integrity, opportunity, progress, freedom, efficiency, enterprise, achievement, equality, tradition, respect, justice, fairness, diversity, education, security, leisure, the rule of law, and accountability. Underpinning the American way of life, to most people, is some combination of these "soft" values, which may not be legally enforceable—a person can't be put in jail for being disrespectful or lacking ambition, for example—but they are brought forth in times of strife and chaos as a clarion call for politicians to make decisions that adhere to shared social values.

Many people just assume that these values are contained somewhere in the Constitution or some other foundational document. We have all heard of the Equal Protection Clause and the preamble to the Declaration of Independence, which states that "all men are created equal." But these examples are exceptional. Scholars look to the contemporaneous writings of the framers of the Constitution in order to understand it, and such writings—collectively known as the Federalist Papers—contain discussions on many of the soft values we expect our government to live by today. But they are *not* all spelled out in the founding documents of our democracy.

To be sure, some of these values have been enacted into law by Congress through legislation. The Civil Rights Act of 1964, which ended segregation in public places and banned employment discrimination on the basis of race, color, religion, sex, and national origin, is an example. There was a time in the not-so-distant past that discrimination on the basis of these traits was lawful; morally wrong, yes—but not illegal.

It thus may come as a surprise that the values we consider quintessentially American are not self-executing; that is, you can't walk into court and ask a judge to force someone to do the right thing—unless there is a source of law affording the right to do so. If someone gives you the stink eye on the subway, you may feel wronged, but there is no law on the books that gives you a right to go to court to get a judge to order that person to stop giving the stink eye or to give you money for the pain and annoyance that the stink eye caused you that day. If someone punches you on the subway, by contrast, there *are* laws—state statutes, perhaps, as well as laws made over many centuries by courts (what lawyers and judges call common law)—that give you a right to go to court to get money or other sorts of relief designed to make you whole again. There are also laws that allow the government to put the puncher in jail. But no anti-stink-eye laws.

The same holds true for our political leaders: not everything we expect of them is required by law. The Constitution is the boss of all laws in the United States, but much of its strength is based on social norms and values that many of us wrongly assume rise to the level of rights of citizenship. But as mentioned before, the Constitution is, in fact, fragile—and porous. Many of these values must come from somewhere else—and also be *enforced* by society—if they are to continue to characterize the American way of life. There is no law establishing them, in other words, and no Constitution cop poised to enforce any such laws if they did exist. In today's political climate, we can no longer sit back and take them for granted.

Sixth. No constitutional power is absolute. Because the Constitution contains ambiguous language, it's rare for a court to conclude that a certain enumerated power is absolute, meaning that it is not susceptible to limitation by other provisions of the Constitution. Take the president's power to "execute the laws" under Article II. Some people (like Donald Trump) might take the position that such power *is* absolute—that when it comes to investigation and prosecution of federal crimes, which is a traditional executive power, he calls the shots, full stop. Think about it. What this posture effectively means is that the president can ignore laws passed by Congress and judgments issued by courts if they in any way impact investigations and prosecutions—which is his exclusive turf. Could he ignore statutes governing wiretapping and order a wiretap on a whim? On this broad theory, yes. What about court judgments relating to the Fourth Amendment—could he search a political opponent's home out of bald curiosity? Probably yes again, to the extent that there is no limiting principle to this view of executive power.

Even with respect to pure prosecutorial power, the theory espoused by the Trump team and to some degree by President George W. Bush's advisers before them—known in less extreme variations as the unitary executive theory—is breathtaking. What it suggests is that under our Constitution, the president ultimately picks and chooses who gets prosecuted and who does not—including himself—regardless of whether the criteria he uses are illegal or nefarious, and that those decisions get zero oversight. As a result, he can violate laws with impunity because he can unilaterally decide *not* to enforce criminal laws against himself. *He* also gets to decide not to enforce criminal laws against whomever he handpicks to flout the law—perhaps at his own direction. An extreme unitary executive view likely means, as well, that any prosecutions that happen to slip through the cracks against a president's personal judgment could be pardoned on a similar theory, i.e., the pardon power is absolute. In other words, the president *is* justice.

Of course, this theory of absolute executive power cannot be correct. Ignoring a federal court's decision on the Fourth Amendment would elevate the power to execute laws above other provisions of the Constitution, including the judicial power as well as the Fourth Amendment itself. But from a structural standpoint, it also means that the president could run the Oval Office like a dictatorship or Mafia ring—those people who line his pockets with enough cash can commit crimes, while those who turn him down get prosecuted and potentially jailed.

That's ridiculous, some might say. *How could it possibly happen?* The answer is that on a very broad theory of executive power, the president has unlimited discretion to "call off the dogs" on himself, so anything goes. Assuming he has physical access as president, he could empty the federal treasury into a bank account in his own name and get away with it. Pretty soon, the theory must go, we would find ourselves living in a lawless country under a government that looks like an autocracy.

Instead, the powers vested in Article II must be construed in a way that acknowledges the entire premise behind the founders' drafting of the Constitution: no more kings! Most other provisions of the Constitution work like Article II—they are limited. There is the First Amendment free speech right, but not if someone "speaks" through child pornography. There is the Second Amendment right to bear arms, but not for juveniles. There is a right to be free from unreasonable searches and seizures, but some searches *may* be conducted without a proper warrant. A court's interpretation of the word *unreasonable* requires some kind of balancing under the Constitution. So, too, does much of constitutional law. Courts look at the various competing policy issues at stake and strike a balance that considers the language of the Constitution as well as macro rationales for structuring the government into three distinct, somewhat overlapping parts. That rationale, in a word, is accountability.

Seventh. With law, it all depends. Cue the eye rolls. Of course we all like to get answers, but the fact is, the law is not a calculus proof. A legal question depends on two things: the law (i.e., the rules governing certain conduct) and the facts (the story that gave rise to a particular lawsuit). The story involves at least two parties, and it is unique. No two car accidents are exactly the same. Sometimes, one driver screwed up to cause a crash. Sometimes, both drivers screwed up. Sometimes, nobody screwed up—there was a horrible windstorm that caused the collision and nobody but Mother Nature was at fault.

Imagine, then, a car accident in which the driver of a red car runs a red light and hits a blue car that was entering the intersection on a green light. In this story, it looks like the red-car driver screwed up. But courts want proof before they give the blue-car driver any relief. The story alone doesn't constitute proof. Of course, if the blue party wants to invoke the court system, she will tell her side of the story on a piece of paper, called a complaint. The red-car driver will tell his side of the story on a piece of paper, called an answer. Then there will be a period of fact-finding, called discovery. Both parties will talk to witnesses, in what are called depositions, and collect documents and other information from each other (like photographs, police reports, and medical records) and from other sources.

Once that is done—and after a few more procedural maneuverings—the case might go to trial. The blue-car party will have to prove that the red-car party screwed up, i.e., that he was negligent. Negligence is a legal concept that has four parts, each of which must be proven at trial: the red-car driver had a duty to drive safely, he violated that duty, his violation (or breach) caused the car accident, and the plaintiff suffered damages as a result. If the blue-car party proves each of these four parts with facts uncovered during discovery (which at trial are called evidence), she can get money to make up for her injuries. In sum, the *law* in this instance is made up of the four elements of negligence. The *facts* amount to proof of this particular story—one way or another.

Whether something is legal depends on *both* the law and the facts. The red-car driver was negligent if he caused the blue-car driver's injury. Say, however, that she is suing for emotional pain and suffering caused by the incident. She claims she cannot sleep and uncontrollably flies into fits of rage. During discovery, the red-car driver finds out that the plaintiff has bipolar disorder and is on medication. This is a sad state of affairs, to be sure, and the red-car driver knows he did in fact run the red light. But the blue-car driver probably cannot get money from him for her bipolar disorder—unless his red-light running *caused* that disorder.

Now consider the Constitution. Whether an action by the government violates the Constitution also depends on a number of factors. Recall the Fourth Amendment's ban on unreasonable searches and seizures. To be sure, the FBI cannot bang down a front door while you are at work and ransack your house just because you have blue eyes and the agents in charge hate people with blue eyes. But what if instead of banging down your door, they run a search of your data online and piece together that you like heavy metal music, that your best friend is a Muslim, and that you recently read Karl Marx's *The Communist Manifesto*? Is that a search?

Again, it depends on the facts of this particular story—specifically, the use of the Internet to get information about someone (rather than banging down his or her front door). If no court has considered whether an Internet search is a Fourth Amendment violation, then there is no law banning such a search—the court will *make* that law based on the facts of your particular case. This is so even though there *is* a law banning unreasonable searches and seizures in general.

Lawyers drive nonlawyers crazy by hedging their answers with tons of caveats. People want the bottom line on questions like: Can the president tell his subordinates not to talk to the grand jury on executive privilege grounds? The answer to this one is easy: no blanket ban applies, because the law of executive privilege does not allow that. But certain information *may* be protected, and that question depends on the person who is testifying and what she is testifying about. It is a fact-specific, situation-by-situation inquiry. The answer is that "it depends" on many factors; there is usually no one answer to "is it legal?"

The Constitution is just 230 years old—a wee babe in the broad arc of human history. It could falter. The drafters of the Constitution knew this. They were deeply influenced by the French philosopher Montesquieu. He wrote that "[w]hen the legislative and executive powers are united in the same person, or in the same body of magistrates, there can be no liberty; . . . lest the same monarch or senate should enact tyrannical laws [or] execute them in a tyrannical manner."[6] This dark proposition is not a partisan or ideological one. The Constitution was set up to prevent any one person or branch of government from having too much power. Each branch must be made to answer to the other two, regardless of who is in the White House or Congress. If the Constitution's system of checks and balances is allowed to lapse or weaken, another governmental structure will emerge to fill in the gap. And rest assured: it will not be superior to the one that has operated to protect individual liberties and freedoms since 1787, albeit imperfectly. It is human nature to amass power.

Now, let's get started on excavating the Constitution.

PART I

$\mathfrak{Structure}$

It is no exaggeration to say that in the twenty-first century, the structure of the Constitution is being tested like never before. There are several reasons for this—a number of which I discuss in part three—including defects in how Congress operates, the flood of money in politics, the way the election process functions, and the creeping influence of technology and big data on how government does its business and how people live their lives.

But mostly, the Constitution's structure is being tested by the absence of accountability. The Constitution sets up three branches of government—the legislative, the executive, and the judicial—and makes no one person or group of persons in charge of everyone. If one branch breaks rules, the other two stand ready to hold the rulebreaker accountable. That way, nobody amasses too much power, which would be a recipe for tyranny.

But these days, rules are being broken without a whole lot of consequences. The key question is not the ubiquitous one we're hearing: whether an action by a sitting president is constitutional. As we shall see, nine justices on the Supreme Court can sharply disagree on such things, which means that there is usually no one definitive answer to the vast majority of legal questions—particularly constitutional ones. The correct question is: When the president does something that pushes boundaries, breaks norms, or maybe even breaks the law, what happens? If the answer is that nothing happens, then the boundaries, norms, and laws themselves—even those enshrined in the Constitution—lose their meaning and their force. They become like graffiti on a concrete wall—curious enough to shrug at, but not worth a meaningful modicum of attention.

In thinking about constitutional structure, it may be helpful to picture a magnificent bridge across a wide river. Imagine a toll booth on one end with uniformed police officers directing traffic. Suppose that, as a group, the police officers on duty happen to be politically biased against red cars. Anyone in a red car gets pulled over and harassed. That's not fair, of course. It's a terrible thing for drivers of red cars, who call the precinct and complain. The police officers get fired and replaced. It turns out that the replacement officers happen to hate blue cars. They do nasty stuff to those drivers—just like the last team did to red-car drivers.

Meanwhile, as everyone is busy arguing about which team of police officers gets all the power on the bridge, the bridge itself is in decay. It hasn't been tended to for decades. The bridge's structure depends on large cement pillars lodged in the riverbed. The cement is cracking. River water is rushing through the cracks, weakening the bridge. But nobody cares enough to notice. While the bridge's infrastructure is failing, people focus all their attention on other important issues like fairness to car drivers and crooked cops on the beat. They simply assume the bridge will continue to hold for the next generation and the next—just as it has for decades.

But one day, the stresses on the bridge's structure overwhelm it. The bridge collapses. Everyone on the bridge goes crashing to their deaths—including, of course, everyone in both red and blue cars.

You see, it doesn't matter which band of cops is directing bridge traffic on a particular day. If the bridge's structure is neglected to the point of destruction, everyone will go down with it—regardless of political party or ideology.

CHAPTER 1

The Basics:
Each Branch Has a Job
Description—and Two Bosses

I talk to people about the Constitution a lot. What strikes me is that everyone knows they have rights. They know there is something called the Constitution that contains those rights. They know that the Constitution says how people get into office, and that it has some rules about what the president, members of Congress, and other officials can and can't do. But when an issue of constitutional law comes up on the news—such as whether the president can pardon himself, or whether he can drop stealth bombs somewhere without Congress first declaring war, or whether only Congress can decide to separate children from their mothers at the US border—the first question that pops up is, *Is that legal under the Constitution?*

This chapter gets out a few basic ideas about how to approach questions of constitutional law—ideas that are explored more deeply in later chapters. The chapter divides constitutional law into two axes and suggests that the first thing you do in thinking about a constitutional law question is to decide which camp it falls into: a rights-based constitutional law issue or a structural constitutional law issue. This chapter then lays out a few things about both axes.

Second, it introduces the concept of plain-language reading. I tell my first-year law students that they will be learning *how to read*. "Huh? We've known how to read since we were six!" Sure, that's true, in the sense that students come to law school knowing cognitively how to translate black-and-white marks on a page into words. But what I mean by *read* is different. It requires you to isolate phrases, then individual words, and then figure out as many interpretations of those words as possible. Once you have the various options on the table, you can start to prioritize the options and choose which is best—or at least how to argue for one over the other on behalf of a client. This is a *skill*, and one that is becoming increasingly rare in a world of information overload, texts, tweets, and sound bites.

Third, this chapter introduces a handful of core constitutional ideas that operate as guideposts for deciding which interpretations of important words are the best ones. Those concepts include the separation of powers, checks and balances, and the truism that the respective powers of government overlap and blur.

Fourth, this chapter explains in commonsense terms how the government gets its power in the first place—that it comes from "We the People," not some piece of paper—and why that matters for our enduring democratic legacy.

One of the two constitutional axes—the one we hear a lot about in the news media and on cable TV shows—is the so-called rights-based Constitution.* The Constitution gives certain rights to every citizen and to some noncitizens. It's as if we each walk around with a backpack containing a bundle of rights that we can pull out to defend ourselves if the government does something to us that the Constitution says it is not supposed to do. The possession of a constitutional right isn't a "goodie" from the government.

---

*   There is a third axis, which is the separation of the federal government from that of the individual states. The proper demarcation between the balancing of federal and state power is known as federalism, and it is a critical component of ensuring accountability for elected officials. Chapter 9 discusses what the Constitution says about the states.

Say the government tries to take away our property, or mucks around with something we are lawfully trying to do (like speak about religion) because it dislikes a particular political view. We can reach into our respective backpacks and pull out a constitutional right—as if it were a badge—and get the government to stop. We might even use our "rights badges" to get money from the government to compensate us for its violation of those rights. We get these things by going to court and persuading a judge to issue a piece of paper called an order, which directs the government to either do something or stop doing something, or to pay us money damages to make us whole again.

It also happens that the bare knowledge of the threat of a lawsuit may force the government to act a certain way because it doesn't want to get pinged with a court order saying it violated a right. So, for example, if a person is arrested, the police officer will read him what is known as *Miranda* warnings, explaining that he has the right to remain silent, etcetera. This speech derives from a Supreme Court case holding that the Constitution requires police officers to do that when they arrest people.[1] If an officer doesn't do it, she won't go to jail, but she might get in trouble in court—trouble that could ultimately result in her having to pay the person she arrested some money. Or the court just might throw out the arrestee's conviction later because the officer messed up. That's a bad outcome for law enforcement: it means a lot of time and effort down the drain, in addition to the fact that a bad guy is back on the streets without having paid his dues for breaking the law. Either way, the threat of a lawsuit to enforce constitutional rights creates an incentive for the police to avoid violating those rights. The existence of rights under the Constitution is accordingly important for purposes of forcing government to do the right thing without being reminded each time.

The Constitution was ratified in 1787, but most provisions governing individual rights were added in 1791. (Others came later.) The list of amendments to the original Constitution (the Bill of Rights) is where one finds the rights to free speech, assembly, and religion (First Amendment); the right to bear arms (Second Amendment); the right to be free of unreasonable searches and seizures (Fourth Amendment); the due process clauses (I frankly didn't realize there were two due process clauses—in the Fifth and Fourteenth Amendments—until I was out of law school), and so on.

Before we talk more about rights, let me share one basic thing about the law that many people don't really "get." Before anyone can go before a court, they need what is called a cause of action. In order to possibly get relief from a judge, one must prove that a list of particular things occurred that broke a law. For example, there are laws establishing what turns an agreement into a contract that can be enforced in court. Jane must prove that she has a contract with Joe to renovate a kitchen before she can sue Joe for failing to renovate the kitchen after she gave Joe money. There are rules that define what it means to have a contract; let's call those rules laws. If Jane just happened to give Joe money on a generous whim without a contract or other cause of action requiring him to renovate Jane's kitchen in exchange for that money, she can't sue Joe to get the money back. It doesn't matter how "unfair" it is that Joe refuses to give Jane's money back—maybe she was half asleep when she opened her checkbook and confused Joe for her doppelgänger grown son. She can complain to Joe, or to her sister, or to her neighbor, but she can't formally complain to a judge. In general, people can't just run to a judge and gripe about anything that bothers them; there has to be a law stating that a certain complaint amounts to something that gives rise to a legitimate legal claim in court. That law can come from a statute or, historically speaking, from a line of prior decisions by courts.

Somewhat amazingly, the Constitution is *not* one of those laws that uniformly gives citizens a cause of action to sue if their rights are violated. A person cannot walk into court and wave around the Constitution whenever the government does something that might offend it. Only some—not all—of the Bill of Rights can be enforced in a court. If a person is upset with a federal official—say, an FBI agent who raided that person's office and took his laptop—that person would have to look to Supreme Court cases to see if he can use the Constitution to get money from the government. The Supreme Court created causes of action against federal officials in a series of decisions resolving individual cases. The ability to sue a federal official for violating a constitutional right is known as a *Bivens* action, named after the first case in which the Supreme Court held that an individual could sue federal officers for violating Fourth Amendment rights.[2]

However, if the raid was conducted by state or local officials—say, the county sheriff or a city police officer—*Bivens* would not apply. To sue a state or local official, the person whose office was raided would use a statute passed by Congress.[3] A statute is a separate source of law (remember the others, so far, are the Constitution or decisions by courts, known as case law) that, in this instance, contains a law allowing people to file lawsuits to enforce their individual constitutional rights against state or local officials. Such lawsuits are known as 1983 actions because of the numerical section of the US code that contains that particular law. Prior to the enactment of that law, which was passed in reaction to police tolerance of hateful activities in the South by the Ku Klux Klan, people could not sue in court to obtain relief for state and local officials' violations of their constitutional rights. There was, in other words, no such cause of action.

The next axis of constitutional law concerns itself with the Constitution's structure.

The Supreme Court's decisions regarding the structural Constitution seek to ensure that the federal government is erected and operates according to the architectural blueprint set forth in the Constitution. That blueprint lays out rules for how the United States government must function. In theory, those rules make the US government impervious to dictators. If a would-be dictator tries to take over, he will inevitably bump up against structural barriers. Ultimately, he will lose his power grab *not* because the American people are smart enough to elect only good people but because *the system* will (or should) inevitably force unethical, power-hungry people out of power one way or another. The structural Constitution assumes that human beings will continue to act like human beings—meaning some will seek more power regardless of the external costs. The structural axis of constitutional law kicks *in* when it needs to kick *out* those people who are trying to violate democratic norms.

Think of an ice-cream shop. The owner might set up the structure of the business to include a general manager, an assistant manager, individual workers, and maybe a contractor or two to maintain the equipment. That structure will include a system of wages, hours, and benefits and criteria for termination (such as stealing) and possibly even for receiving bonuses for a job well done. It might have a security system and a detailed method for counting and depositing money and for keeping track of inventories so that the owner can get ahead of employee theft.

Surrounding that system are various state and local laws governing food safety, permitting, noise ordinances, and whatnot. The people who come and go into the system (the employees) might change, but the system itself will endure—possibly with a few tweaks along the line. The idea is that, if the ice-cream shop is to be sustaining and profitable, there must be a system in place to guard against abuses and to reward those who follow the rules. Those rewards could simply include the ability to keep a job.

Of course, we can assume the shop owner takes care to hire ethical people. But if a dishonest one slips through the cracks, the ice-cream shop's organizational structure will continue to function to ensure that the operation survives. An employee who is stealing $100 from the cash register every week might be caught by surveillance cameras, or by another employee who sees him and tattles, or by an outside accounting firm who notices that the books aren't balanced and the shortfall always occurs on that guy's shift. There are many ways that the structure of the organization will catch and do away with troublemakers. The shop owner doesn't have to lose sleep simply hoping he got lucky and took on only ethical people. The organizational structure is critical to ensuring that the shop stays open.

The Constitution has a structure that's like an ice-cream shop but a lot more complicated. The Constitution does not put a single person in charge. It is decidedly not a hierarchy with upper management at the top. The framers instead took the job description of a monarch and broke it into three parts—it gave each part, or branch, a distinct task. It then gave each branch some tools to oversee or check how the other two are doing. It's ingenious, really, as it doesn't have many analogues in everyday life. By comparison, most organizations that we encounter—like corporations, schools, and churches—are designed as pyramid-like hierarchies. Only a few innovative companies have attempted to disseminate power *among* the members of an organization.

In 2014, for example, the online shoe and clothing retailer Zappos implemented a holacracy, getting rid of bosses and titles. Workers instead began tracking strategy decisions and results on an app. The shift was risky and bred confusion because people weren't sure what they were supposed to do. Human resource personnel couldn't ascertain salaries without job titles, and there was nobody higher in the chain of demand to make the hard calls. In 2016, Zappos reportedly experienced huge attrition rates.[4] Let's face it: people tend to like pecking orders.

Although the Constitution does not establish a straight-up hierarchy, its blueprint for government is vital to ensuring that bad apples don't last long. The animating principle behind the Constitution's structure is well-known. It's called the separation of powers. Although the term *separation of powers* is nowhere in the Constitution's text, the idea stems from a rejection of England's King George III and the model of an all-powerful sovereign who can exercise his authority arbitrarily and with virtual impunity. If the government is separated into three branches, the theory goes, no one branch has all the power, and tyranny—which the framers thought was inherent and unavoidable in human nature—can be evaded. Unlike under Zappos's holacracy, there are hierarchies within each branch of government, and everyone at the top of each branch gets a boss: the other two branches. Each branch checks the other two branches' powers, and if those powers have somehow gotten off-kilter, the system operates to rebalance the dynamic so that power is more equally distributed among the three branches.

This parallel notion of checks and balances derives from the separation of powers.

Once again, the term *checks and balances* is not in the Constitution. Yet it functions as a foundational tenet of American democracy. Each branch supervises the other two branches, so everyone's papers get graded, so to speak. No government actor is unaccountable. No more kings.

Another way to think about the separation of powers is to treat the Constitution like a company's employee manual. It gives each branch a job to do. The branches' job descriptions are set forth in one of three articles of the Constitution. Each branch has articulated ways of stopping bad behavior if things get out of sync within the other branches—at least in theory. Following is a chart a colleague shared with me.

By nature of a particular branch's power, the chart refers primarily to the contents of what are known as the vesting clauses of the Consti-

Power	LEGISLATIVE Article I	EXECUTIVE Article II	JUDICIAL Article III
Nature	Make laws	Implement laws	Apply laws; resolve cases and controversies
Body	Congress	President and executive officers	Supreme Court and lower courts
Selection	Elected by state (Senate) or district (House)	Electoral College	Presidential appointment with Senate consent; life tenure and salary protection
Checks	**Executive:** Veto, pardon power, prosecutorial discretion **Judicial:** Judicial review	**Legislative:** Impeachment, veto override, budget control, oversight, statutory limitations **Judicial:** Judicial review	**Legislative:** Impeachment, amendment, and jurisdiction **Executive:** Appointment, removal, pardon power, prosecutorial discretion

tution. To visualize the vesting clauses' function, imagine a sovereign dressed in lavish finery, scepter in hand, "knighting" Congress with the pronouncement "All legislative Powers herein granted shall be vested in a Congress of the United States, which shall consist of a Senate and House of Representatives." The sovereign's official secretary might memorialize her words in ink on a roll of parchment under the heading, "Article I, Section 1 of the Constitution."

Now imagine that the sovereign directs under Article II that "[t]he executive Power shall be vested in a President of the United States of America." And finally, she announces that "[t]he judicial Power of the United States, shall be vested in one supreme Court, and in such inferior Courts as the Congress may from time to time ordain and establish," a proclamation that winds up in Article III of the Constitution.

Note for a moment that something is conspicuously missing from the vesting clauses' language: a written definition of what each power means. The Constitution does not define the terms *legislative*, *executive*, or *judicial*. This is where the notion of careful reading comes in.

Strange as it sounds, reading the Constitution is a lot like reading poetry. Why? Because poetry requires careful focus on individual words as well as analyses of competing meanings. Consider the following poem by Wallace Stevens. I have bolded the words (including the title) that are particularly important to the point I'm trying to make here.

The Snow Man

One must have **a mind of winter**
To **regard** the **frost and the boughs**
Of the **pine-trees crusted with snow;**

And have **been cold a long time**
To behold the **junipers shagged with ice,**
The spruces rough in the distant glitter

Of the January sun; and **not** to think
Of any **misery** in the sound of the wind,
In the sound of a few leaves,

Which is the sound of the land
Full of the same wind
That is blowing in the same bare place

For **the listener,** who listens in the snow,
And, **nothing himself,** beholds
Nothing that is not there and the nothing that is.

What does this poem mean? One interpretation is that a person—"one"—who "regards" or observes nature must do so disinterestedly; the frost and snow on the trees do not reasonably reflect human emotions like misery. A "mind of winter" instead knows that nature is just nature, e.g., a "pine-tree encrusted in snow," "boughs covered in frost," or "junipers shagged with ice." Everything exists in black-or-white terms. A snowman is just a pile of snow. It is not a person, and it doesn't have a soul. The poem's title—"The Snow Man"—refers to wads of snow stacked on top of each other in someone's front yard. Or, shifting the meaning slightly, the snow man could be a crude description of a person who happens to spend a lot of time amid the snow—someone who has "been cold a long time" and is used to it.

Or the poem's words could mean something more abstract, erecting a metaphor for a cold, disinterested person. Someone who is icy and devoid of emotion as he goes through life. For this interpretation, the word *not* is critical. In other words, one would have to be pretty coldhearted—to have "a mind of winter"—to *not* look at the barren landscape, with its sparse leaves, and think of human emotions like "misery." Under this interpretation, the *listener* has an active approach to nature and constantly seeks a deeper meaning in it. The word *misery* activates a very human feeling rather than deactivating it, as the prior interpretation would aim to do.

A related question in reading this poem has to do with the broader takeaway message. On one hand, the poem endorses an approach to life that is like that of the disinterested snow man: that is, taking life at face value for what it is and is not, and not reading into things too much. On the other hand, the poem could be read as saying that people should not live as if freezing and desperate for emotional warmth. We should look for human emotion—even in a barren landscape—and constantly listen for what nature aims to teach us about the art of living. We might even find a third reading—that is, don't sweat the small stuff. Live in a way that is akin to nature. Focus on the moment. Be mindful, authentic, and honest with every breath.

Let's next consider the notion of context. Imagine that the reader of the poem is a marketing executive seeking to push a client's aromatherapy products. The last interpretive option outlined happens to jive with the message behind today's multibillion-dollar wellness industry. Live in the moment, people! A person looking for this message in her personal or professional life is more likely to find it embedded in the poem. The context in which a reader approaches poetry will deeply affect which reading she adopts as the best one.

We could go on with the various possible meanings of this short poem. Inevitably, whether one reading is better might turn on factors beyond the text itself—such as the reader's personality and experience, the weather, current events, or whether profit margins hang in the balance. The bottom line is that there is no single, correct, enduring answer to the precise meaning of this particular text.

Reading the Constitution works in much the same way. The text contains a handful of clues but nothing definitive or exhaustive. Additionally, context and purpose matters. As with reading a poem, we start with the language itself. We might construe "All legislative Powers" to literally mean *all*—in other words, that Congress has a mandatory lock on the legislative power. Nobody but Congress can exercise it. We might also read the term *legislative* as necessarily having a meaning that is separate and distinct from the other two. In other words, whatever the legislative power is, it does not include the unique powers of the judicial or executive branches, and so forth. They are all mutually exclusive.

But it should come as no surprise by now that the term *legislative* is not defined in the Constitution, and there is no list on the door of the constitutional fridge. A person applying the term's plain meaning might naturally think of *legislative* as meaning lawmaking, and a law as meaning something that governs or limits the behavior of individuals or entities. A law against trespass limits my ability to drive a truck through someone's backyard as a shortcut on the way to work. Laws against negligence also constrain such behavior to the extent that tires end up damaging lawns or knocking over personal property such as a bird feeder. The Constitution seems to say that only Congress can do such a thing as make laws for the federal government; neither the courts nor the president can.

Beyond that, someone reading the vesting clause language for the first time and assigning its plain meaning might assume that *judicial* has something to do with judges and trials and disputes among individual parties. We have all seen courtroom dramas or *Judge Judy* on TV, or have participated in jury duty or a real-life lawsuit. We can envision a courtroom with two tables at which each side sits. The sides—called parties—have a dispute. They can't resolve it, so they go to court. The judge has the power—the power of the government, to be precise—to resolve the dispute with something we call a judgment. A judgment is a decision pertaining to those two parties. It doesn't bind anybody else.

Note that in no circumstance does the court—or *can* the court—simply say, "I hereby pronounce a rule for everyone in this courtroom that the hotel owner must pay you money if you had a contract with this particular luxury hotel that remains unpaid." This would smack of lawmaking. Judicial decisions are not legislation; they are generally backward-focused, and they resolve fights about things that happened in the past. Lawmaking is generally forward-focused, and it sets forth rules aimed at managing or restricting conduct that has yet to occur.

Last, let's talk about *executive* power—the power of the president of the United States.

And again, let's do it first from the standpoint of attempting to divine the plain meaning of the words of the Constitution. The term *executive* sounds a lot like the word *execute*, which in turn assumes that there is some separate body of something that needs executing. A teenager might execute her chores after school. In order to do that, she needs to know what the chores are. With respect to the Constitution, the words *execute* or *executive* do not help in this regard. But Article II does contain a couple of clues. Article II, Section 3 provides that the president "shall take Care that the Laws be faithfully executed." This language confirms that laws come from somewhere else—let's assume for now that it is Congress—and the president must (i.e., *shall*) take care to execute them faithfully. He cannot ignore them, at least in theory. (Remember we need a police officer for words to mean more than the parchment they were written on.)

As for Congress, among its many expressed powers (such as the power to establish post offices and the power to declare war), Article I gives it "clean up" authority that, by virtue of the powers it implies, is grander than the legislature's delineated powers combined. Congress can "make all Laws which shall be necessary and proper for carrying into Execution the foregoing powers, and all other Powers vested by this Constitution in the Government of the United States, or in any Department or Officer thereof." This is known as the Necessary and Proper Clause.[5] Congress, therefore, makes the laws that the executive branch must take care to faithfully execute, and the president is at the helm of the executive branch. To revert to the teenager scenario, Mom makes up the list of chores for the teen to execute. Now remember—if the teen fails to do that, Mom had better be prepared to impose a consequence, or the chores will quickly become meaningless and remain undone.

So far, the Constitution's text appears pretty straightforward regarding the structure of the federal government. Affording each branch an exclusive job description is a logical approach, which is respectful of the framers' original words and neatly ensures that each of the three major federal players stays in its respective sandbox. Mom makes the laws; the teen executes them. If there is a dispute about the meaning of the law (does "clean the bathroom" include scrubbing toilets or just wiping down the sink?) perhaps the dispute can be brought to Dad, the arbiter or judge. When Dad resolves the dispute (likely in Mom's favor—but let's set aside judicial bias for now), the entire family respects and adheres to that judgment, or rule of law. If the teenager refuses, then the ante is upped—maybe her phone goes away for a week—until she is willing to adopt the family's norm of adhering to parental decision-making. From the standpoint of the US Constitution's separation of powers, however, things rapidly get tricky.

Fast-forward from 1791—where we last left off—to 2019. A drive through downtown Washington, DC, takes tourists past numerous national monuments and the many structures that house the Smithsonian Institution; along the Potomac River; past the Capitol, where Congress does its work; by the White House; and alongside a number of courthouses, including the United States Supreme Court. In less than an hour, the tour touches down on all three points in the system of separated powers. Many of these places are along Independence or Constitution Avenues (two key thoroughfares in downtown Washington, DC), which also have many gray marble buildings housing federal agencies, such as the Department of Justice (DOJ) and the Department of the Treasury. (Keep in mind that federal agencies with the word *department* in their names are each headed by a secretary who is appointed by the president and confirmed by the Senate. Taken together, the secretaries form the president's cabinet.)

As a matter of common sense, it is reasonable to assume that the existence of these buildings must mean that the agencies' collective job is to help the president take care that the laws are faithfully executed and otherwise effectuate his *executive* authority under Article II. Like the legislative authority, the executive power under the Constitution has a handful of components that are expressly stated, such as the power to veto legislation or command the armed forces, but otherwise undefined.

Generally speaking, if we read the president's job description, it is fair to assume that everyone who works for him is confined to executive and take-care duties, right?

Wrong. Federal agencies in fact dip their toes into each of the three constitutional sandboxes—they execute laws, to be sure, but they also make them and adjudicate them. A bit of history helps explain why. With the stock market crash of the 1920s, President Franklin Delano Roosevelt decided that the economy was massively underregulated. The idea was that if the government played a greater role in managing the economy by passing rules of the road for banks and other players in financial markets, future fiscal catastrophes and consequential mass suffering could be avoided. Aided by a compliant Congress, an alphabet soup of federal agencies was born in the 1930s.[6]

Federal agencies have thus been around for nearly a century, and they are here to stay—which presents a problem for someone who wants to stick to the plain language of the Constitution. If the vesting clauses mean what they say, agencies that make laws (Congress's job) and adjudicate disputes (judges' job) are unconstitutional from the point of view of the Constitution's architectural blueprint. Put another way, if agencies are located within the umbrella of the executive branch (since they are headed by individuals hired and largely fired by the president), but exercise powers that exclusively belong to the other branches, then their activities violate the basic structure of the Constitution every working day of the week.

In these circumstances, under the system of separated powers and its implied checks and balances, it would be up to the other two branches to tamp down what appears to be a power grab by the executive branch. How the other branches do this is a question that sends us back to the handy chart provided on page 41.

By this point, we have walked through the first three topics of this chapter: the two axes of constitutional law (rights-based constitutional law versus structural constitutional law); how lawyers must learn to "read" ambiguous language; and how constitutional law is guided by foundational concepts that include the separation of powers, the system of checks and balances, and the blurring of powers within a branch (despite a constitutional job description that is much narrower). The chapter's final task is to explain what the power of the US government really means. For this, we must dabble a bit in theory.

Here's a question of everyday life that you may not yet have pondered: Why do we even bother to pay attention to what the government says we can and cannot do? The simple answer is that we don't want to get in trouble. Every driver has gazed in a rearview mirror to see a cop car with flashing lights. An irritating *blip-blip* follows—an order to pull over and produce a license and automobile registration to check. Most of us go along with this scenario, even though it's pretty stressful, it delays plans, and it may trigger a fine or points on a driver's license. We cooperate because a police officer has powers that ordinary people do not, i.e., the power to make arrests and put people in jail. Which nobody wants to experience.

Note, however, that this system is very different from one in which abject fear of government brutality governs individual behavior. As Americans, we generally do not fear that the government will arbitrarily throw us in jail based on our political views or the company we keep. We are a society in which "the rule of law" governs. What that means is that we as a society have agreed on a series of rules of conduct. If we comply with those rules, we can stay out of trouble. If we don't, we agree that the government can take steps to hold us accountable.

What is important to keep in mind in this regard is that we generally trust the legitimacy of government. Legitimacy is an important concept here. We have all had bosses or teachers or family members whom we respect; we go along with their way of doing things because it matters to us if they are displeased. On the flipside, we have all had people in our lives whom we do not respect—the professor or boss or colleague who lays down a rule that is immediately shrugged off. "That guy is a total joke," we say.

There are numerous reasons why we might respect one person in a position of authority but ignore another. We respect those who have a legitimate claim to authority—if the lady who shushes you during a ballet performance is the theater manager, you are more likely to pay attention than if she is just a grouchy person in the seat behind you who gets annoyed with your coughing. The same holds true for government. It's considered legitimate "if the people to whom its orders are directed believe that the structure, procedures, acts, decisions, policies, officials, or leaders of government possess the quality of 'rightness,' propriety, or moral goodness—the right, in short, to make binding rules."[7]

In my theater example, one reason why a patron is more likely to comply with a manager's shushing than an angry bystander's is that the manager is employed by the theater. We are guests of the theater, and the manager has been given the authority to enforce the rules of her employer.

Where, by contrast, does the government's power actually come from in America? In a monarchy, the sovereign's power theoretically comes from God. If a warrior won a battle against an incumbent monarch on the bloody shires of England, the notion was that God anointed that person to be the king. It's not unlike the Catholic pope, who is—again in theory—chosen by God to lead the Church on earth. The pope is deeply revered and deferred to because he is handpicked by God.[8]

Our government, by contrast, is secular. We have the so-called separation of church and state—another concept that's nowhere explicit in the Constitution (but considered implicit in the First Amendment's text)—which keeps government from interfering with religion and vice versa. In short, God has nothing to do with why police in America can throw you in jail.

We should think pragmatically of the federal Constitution as simply a piece of paper. It isn't a source of divine power. It is not a *source* of power at all. States constitutions aren't either. A constitution is just a set of rules for how power must be shared and executed. The power comes from somewhere else. Although we won't get deep into constitutional theory here, most readers will instinctively know what that somewhere else is. The US government's power comes from the people. The ability of the people to elect and replace representatives via valid electoral processes is a key reason why Americans treat our government as legitimate. It is arguably why many of us go along with a routine traffic stop without much ado over the authority of police officers to interrupt our daily lives.

This is all precisely as it was meant to be. Having fled a tyrannical monarchy, the framers of the Constitution wanted a government *by the people*—meaning a government that accordingly responds *to the people*. It is the Constitution's opening salvo: "*We the People* of the United States . . . do ordain and establish this Constitution for the United States of America" (emphasis mine).[9] The concept of "We the People" is scattered throughout Supreme Court case law interpreting the Constitution as well.[10] The Declaration of Independence likewise provides that "to secure these rights, Governments are instituted among Men, deriving their just powers *from the consent of the governed*," and "whenever any Form of Government becomes destructive of these ends, it is the Right *of the People* to alter or abolish it" (emphasis mine).[11]

In Federalist No. 49—one of a series of papers in which three of the Constitution's framers promoted its ratification—James Madison explained that "the people are the only legitimate fountain of power."[12] Alexander Hamilton relatedly emphasized in Federalist No. 78 that elected representatives cannot act in a manner that contradicts the Constitution. "To deny this, would be to affirm, that the deputy is greater than his principal; that the servant is above his master; that the representatives of the people are superior to the people themselves."[13]

Ultimately, however, the founders did not craft a true democracy, whereby citizens would assemble and participate personally in elections. The Constitution's drafters were worried that a direct democracy would allow irrational, ideological, or political factions to effectively take over, with no means of putting things back on track. The founders instead opted for a republic, whereby power is run through a small number of presumably wiser government representatives.[14] As Madison explained in Federalist No. 37, "The genius of republican liberty seems to demand on one side, not only that all power should be derived from the People, but that those intrusted with it should be kept in dependence on the People."[15] The Supreme Court has repeatedly reinforced that our republican government can only exercise delegated powers that are channeled from the people through the Constitution. "To hold otherwise is to overthrow the basis of our constitutional law."[16]

Of course, problems occur when the people's representatives cease to respond to their constituents—if that part of the republic breaks down, so does the system as a whole. It is therefore no cliché to say that the people must hold elected representatives accountable for violations of the Constitution. The idea that the government's power flows from the people means that those who exercise power in the people's name *must* be reciprocally accountable to them. The mechanism for such accountability lies in the Constitution, which reflects a consensus that "We the People" agreed on certain terms, which operate to check against the illegitimate exercise of power.[17]

Importantly, the Constitution binds generations to this way of doing business.

If a generation of Americans comes along and happens to allow elected representatives to flout the Constitution's terms, then the structure for holding government accountable to the people could fall apart for good. It's like a no-jumping-on-the-couch rule for children. If a parent allows the kid to jump—just this once—then the no-jumping rule ceases to exist. The child knows this instinctively. She knows that the parent is no longer a *legitimate* authoritarian, with respect to the rules of the couch, at least.

Similarly, if the people ignore representatives' failure to uphold the Constitution—or even the norms underlying the Constitution—just this once, future officeholders will understand that they can get away with violating the same rules and norms in the future. This theoretical use-it-or-lose-it concept is immeasurably important. If you don't *use* the rights and rules that the Constitution provides, you will lose them.

If you take nothing else away from this book, I hope you take away an appreciation for how we cannot take the Constitution for granted. It works only insofar as we enforce it—that is, we throw our elected leaders out of office if they ignore the terms of their representation—and that we do this consistently, from generation to generation, so that our children are not left with a replacement that is far inferior.

CHAPTER 2

Congress:
Lots of Power to a Herd of Cats

No definition of legislative power.

Article I, Section 1.

All **legislative Powers herein granted shall be vested in a Congress** of the United States, which shall consist of a Senate and House of Representatives.

Section 3.

The Senate shall have the **sole Power to try all Impeachments**. When sitting for that Purpose, they shall be on Oath or Affirmation. When the President of the United States is tried, the Chief Justice shall preside: And no Person shall be convicted without the Concurrence of two thirds of the Members present.

Impeachment is mentioned in Article II as well, but the power belongs to Congress.

Judgment in Cases of Impeachment shall not extend further than to removal from Office, and disqualification to hold and enjoy any Office of honor, Trust or Profit under the United States: but the Party convicted shall nevertheless be liable and subject to Indictment, Trial, Judgment and Punishment, according to Law.

Section 8 expands Congress's powers, while Section 9 limits them.

Section 8.

The Congress can have Power To **lay and collect Taxes**, Duties, Imposts and Excises, **to pay the Debts and provide for the common Defence and general Welfare** of the United States; but all Duties, Imposts and Excises shall be uniform throughout the United States;

What does general welfare mean, and who gets to decide?

Three pillars of congressional power: to tax, borrow money, and regulate commerce.

To **borrow Money** on the credit of the United States;

To **regulate Commerce** with foreign Nations, and among the several States, and with the Indian Tribes;

. . .

To **constitute Tribunals** inferior to the supreme Court;

If Congress wanted, there could be just one Supreme Court justice and no lower federal courts. To be addressed in chapter 4.

This power has been neglected and largely yielded to the president, as will be discussed in chapter 3.

. . .

To **declare War**

. . .

To raise and support Armies . . .

To provide and maintain a Navy

. . .

To make all laws which shall be **necessary and proper** for carrying into Execution the foregoing Powers, and all other Powers vested by this Constitution in the Government of the United States, or in any Department or Officer thereof.

This is very open-ended language that, along with the Commerce Clause, is the basis for lots of congressional power.

We will talk about the "Great Writ" in chapter 3.

Section 9.

. . .

The privilege of the **Writ of Habeas Corpus shall not be suspended**, unless when in Cases of Rebellion or Invasion the public Safety may require it.

No Bill of Attainder or ex post facto Law shall be passed.

. . .

No Money shall be drawn from the Treasury, but in Consequence of **Appropriations** made by Law . . .

> This is one way Congress controls the executive branch: the purse strings.

No Title of Nobility shall be granted by the United States: And no Person holding any Office of Profit or Trust under them, shall, without the Consent of the Congress, accept of any present, **Emolument**, Office, or Title, of any kind whatever, from any King, Prince, or foreign State.

> Here is the Emoluments Clause, which has been in the news during the Trump administration.

When it comes to the powers of Congress, there are two ideas to bear in mind. The first is that Congress is, of course, constrained by the other two branches. The framers were particularly worried about too much power accumulating in the legislature, which James Madison characterized as "everywhere extending the sphere of its activity and drawing all power to its impetuous vortex."[1]

The second is that, unlike the other branches, Congress is hemmed in by the competing sovereignty of the states. We will return to what the Constitution says about the states in chapter 9, but for now keep in mind that there is another power struggle going on here: if Congress can't do something "governmental" under the Constitution, that power goes to the states. This concept of sharing power between sovereigns is known as federalism, and it's an important one for limiting what could otherwise be an overpowering Congress.

As with most other questions of constitutional interpretation, however, the Supreme Court has not taken a consistent approach to federalism. Do we need a strong national government to address modern problems in a consistent way for *all* people involved? Or should key issues of personal consequence—such as health care, safety, education, immigration, abortion access, and voting procedures—be left primarily to the individual states to address? Because the Constitution does not have clear answers, how the Supreme Court construes its ambiguity can translate into real consequences for the everyday life of a Texan versus a New Yorker versus a Californian.

As this chapter explains, Congress has a number of expressly delineated powers in the Constitution—the power to legislate, to tax and spend, to regulate commerce, and to declare war, for example—but it also has *implied* powers that it can exercise (or not) with rigor. The Constitution says nothing about Congress's ability to haul people before its chambers for a public grilling, for example. The idea stems instead from the vesting clause—Congress needs to investigate in order to legislate.

But consider the Red Scare of the 1950s—also known as McCarthyism after the senator who drove that quest. Under Joseph McCarthy's leadership, the House Un-American Activities Committee conducted wide-scale character assassinations on the assumption that subversives sympathetic to the Soviet Union had infiltrated government. Because this was done in Congress, witnesses did not get the full procedural protections that would apply if they were tried in a court of law. This is not to say that congressional oversight is unwarranted at times—Congress does have an obligation to investigate perceived improprieties by the executive branch—but voters must be vigilant in ensuring that Congress does not go too far.[2]

Of course, Congress's implied powers have only vague constitutional limitations. For example, the Constitution imposes no clear limits on Congress's ability to gift its legislative powers to another branch of government—or even to a private corporation or lobbyist. Justice Clarence Thomas has expressed strong views that federal agencies are unconstitutional to the extent that they pass rules and regulations that function like laws.[3] Lawmaking is Congress's job, for sure. But what if a favored lobbyist for the coal industry drafts a law deregulating mining and slips it to a member of Congress for consideration? What if that member then simply cuts and pastes the "law" into a bill for consideration by the House of Representatives? One could argue that there's nothing problematic about this scenario because the member of Congress could be voted out by his constituents for caving in to monied interests rather than actually legislating based on the preferences of the electorate he represents. But there is nothing requiring that the lobbyists' draft be made public—so would voters even know? One irony about separation-of-powers questions, therefore, is that they don't address governing by nongovernment workers. As corporate interests become more and more powerful, a fair question to ask is whether this talk about the powers of the branches is, as a practical matter, beside the point.

Legislative Vesting Clause

The vesting clause of Article I states that "[a]ll legislative Powers herein shall be vested in a Congress." The Supreme Court has decided that *all* does not mean "in its entirety, with no exceptions" in this instance. But, for now, let's consider what *legislative* means on its face: it likely means making laws. But what is a law? Using logic and everyday experience, we might conclude that a law is a rule for everyone: For example, smashing other people's property is against the law, and if you do it, you must pay for the damage. This kind of law is distinct from a rule that applies to just one person: for instance, Fred must pay Bernice $1,000 for having damaged her parked car during a hit-and-run. That's a rule for courts.

Consider a case in which President Harry Truman tried to do something that looked like legislation. (It is also the key case that sheds serious doubt on the constitutionality of President Trump's declaration of a national emergency in order to build his so-called border wall.) In 1952, the United Steelworkers union announced that its members were going to go on a nationwide strike for higher wages. This occurred during the Korean War, and the Truman administration was worried about inflation. Truman believed that a strike of all the major steel producers could hurt the defense contracting industry because weapon production requires steel. To avoid a strike, Truman seized control of the steel mills to keep them running. He did this via an executive order, which we will discuss in chapter 3. Congress sat idly by and let it happen.

The steel companies sued, arguing that the president lacked the power to take private property without Congress saying he could. If the president had the power to do something as significant as unilaterally taking over the steel industry, the argument went, what's the point of even having a Congress with the power to legislate? Congress had not declared war, so there was no special circumstance that might have triggered greater presidential powers. The case went to the Supreme Court, which agreed with the steel companies. It held that Truman had acted unconstitutionally and barred him from seizing the steel plants.[4]

There are many thorny subissues here, but the main one is this: As a matter of the separation of powers, can the president act *only* if Congress gives him the specific authority first? In other words, does Congress have to pass a law—to legislate—before the president can execute or enforce it? Or is there something about law execution that allows the president to create his own rules from time to time?

Remember that the vesting clauses give each branch its exclusive job description. Each branch also checks the other branches—it grades their papers, so to speak. These two concepts are often at odds. Think of a professor in a university. If she is uncomfortably innovative but extremely good at teaching—like Robin Williams in the movie *Good Will Hunting*, perhaps—we don't want much checking of her actions by school administrators. We want to let her do her thing. But if she's a terrible teacher, even if she sticks to conventional methods, we want checking. We want accountability.

By the same token, if the president is doing something we don't like, we want the courts and Congress to check, check, check. But if we like what he's up to, we want separation—we want the other branches to leave the guy alone and let him do his job. There are lots of justifications implicit in the Constitution's text for one route or another, but none is definitive. And if power goes unchecked, it's harder to check the exercise of the same power by a different person later. Drawing clear boundaries around the vesting clauses—keeping each branch in their respective sandbox—is one mechanism for checking and separating. We will return to the difference between law execution and lawmaking in more detail when we talk about the president's powers under Article II. For now, the long and short of the meaning of *legislative* under the vesting clause of Article I is that the president makes laws too.

In 1952, the court wasn't so willing to bless Truman's broad exercise of presidential power. In that case—known as *Youngstown Sheet & Tube Co. v. Sawyer*—the justices issued seven separate opinions, which most scholars summarize into four distinct views of the line between legislating and executing. The first theory, reflected in the majority opinion by Justice Hugo Black, is that the president can act only if there is clear constitutional or statutory authority. Think of a police officer. She can ticket someone for driving at 65 mph if the speed limit is 55, but she can't issue a ticket for driving 65 if the limit is 70. The speed limit is established by the legislature. It's a rule that applies to everyone, prospectively, from the time it is created. The police enforce that law. Likewise, theory one goes, Congress creates binding policies and the president carries them out. Vesting means exclusivity—not sharing.

The second theory is that the president can do what he wants so long as it doesn't actually step on the toes of another branch. Is taking over a steel mill creating a new law? If not—if what the president was doing wasn't really lawmaking—then Congress has no right to complain. In a concurring opinion, Justice William Douglas agreed that Truman acted unconstitutionally but not because he exercised legislative power. Rather, by taking this action, the president was spending money that wasn't authorized by Congress. This view recognizes that the president has implied powers. The Constitution inevitably leaves voids, and they need to be filled so the presidency can function.

The third theory agrees that the president has implied powers, but if Congress contradicts them by statute—even by implication—the president loses that battle. This opinion, authored by Justice Robert Jackson, is perhaps the most famous accounting of the president's powers vis-à-vis Congress. But it leaves many questions unanswered—and thus a lot of gray area for judges to fill in. How does one know when Congress *impliedly* contradicts what the president is doing?

The fourth view holds up executive power above that of Congress, full stop.[5] It seems to put the presidency above the other branches too by confining the judiciary's power to check a president if a case reaches the courts. Chief Justice John Roberts may have embraced this theme of presidential power in *Trump v. Hawaii*. He ignored Trump's public statements regarding the so-called travel ban, which limits individuals' entry into the United States if they are from certain countries (which happened to have a large percentage of Muslims). So long as at least one stated rationale for the president's action on immigration is legitimate, Roberts therefore indicated, it is likely constitutional. Whether the ban violates other parts of the Constitution—such as the due process or Equal Protection clauses—was beside the point. Roberts erected a high barrier for challenging presidential actions around immigration.[6]

Somewhat incredibly, *all* four views from *Youngstown Sheet & Tube* can be found sprinkled in later Supreme Court cases, underscoring how judicial philosophy matters. A group of people can agree on one thing in 1952, and a different group of people can take an entirely different view in 2019.

In the early 1970s, for example, President Richard Nixon took money appropriated by Congress, impounded it, and refused to spend it—which was arguably an abdication of his obligation to take care that the laws are faithfully executed. Under theory one of *Youngstown Sheet & Tube*, this was unconstitutional, as the president can't impound money without particular constitutional or statutory authority. Under theory two, impoundment is okay unless it interferes with the power of Congress—a conflict that courts get to decide. Under theory three, impoundment is an implied power that the president can exercise unless Congress says no, which it did with the Impoundment Control Act of 1974. Yet under theory four, the president has implied power to impound money. So we have four theories—two giving Nixon the constitutional thumbs-up, and two giving him a thumbs-down. The Constitution, in short, is not set in stone. There is no singularly proper way to read it, which has massive implications for generations to follow.

Affirmative Powers: Taxing and Spending

Under the Articles of Confederation—the blueprint for American government prior to the Constitution—the federal government had very limited powers. It had no power to tax, and therefore no money to spend.

The Constitution changed that by allowing Congress to "lay and collect Taxes, Duties, Imposts and Excises, to pay the Debts and provide for the common Defence and general Welfare of the United States."[7] Today, one of the biggest gripes people have about the federal government is that it taxes and spends too much.

The Supreme Court long ago construed the taxing-and-spending powers broadly—meaning that Congress can use them so long as it does not violate some other provision of the Constitution.[8] Congress is not allowed to tax only white people, for example, as it would violate the Equal Protection Clause, which we will discuss in chapter 8. Otherwise, Congress can decide for itself whether a tax or an expenditure benefits the "general welfare."[9] Congress's power to tax formed the basis of the Supreme Court's 5–4 decision to uphold the constitutionality of the "individual mandate" in the Patient Protection and Affordable Care Act, i.e., the penalty it places on people who don't buy health insurance. Congress has "influence even in areas where it cannot directly regulate," explained Chief Justice Roberts, and the Obamacare mandate "looks like tax."[10]

This broad reading of Congress's ability to tax and spend for the general welfare makes it possible for Congress to impose taxes for reasons other than to raise money. Congress can pass laws that require people to turn money over to the federal government so that it can achieve other policy objectives—such as regulating firearms by requiring dealers to pay an annual tax, for example.[11] The Supreme Court has declared that "[i]n considering whether a particular expenditure is intended to serve general public purposes"—i.e., the general welfare outlined in Article I— "Courts should defer substantially to the judgment of Congress."[12]

The Supreme Court once determined that Congress could pass a statute directing the secretary of transportation to withhold federal highway funds from states where the drinking age was under twenty-one. "We can readily conclude that the provision is designed to serve the general welfare," the court wrote, as "Congress found that the differing drinking ages in the States created particular incentives for young persons to combine their desire to drink with their ability to drive, and that this interstate problem required a national solution."[13]

It didn't have to go this way. The court could have read the taxing-and-spending power more narrowly, limiting it, for example, to revenue raising and inherently federal spending (which the drinking age doesn't seem to entail). Like many other battles around constitutional language, this one does not involve lines drawn by the text itself. The text is silent. Opposition camps cluster around other battle lines, such as the power of the states versus that of the federal government, the dangers of underage drinking versus the ability of individual states to regulate themselves, the ability of Congress to construe its own general-welfare power versus looking to an independent source of that definition, and so on.

Oftentimes, which factors matter *to you* most are what determine which side you are on in a constitutional case—not the plain language of the Constitution. So when people talk about the benefits and downsides of appointing judges who will rely on policy judgments rather than on the Constitution's plain text and tradition, they are setting up a false dichotomy. You now know why.

The Big Enchiladas: Regulating Commerce and the Necessary and Proper Clause

In defending Obamacare, the government also argued that the individual mandate was legal under Congress's powers, first, to "regulate Commerce" and second, to "make all laws which shall be necessary and proper for carrying into Execution the foregoing Powers." I call these the big enchiladas because they together form the basis for a significant exercise of nationwide power by the US Congress—power that would otherwise be left to the individual states.

Let's start with the Necessary and Proper Clause of the Constitution. In a case called *McCulloch v. Maryland*, the Supreme Court decided that Congress has lots of implied power under the Constitution—including the power to create a national bank of the United States, which the states could not tax or regulate. Keep in mind that in 1819, there was a power struggle going on between the newly formed federal government, barely thirty years old, and the states.[14] States had adopted laws taxing the US bank or banning it within state borders. Maryland's attempt to tax the US bank reached the Supreme Court. Chief Justice John Marshall took the opportunity to pontificate on the powers of Congress to create the bank in the first place.

Justice Marshall pulled out a tool of constitutional interpretation that judges rely on to this day: invoking historical experience as a gloss on what the Constitution means. Because Congress created the bank after much debate, he reasoned, the bank was probably valid. Of course, the use of history is an interpretative tool like any other tool—not one required by the Constitution but one that can have a profound impact on outcomes. "[T]o contain an accurate detail of all the subdivisions," Marshall explained, a Constitution "would partake of the prolixity of a legal code, and could scarcely be embraced by the human mind."[15] In other words, Chief Justice Marshall pointed out as early as 1819 that the Constitution leaves lots of things unsaid and judges must fill in the blanks.

Marshall went on to invoke the Necessary and Proper Clause to justify a broad reading of congressional power that enables an old document to adapt to modern challenges. In his view, Congress must act within the other limits of the Constitution, and consistent with its "spirit"—an approach to constitutional interpretation that looks to its underlying values and objectives as well as its plain language.

Marshall could have instead looked to the word *necessary*—as in "required" or "essential"—and decided that a federal bank would be constitutional only if it was essential. Of course, what is and is not essential is itself a squishy question. But to this day, the Supreme Court has mostly equated *necessary* with *useful*—not essential. This more flexible reading of the term has enabled Congress to do things like create the vast administrative bureaucracy—i.e., federal agencies—that sprawls across Washington, DC, among many other things.[16] Marshall construed the word *necessary* to give Congress and judges lots of leeway on the rationale that it "is made in a constitution, intended to endure for ages to come, and consequently, to be adapted to the various crises of human affairs."[17]

Now back to Obamacare. Remember, it requires insurance companies to provide coverage regardless of preexisting conditions and forbids them from capping lifetime payments.[18] Without the individual mandate, these requirements could have set up a lose-lose proposition for insurers. People would just wait to get insurance until they got sick.[19] The statute would still protect them against insurance companies cutting off benefits. And people could achieve this benefit without paying premiums into the system, which insurance companies need in order to afford the statute's mandates in the first place.

So would Marshall's construction of the Necessary and Proper Clause authorize the individual mandate? One can certainly argue that it's useful for creating a health care system with greater access. Enhancing health insurance coverage for all Americans is also arguably within Congress's broad general welfare powers to do. In an opinion written by Chief Justice Roberts, however, a 5–4 majority of the court said no—and put a caveat on the Necessary and Proper Clause that clipped Congress's wings. Congress can't use the necessary-and-proper power, the court decided, unless it's tied to *another* power in Article I. The necessary-and-proper power could be "added on" to another power—like a piggyback power—but it isn't a stand-alone source of congressional power to do things.[20] (I raise this as a reminder that conservative and progressive justices alike make brand-new laws—or reverse old laws—under the Constitution.)

Next, let's turn to the Commerce Clause, which is also a biggie. It's how Congress has found its way to passing laws creating federal crimes, protecting civil rights, staving off monopolies, and regulating how people can invest their own money, among many other things. The Supreme Court's construction of the Commerce Clause has fluctuated over the years, from restrictive to expansive and back again. In the Obamacare case, the majority held that the Commerce Clause did not authorize the individual mandate (the requirement that individuals pay into the system), although it did give Congress the power to tell the insurance companies what to do.

Let's start with a close read of the Commerce Clause. Ask yourself: Where is the squishy language, and what is the best way to give it meaning? Consider *commerce*. Our friend Chief Justice Marshall began that very conversation nearly a hundred years ago in a case called *Gibbons v. Ogden*.[21] New York had given two guys a monopoly to operate steamboats in New York State waters. A competitor jumped in with his own ferry, claiming that a federal law licensed him to operate "vessels in the coasting trade," and that the federal law overrode the monopoly allowed under New York law. New York's courts ruled for the monopoly, and the Supreme Court reversed the decision—finding that the federal law was the boss, so the competitor could run his ferry without worrying about the state law monopoly. To achieve this, Marshall construed *commerce* to mean not just buying and selling commodities, but also "commercial intercourse," including the navigation of boats.

After the Civil War, however, the Supreme Court started invalidating legislation under the Commerce Clause. During this period, the court was dominated by people who believed strongly in an unregulated economy. To tamp down on Congress's power, the court drew what looked like arbitrary distinctions between *early* stages of commerce and *later* stages. To strike down wage and hour legislation for coal miners, for example, it reasoned that "[p]lainly, the incidents leading up to and culminating in the mining of coal do not constitute . . . intercourse" for the purposes of trade. "The employment of men, the fixing of their wages, hours of labor and working condition . . . constitute intercourse for the purposes of production, not of trade."[22] In a word . . . *huh?* The difference between production on the one hand (not okay for Congress to regulate) and trade (good to go) can hardly be drawn from the text of the Commerce Clause itself.

So imagine that Congress passes a criminal statute that makes petty theft a federal felony (meaning the perpetrator could land in jail for a year or more) if the person doing the stealing has a firearm. Usually theft within state borders is handled by state law and state courts. A seventeen-year-old kid robs a local convenience store in Orlando. He is arrested in the parking lot with a gun in his jacket and charged with a federal crime, which carries a longer potential prison sentence. Did Congress have the power to pass the law he was charged under to the extent that it converts basic theft into a federal crime? Well, the gun came from out of state and the store sold imported beer. That's "trade," right? So even though the robbery occurred entirely within Florida and the money was immediately returned to the store owner, the kid was charged with a federal crime.[23] This is a pretty vast conceptualization of Congress's power over commerce.

The rub with the Commerce Clause is that courts cannot legitimately read it to capture *everything* that has a tangential impact on commerce; that would leave little for the states to regulate. But sometimes Congress passes national legislation that's not expressly authorized in the Constitution but is good for the country. Such power is often found in the Commerce Clause. We want Congress to have enough leverage over national commerce to do good things, but not so much that its power becomes unlimited. Drawing meaningful and intellectually honest limitations is hard.

For a chunk of the twentieth century, the Supreme Court again tolerated an expansive view of Congress's power on the theory that all stages of business are fair game. As a result, Congress pretty much did what it wanted for several decades. To many, this was a good thing. Congress passed the Civil Rights Act of 1964, which prohibits private employers from discriminating on the basis of race, gender, or religion. The government is already prohibited from engaging in such discrimination under the Constitution itself. But the Supreme Court held that the Equal Protection Clause and other parts of the Bill of Rights don't bind private parties, so companies were free to discriminate prior to 1964. The court upheld the Civil Rights Act on the rationale that "voluminous testimony [before Congress] presents overwhelming evidence that discrimination by hotels and motels impedes interstate travel."[24] This interpretation—that people traveling from one state to another to purchase time in a hotel room is in fact participating in commerce—was key.

The hands-off approach to the Commerce Clause lasted until 1995, when the court again narrowed its definition of *commerce*, at least for certain things. In a case called *United States v. Lopez*, for example, the court held that Congress could *not* use the Commerce Clause to pass a law prohibiting people from carrying firearms within one thousand feet of a school.[25] And with the Affordable Care Act, the Supreme Court rejected the government's attempt to justify the law using the Commerce Clause. It held that Congress could use the Commerce Clause only to regulate *activity*. Regulating *inactivity*—such as a decision *not* to purchase health insurance—was off-limits. This distinction was new. But as the dissenting justices argued, getting uninsured medical care in emergency rooms *does* constitute "activity." And Congress "estimated that the cost of uncompensated care raises family health insurance premiums, on average, by over $1,000 per year."[26] Why wasn't that price tag treated as commerce? Given the squishiness of the Commerce Clause, why didn't the court just bow out and have Congress's back on this one? The answer probably has something to do with the fact that judges are people with their own views on what the Constitution *should* say.

Keeping Tabs on the Executive: Emoluments and Impeachment

Article I also has some provisions that allow Congress to keep tabs on the other branches. These are summarized in the separation-of-powers chart contained in chapter 1. Here's a bit on two other ones: the Emoluments Clause and the impeachment power.

The Emoluments Clause states that "no Person holding any Office of Profit or Trust under them, shall, without the Consent of Congress, accept of any present, Emolument, Office, or Title, of any kind whatever, from any King, Prince, or foreign State."[27] The Constitution therefore allows Congress to consent to emoluments. It doesn't ban them outright. But without the consent of Congress, they are a no-go.

It is impossible to talk about the Emoluments Clause without picking on President Trump. There's certainly money to be made from his many private holdings bearing the Trump brand, and he knows it. With his predecessors, the emoluments issue didn't come up because they adhered to soft norms of financial disclosure and divestiture of holdings in order to avoid conflicts or perceived conflicts of interest.

Team Trump has tried to get around the Emoluments Clause by arguing that the term *present* doesn't mean income from foreign governments who book stays at one of Trump's hotels. Can this be correct? For starters, we might look to a common definition of the noun *present*—a thing given to someone as a gift. This definition might exclude commercial transactions such as securing a place to sleep for the night in exchange for money. After all, as a standard political gift at the time of the Constitution's founding, Louis XVI offered a portrait surrounded by diamonds, which was perceived as a potential bribe.[28] Paying to stay at a commercial hotel is not the logical equivalent of diamonds.

But if we add to the common definition of *present* the idea of a benefit or advantage—which is a reasonable addition from a plain-language perspective—Trump's hotel profits become problematic. After all, the clause itself forbids the acceptance of "any present, Emolument . . . *of any kind whatever*" (emphasis mine). The language suggests that the terms *present* and *emolument* are to be broadly construed—no exceptions. It may count, then, if foreign diplomats seek to curry favor with the president by choosing Trump's hotel over other hotels in Washington, DC, and Trump personally stands to profit from that choice.[29]

The practical answer to the meaning of *present* might be "let's just let the courts decide." If we pick the right judges, who are fair and impartial and don't politicize their role, we can rely on them to read the language properly. There are a few problems with this solution, as we will discuss in chapter 4. Because the Constitution limits judicial power to Article III's sandbox, Supreme Court case law over the course of decades has developed so as to ensure that only parties with a proverbial broken arm can bring such a lawsuit, not just a generically concerned—but not individually injured—citizen.

Concerned citizens must go to Congress, but it already has a law on the books called the Foreign Gifts and Decorations Act. Since its enactment in 1966, the law and its regulations have provided guidance on what types of gifts federal officers or employees can receive. Violations carry up to a $5,000 penalty.[30] During much of the Trump presidency, Congress has been on the sidelines when it comes to the Emoluments Clause and has failed to legislate a requirement that presidents release their tax returns to the public. Moreover, Congress has a lot on its plate; constituents have many pressing concerns that they expect elected officials to address—a president's conflicts of interest may be so far down the priority list that galvanizing a coalition of enough members of Congress to make a concrete difference on this issue becomes a lofty—if not impractical—goal.

Thus, the federal courts appear to offer the most viable avenue for getting today's presidents to pay attention to the Emoluments Clause.[31] Let's assume that a proper plaintiff is found, and that after months of hard-fought and expensive litigation, a judge issues a ruling that President Trump has violated the Emoluments Clause by retaining a financial interest in his DC hotel while in office. Maybe the Trump organization would divest itself of everything going forward. But Trump could also refuse to comply with the order on the theory that it's unconstitutional, or comply very narrowly—leaving many of his conflicts of interest in place unless and until more litigation is won against him.

The question lingering over the Emoluments Clause is whether it has any meaning today. If the term *present* doesn't include more modern means of wealth transfer, we might as well put a red line through this part of the Constitution. That's because if the Emoluments Clause is not enforced, it is meaningless, and likely unenforceable the next time a president decides to push the limits of what it could mean.

Last, a few words about impeachment. The ultimate check on any employee—including the president—is termination of employment. Congress gets to fire the president by impeachment. Some people believe that any other sort of process such as a criminal indictment and possibly a jury trial—would be unconstitutional, even if a president clearly committed offenses that amount to crimes under state or federal laws.[32] There are few hard-and-fast rules in the Constitution, but there is little question that the framers wanted to counteract corruption by officeholders.[33] If a criminal indictment is necessary to effectuate that overall objective, the counterargument goes, so be it.

Note that Congress can impeach a number of different people— "[t]he President, Vice President and all civil Officers of the United States."[34] The House of Representatives has the actual power to impeach, which basically means that it can issue charges that go to a quasi-trial in the Senate. For presidents Nixon and Clinton, things went beyond the articles of impeachment. Nixon resigned when it became clear that he would lose in the Senate. In Clinton's case, the Senate acquitted him.[35]

The Constitution provides the standard for impeachment: "high Crimes and Misdemeanors." But it provides no definitions. A narrow view of this language might tie the Impeachment Clause to actual crimes—that is, Congress can only impeach a person if he could be tried and convicted in court under a statute or other law that makes what he did a crime. But impeachment is a political decision—so Congress decides what counts.[36]

The Constitution doesn't give much guidance about how an impeachment process must go. We know that two-thirds of the Senate must agree to convict. And if the president is the subject, the Constitution makes clear that the chief justice of the Supreme Court presides over the process. For impeachment of other officers, the Constitution is silent. There are lots more unanswered questions here. Can the Senate select a representative number of senators to hear the evidence submitted during the impeachment trial—much like a jury? Does the evidence submitted to the Senate have to comply with some set of rules to ensure that it is reliable and accurate (versus the dreaded "fake news")? Must the proceeding be public? And if so, should cameras be allowed? In making these calls, how much does Congress have to adhere to historical practice? President Clinton's impeachment trial was conducted behind closed doors.[37] And the one time the Supreme Court was asked to weigh in on these kinds of questions, it refused, reasoning that the topic was too political for the courts.[38]

But imagine a hypothetical scenario under which a president was quietly backed by a multibillionaire. That person pays off more than one-third of the Senate and tells them to vote against impeachment no matter how deep the corruption in the White House. Everyone knows about the illegal payments. The voters can't do anything until the next election, which could be years away. The DOJ does nothing to investigate or prosecute the bad deeds because the president is in charge of the executive branch and, therefore, the DOJ. Should the courts refuse to do anything on the vague theory that it's all too political?

The no response would again find support in the notion that the Constitution must be enforced for it to have any meaning. If it takes something other than impeachment to achieve that with respect to a particular president, the integrity of government is worth it. But the DOJ has taken the written position that a criminal trial of a sitting president would be unconstitutional. Both special counsels who investigated President Nixon (a Republican) and President Clinton (a Democrat) disagreed. In all likelihood, it is Congress that will—and should—remain the sole cop on the block when it comes to holding presidents accountable for wrongdoing between elections. And Congress answers to the voters. So if accountability is to be had at the upper levels of the executive branch, individual voters need to care enough to make that urgency clear to their elected representatives.

CHAPTER 3

The (Real) Powers of the President: No More Kings

Note, again, there's no definition of executive power.

Article II, Section 1.

The **executive Power shall be vested in a President** of the United States of America.

How does this jive with Congress's war power?

Section 2.

The President **shall be Commander in Chief of the Army and Navy of the United States**, and of the Militia of the several States, when called into the actual Service of the United States; . . . and he shall have **Power to Grant Reprieves and Pardons** for Offences against the United States, except in Cases of Impeachment.

Is the pardon power unlimited under this language?

He shall have Power, by and with the Advice and Consent of the Senate, to **make Treaties, provided two thirds of the Senators present concur**; and he shall nominate, and by and with the Advice and Consent of the Senate, **shall appoint** Ambassadors, other public Ministers and Consuls, Judges of the supreme Court, and all other Officers of the United States . . . but the Congress may by Law vest the Appointment of such inferior Officers, as they think

What does *Treaties* mean? And can the president do treaty-like things without Congress?

Says nothing about removal, although it's a critical presidential management tool.

proper, in the President alone, in the Courts of Law, or in the Heads of Departments.

Section 3.

Shall suggests the take care prerogative is mandatory.

[H]e **shall take care that the laws be faithfully executed**, and shall commission all the Officers of the United States.

Section 4.

Recall chapter 2: Does this imply immunity from criminal process?

The President, Vice President and all Civil Officers of the United States, shall be removed from Office on **Impeachment** for and Conviction of, Treason, Bribery, or other **high Crimes and Misdemeanors**.

We don't have a king. But the president can do a lot.

The core function of the executive branch is to execute the laws—to identify individuals who violate laws passed by Congress, for example, and to prosecute those individuals in courts. Although the courts exist to ensure that the process is fair, the decision whether to investigate, arrest, and prosecute someone for allegedly violating laws rests exclusively within the executive branch. The Constitution thus gives the executive relatively extraordinary power to affect the liberty of specific individuals. And importantly, Article II's mandate that the president take care to execute the laws faithfully implies that the president must have enough authority to manage those who exercise executive authority. There are more than seventy-three federal agencies with law enforcement power.[1] The thousands of people employed by those agencies ultimately answer to one person: the president.

The president gets to do even more hefty things. He has the exclusive power to issue pardons for federal crimes; he can make treaties with the advice and consent of the Senate; and he is "Commander in Chief of the Army and Navy of the United States, and of the Militia of the several States."[2] The president can appoint executive branch officers—he can pick and choose who gets hired to make important decisions within the scope of executive power and, impliedly, he can remove officers at will in order to effectuate his own political agenda (and for other reasons). The president has other implied powers: he can also order military action and engage in foreign policy on behalf of the United States, for example, even though neither of these functions is spelled out in the Constitution.

Thus, although the president is not a king, nobody is directly above him in the chain of command either. Preventing American presidents from amassing the power of a king requires that the other two branches of government—Congress and the courts—be vigilant in checking the power that the president does have. Courts can exercise their checking function only in connection with individual cases. They have no say as to whether, and if so which, individual cases come before them. As a consequence, Congress must embrace its vital oversight role if "We the People" are to keep presidential power in check.

Executive Power and the Take Care Clause

To understand the president's "executive" powers, let's start by asking a basic question: How does a person land in jail?

First off, someone had to pass a law. Suppose that someone is the US Congress. And suppose the law it passes states that "[w]hoever knowingly develops, produces, stockpiles, transfers, acquires, retains, or possesses any biological agent toxin . . . shall be fined . . . or imprisoned for life or any term of years, or both.[3] The law does not mention any one individual by name. It applies to everyone—"[w]hoever," to be precise. It's a general, prospective rule that Congress enacted pursuant to its legislative power under Article I.

Now let's say John Doe violates the law by stockpiling anthrax in his garage. The FBI is tipped off, gets a warrant to search his residence (more on that later), and arrests him. The FBI is part of the executive branch. It is a subentity of the DOJ.

Next, the prosecutor brings an indictment—a piece of paper containing criminal charges—before the grand jury. A grand jury is a group of individuals tasked with considering documents, testimony, and other evidence presented by prosecutors regarding an individual or entity's bad deeds, and deciding whether that party should be charged with a crime. It has more members than a regular jury, which decides facts.[4] The grand jury has the power to subpoena documents and testimony—to force people to show up and explain what they know, but without an attorney present. If a subpoena recipient refuses to comply, she can be sent to jail until she changes her mind. So without that particular "cop on the block" (i.e., the subpoena power), nobody would bother to heed the grand jury's requests, the prosecutor couldn't collect the evidence she needs to try and convict bad guys, and the streets would be less safe as a result of criminals running around with the knowledge that they can't really be held accountable.

Let's assume that the grand jury determines that there is probable cause to indict John for violating Congress's statute banning the stockpiling of chemical weapons such as anthrax.

John is prosecuted for that crime in court. The prosecutor is part of the executive branch—an assistant US attorney employed by the DOJ, to be precise. The jury (a "petit" jury, which is smaller than a grand jury and serves a different role of convicting or acquitting a defendant after a trial) sits in a federal courtroom. A federal judge, a member of Article III's judicial branch, presides over the trial. The trial's function is to resolve what amounts to an individual dispute between the government (represented by the DOJ) and John Doe. The prosecutors present much of the same evidence that went to the grand jury. And maybe more. That's because the standard for conviction—the rubric against which the petit jury must weigh the government's evidence—is much higher at trial. Instead of probable cause, the jury must determine that the evidence presented by the prosecution is beyond a reasonable doubt that John violated the statute. John is convicted.

John goes to prison. He is escorted there by a US marshal, a member of another federal law enforcement agency within the DOJ and thus within the president's chain of command. The Federal Bureau of Prisons, still another arm of the executive branch, runs the prison.[5]

We can conclude from this scenario that the executive branch does a lot. And that Congress doesn't do much. Congress essentially sets the toy boat to sail on the pond (by passing a law). Then, for the most part, Congress is done. It can't take action against particular individuals. Congress *needs* the executive branch to bring individual cases. Without police and prosecutors, laws passed by the legislature are nothing more than words on a page.[6]

The president must take care that the laws are faithfully executed. In Article II, the Constitution says *shall*; it does not say *may*. But such apparent rhetorical clarity quickly confronts a roadblock. What does *taking care* mean? We know that Congress creates federal laws. We also know from our hypothetical that the executive investigates, makes arrests, prosecutes, and jails those convicted of violating the laws. Whatever law execution is, therefore, it must include those steps in the criminal justice process—because Congress expressly *cannot* do them in the president's stead.

But it's unreasonable to suggest that *shall* necessarily requires that the executive branch prosecute *every single conceivable* violation of the laws. Indeed, one reason we might elect a particular presidential candidate over others is that she promises to be tough—or relatively lax—on a particular category of crime. Upon taking office in 1981, for example, Ronald Reagan continued President Nixon's war on drugs initiative. Instead of worrying out drug suppliers from other countries, he deliberately focused on the internal *demand* for drugs, promising to arrest, prosecute, and jail more users on the rationale that "[i]t's far more effective if you take the customers away than if you try to take the drugs away from those who want to be customers." Some criticized Reagan's zero-tolerance policies as having a racially discriminatory impact, but there is little question that it produced more drug arrests, convictions, and incarcerations—the very kinds of things that the executive branch controls.[7]

By contrast, when President Bill Clinton took office, he was criticized for allegedly planning to "effectively abandon leadership of America's anti-drug effort," "cut federal enforcement personnel," and "seek to pour over $300 million more into a national drug treatment system" instead of prosecuting drug crimes.[8] Yet as with Nixon and Reagan, Clinton's decisions regarding drug-enforcement priorities fell squarely within the president's constitutional prerogative. Despite its mandatory language, the Take Care Clause reasonably contemplates that presidents will decide which crimes—and alleged violators—should be the focus of law enforcement efforts.

But does that mean that the president can *completely ignore* an act of Congress that declares certain behavior unlawful (or regulates private conduct in some other way)? Can the president simply decide that a statute is dumb or immoral and refuse to enforce it entirely, rendering it dead? Some scholars argue no: "In grammatical form, the Take Care Clause is an imperative: it instructs or admonishes the President to 'take care.'" Among other sources, they cite in support the "1828 edition of Noah Webster's American Dictionary of the English Language," which "explains the meaning of the noun 'care' as including '[c]aution; a looking to; regard, attention, or heed.'" Thus, the argument continues, "[t]he Take Care Clause is . . . naturally read as an instruction or command to the President to put the laws into effect, or at least to see that they are put into effect, 'without failure' and 'exactly.'" What this means is that "the President cannot suspend the law of the land at his whim, as British Kings had."[9] To do so would be akin to giving the legislative branch the proverbial finger—to treat it as if its role were constitutionally irrelevant.

President Barack Obama's Deferred Action for Childhood Arrivals program was criticized for that very reason, i.e., for purportedly ignoring the president's take-care mandate while at the same time undermining the rule of law established by Congress. For years, federal immigration officials lacked clear guidance from Congress regarding what to do about so-called DREAMers—people who were brought to the United States as children by their parents—in light of the laws banning the unauthorized entry of people across the United States border. First introduced in 2001, the DREAM Act bill would have enabled permanent residency for certain people within the DREAMer umbrella. To date, the bill has been introduced every year since 2001 and has repeatedly been killed.[10]

In the wake of congressional inaction, Obama in 2012 issued a memorandum called "Exercising Prosecutorial Discretion with Respect to Individuals Who Came to the United States as Children."[11] As its title suggests, the memo set forth criteria for the Department of Homeland Security to employ in deciding whether to institute removal proceedings for DREAMers. The rationale for declining prosecution was that "[a]s a general matter, these individuals lacked the intent to violate the law." The memo went further, however, and gave "deferred action" to certain applicants, which comes with the government's authorization that they can work, a grant that is not a clear exercise of prosecutorial discretion.

But the memo's primary justification for not enforcing immigration laws against DREAMers was that those who execute the law (i.e., people answerable to POTUS—which is shorthand for president of the United States) get to decide whom to prosecute. We all understand this concept from basic life experience; the cop hiding in the bushes gets to decide which of several motorists to pull over for speeding. In offering a plea deal to a first-time heroin possessor, the prosecutor gets to decide whether to include parole or jail time. Same goes for a sitting president's exercise of the executive power.

Pragmatically speaking, therefore, it is impossible to view the Take Care Clause as mandating 100 percent enforcement of all crimes for all wrongdoers. The resources do not exist to implement such a mandate. There are a finite number of law enforcement agents and prosecutors to go around. The Constitution's use of the word *shall* can't mean *shall* in the very strictest sense.

At a minimum, scholars argue "that the President has no duty to enforce statutory law or treaty provisions that he reasonably and in good faith considers to be unconstitutional."[12] This is undoubtedly correct. The Constitution is the highest law of the land. A federal statute that required the FBI to jail anyone who tweets would violate multiple provisions of the Constitution, including the First Amendment and the due process clause. The president would be duty bound to refuse to enforce it.

A more realistic approach to prosecutorial discretion under the Take Care Clause might be to acknowledge that, although presidents can decide not to prosecute on a case-by-case basis, they must at least prosecute *some* people under every law that they are required to execute. In other words, the president cannot categorically refuse to enforce an act of Congress, but he can make decisions within that outer boundary.

Of course, the question then becomes how many prosecutions are required in order to satisfy this view of the separation of powers. One? Ten? A hundred? Would the president need to pursue a thousand prosecutions to avoid a categorical constitutional failure to enforce a criminal law? To engage in this mathematical exercise seems ridiculous on its face—and completely at odds with any reasonable meaning of the words *take care*, which can't be about counting heads.

Other scholars argue that "[t]he core purposes of prosecutorial discretion—justice, mercy, and societal utility—all necessarily require the President to make independent judgments about the wisdom of prosecution," particularly when it comes to deprivations of liberty. This competing idea of prosecutorial discretion indicates that we elect presidents with the understanding that they will make independent decisions about law enforcement—including whom to prosecute or not prosecute. That's what elections are for.

All told, there is no clear answer on how to read the Take Care Clause. Suffice it to say that when headlines holler, "The President Violated the Constitution," readers can be wary. Like most constitutional issues, the meaning of executive power is not black-and-white—but many variances of gray.

Agencies

A few words about federal agencies are in order here. Agencies are technically part of the executive branch—and thus within the president's chain of command. Agencies are extraordinarily important in American life, yet few people have any clue what they do, how they get the power to do what they do, and how the Constitution makes sure they are held accountable. Agencies do what all three branches do: they create laws, they enforce laws, and they adjudicate laws. They make many, many more laws than Congress does, yet the people who run agencies are not elected. They decide individual disputes, but they are not created under

Article III, and the jurisdictional sandbox rules for courts don't apply to them. They enforce laws too—kind of like prosecutors but without the criminal implications (i.e., they can't send people to jail). They do all three things, yet there is no fourth, "hybrid" branch of government in the Constitution.

It turns out that a number of lawsuits were filed in the federal courts nearly a century ago that complained about newfound agencies having too much power that rightfully belonged to the other branches. The Supreme Court found ways to condone them. And even a solidly conservative Supreme Court would be hard-pressed to dismember the entire administrative bureaucracy, save for its functions that are exclusively executive in nature. Practically speaking, it just wouldn't be feasible. Congress can't do it all. It doesn't have the capacity, the expertise, or the political willpower. It's easier to shrug off work to an agency, which is politically accountable via the president (because voters don't fully understand that a vote for president is a vote for his top officials in federal agencies too—and those people aren't even chosen until after the election).

Because the president appoints heads of agencies under Article II, and has the implied power to remove them, agencies answer to the president. But Congress creates agencies pursuant to the Necessary and Proper Clause. Most agencies get their very own creation statute. Congress also gives agencies their powers. The Environmental Protection Agency has the power to enforce the Clean Air Act, for example, but not the power to enforce the Federal Trade Commission Act; Congress gave that power to the Federal Trade Commission alone.

So, imagine that Congress passes a statute—let's call it the National Internet Crimes Against Children Act (NICAC)—which directs the Federal Communications Commission (FCC) to implement a national strategy for preventing online child exploitation and for protecting children from online sexual predators. The NICAC is full of policy gaps.

The statute leaves it to the FCC to come up with the actual language spelling out the precise rules. The NICAC directs the FCC to work with a number of other agencies—such as the DOJ, the FBI, and the Department of Homeland Security's US Immigration and Customs Division—to formulate policies that take into account several related considerations, such as the needs of law enforcement, the legal expertise of agency officials involved in child pornography sent through the mail, collaboration with overseas regulators and law enforcement partners, and private-sector advancements in online technologies.

There are many possible reasons why Congress left blanks in the NICAC for the FCC to fill. It may be that the highly polarized legislature could not agree on the details of the policy, and its congressional supporters were aware that if anything was to be passed, the only way to do it would be with broad brushstrokes. Members could also have been eyeing the next election and realizing that taking a position on particular elements of a policy—such as banning or not banning certain kinds of online pornography—could prompt an outcry from industry, concerned parents, or some other constituent group, not to mention First Amendment litigation. Or Congress might have insufficient expertise to craft the highly specialized laws. Whatever the reason for the FCC's legislative assignment, the task is a daunting one.

One last global point about federal agencies, and it's an important one: there is a separation-of-powers problem with agencies enacting regulations—another thing that agencies do. Regulations are as forceful as laws passed by Congress itself. In this sense, a regulation is just another word for a law. To someone seeking to apply the Constitution's plain language, agencies' roles as lawmakers—as well as the laws that result from the regulatory process—are unconstitutional. The legislative power is vested in Congress, and the vesting clause does not hedge or equivocate. Justice Antonin Scalia rationalized it this way: when agencies pass regulations, they are not making laws—they are interpreting them, which is an executive function.[13] Of course, *interpret* is nowhere in the Constitution.

At the end of the day, it's a fact that agencies makes laws. So Congress effectively created a statutory "employee manual" for agencies to follow when they make laws. It was enacted in 1946 for the precise objective of keeping agencies from overreaching when they used their newly minted New Deal powers, and it is known as the Administrative Procedure Act (APA). The APA contains an elaborate process that agencies must follow when making laws (euphemistically known as rules or regulations) that have the same force as a statute passed by Congress. The idea behind the process is to give lots of advance notice of the rule to the public and to invite anyone who might have a stake in the rule to weigh in with written comments that are directed at the people within the agency responsible for drafting the rule.

Think again for a moment about the difference between policy and politics addressed in the introduction. Good policy is not purely ideological; it is formed by accounting for lots of information—different sides of the coin, so to speak—and reaching a decision that the policymakers conclude is the very best one, all things considered. An agency regulation reflecting such a policy decision will not be perfect, but maybe we can sleep at night knowing that agencies must at least make rules that are reasoned and supported by sound and comprehensive information—because the rules *have to be* under the APA.

There are numerous additional statutes that agencies must comply with before they can get regulations on the books. In fact, many scholars have bemoaned that so many statutory wickets bog down the process that "paralysis by analysis" ensues, and little gets done.[14] Suffice it to say that agencies are the tail wagging the federal government dog, yet relatively few people know much about what their powers are and how they are kept from going off the rails, so to speak.

Executive Orders

Alas, there is yet one more complicating factor in the seemingly straight-forward question of what it means to execute laws. The Trump presidency has made headlines around this wrinkle in the executive-versus-legislative power struggle: the executive order. The Constitution does not refer to executive orders and there is no statutory authority for them.[15] But historically, any writing by the president giving directives to subordinates constitutes an executive order. In 1873, President Ulysses S. Grant issued an executive order setting forth guidelines for issuing executive orders, which exists today in revised form.[16] The order must go to the Office of Management and Budget and then to the attorney general for approval before it's signed by the president.

Executive orders have the force of law—like statutes and regulations. The sources of their constitutional authority are our old friends the vesting clause and the Take Care Clause of Article II. Under a strict construction of the Constitution, executive and legislative power *must* mean different things. Yet presidents—long before Trump—have used executive orders to create binding rules of general application that govern future behavior (which is our working definition of law). Executive orders now number more than thirteen thousand. President Abraham Lincoln suspended the writ of habeas corpus and issued the Emancipation Proclamation by executive order (more on habeas later). President Dwight D. Eisenhower desegregated schools. Presidents John F. Kennedy and Lyndon B. Johnson barred racial discrimination in federal housing, hiring, and contracting.[17] There can be little question, therefore, that presidents have made laws by executive order without complying with Article I's bicameralism (two houses of Congress must approve) and presentment (the president must sign off) mandate.

Because the guidelines governing executive orders are not statutory or constitutional, presidents are free to ignore them. And presidents can amend or reverse predecessors' executive orders, as President Clinton did with President Reagan's executive order banning the use of federal funds for advocating abortion. Because—tongue-twister alert—the president is *theoretically* exercising executive power by issuing an executive order, Congress can amend the laws relating to an executive order. But the president can also veto any laws that override his executive orders. As was seen with the Trump immigration orders, which were initially stalled on constitutional grounds by federal courts, judges play an important role in making sure that presidents comply with the Constitution in issuing executive orders.

At the end of the day, Congress has a number of other ways to ping the executive branch if it impedes legislative powers. It can impeach the president who presided over the unconstitutional agency activity or an agency head, revoke the agency's legislative charter, hold hearings to find out what the agency is really up to and make a public hullabaloo, or tighten the agency's budget so there simply aren't enough resources for it to continue its bad deeds. Indeed, purse strings are how Congress checks a lot of what the federal bureaucracy does. Or Congress can do nothing. Congress can sit by and let things happen in the other branches that may be bad public policy, unlawful, or even unconstitutional. When Congress as Constitution cop is effectively off duty on its own accord, there is little voters can do other than blast members' offices with angry messages and, barring movement on that tactic, hold them accountable at the voting booth in the next election.

Appointment and Removal

A discussion of the president's power to appoint and remove officials warrants a bit of context regarding what it means to have a single person at the head of the executive branch. At the constitutional convention in Philadelphia in 1787, the delegates rejected the state of New Jersey's proposal for an executive council composed of multiple people. They instead chose a unitary executive, the theory being that a single president would be able to act swiftly, uniformly, and decisively. A unitary executive structure also meant a clear line of accountability. To quote President Harry Truman, if "the buck stops" with the president, then the public will know whom to blame if matters within the president's chain of command go awry.

And things do go awry. In December 2006, George W. Bush's DOJ ordered the dismissal of seven US attorneys, some of the federal government's top criminal prosecutors. The press was all over it. Congress conducted investigations into whether the dismissals were politically motivated. Many people were shocked by the apparent secrecy around how the decision to fire was made and by whom. Yet, as explained in this section of the book, the Constitution is clear: President Bush acted within his constitutional authority in firing these people, even if the motivation was purely political.[18]

President Nixon had tried the same maneuver more than thirty years prior.[19] Attorney General Elliot Richardson appointed an independent special prosecutor to investigate the June 1972 break-in at the Watergate Hotel, during which five Nixon affiliates were caught trying to bug the headquarters of the Democratic National Committee. When the special prosecutor, Archibald Cox, issued a subpoena to Nixon for copies of his taped conversations from the Oval Office, the president refused to comply. An attempt to negotiate a compromise with Cox failed. Nixon ordered Richardson to fire him. Richardson refused, resigning in protest, so Nixon ordered Deputy Attorney General William Ruckelshaus to fire Cox. Ruckelshaus likewise refused and resigned. Nixon then turned to the solicitor general Robert Bork, who finally complied. In a dramatic next act, the White House sent in FBI agents to seal off the offices of Cox, Richardson, and Ruckelshaus.[20]

After this Saturday Night Massacre, public and congressional opinion shifted against the president, and talk of impeachment increased. Relenting to pressure, Nixon appointed a new special prosecutor, Leon Jaworski, who ultimately obtained the tapes after taking the issue to the Supreme Court, which ruled against Nixon's claims of executive privilege. Nixon resigned on August 8, 1974.

Nixon lost the ultimate power struggle—but not because he acted unconstitutionally. Donald Trump dismissed Acting Attorney General Sally Yates for refusing to enforce his controversial travel ban executive order. He also fired FBI Director James Comey. Yet like Bush and Nixon before him, Trump was acting within the purest of his *constitutional* prerogatives to do so (setting aside whether his possible *reasons* for doing so—i.e., hampering the special counsel's probe—separately constituted obstruction of justice). When the president fires a prosecutor, he pulls another crucial lever of presidential power: one lodged in the Appointments Clause.

Recall the ice-cream store hypothetical. The owner wants to run a successful business that turns a profit. To do that, he must establish a coherent structure of accountability, which includes mechanisms for rewarding good behavior and accounting for bad behavior. The very threat of removal keeps employees honest. But hiring decisions are crucial as well. In 2018, basketball player LeBron James signed a stunning $154 million contract with the LA Lakers, presumably because he was considered the best person for the job of helping win basketball games.[21] Although members of a president's cabinet don't make that kind of money, they do wield tremendous discretion to shape matters of national or international importance. A president picks his cabinet with an eye toward achieving his political and policy agenda. He wants people who will implement the objectives that he campaigned on—and do it effectively. Failing that, as for an ice-cream shop owner, the president needs to be able to fire his team if they are not performing.

For its part, the Constitution contains few clues as to what the framers intended the executive apparatus to look like beyond the president and the vice president. What the plain text does envision are executive departments headed by "principal Officers" who are appointed exclusively by the president with the advice and consent of the Senate.[22] The Constitution also allows the president to "require the Opinion, in writing, of the principal Officer in each of the executive Departments."[23] So the text contemplates that the federal government includes executive officials under the president.[24] It also links such officials to an "executive Department" and indicates that there will be a principal officer—"*[t]he* principal Officer*"* (emphasis mine)—in each department whom only the president can appoint. (In addition to "officers," the president appoints ambassadors and Supreme Court justices.)

The language of the Appointments Clause is comparatively straightforward, but not without glitches. Its meaning gets tricky when Congress mucks around with the president's ability to decide who will run the agencies it creates by statute. Keep in mind that any time an agency's name has the word *commission* in it—as in the Federal Trade Commission or the Securities and Exchange Commission—it means that in the statute creating the agency, Congress rejected the "unitary" boss design and instead established a panel to head the agency. In most cases, when Congress does this, it also includes limits on a new president's ability to appoint and remove members of that panel. If the idea is to let the ice-cream shop owner make the hiring and firing decisions that will best enhance his ability to run a successful business, Congress's structural novelties in this regard are a potential problem for the president's capacity to run the executive branch in the way she promised the electorate during the campaign.

Note, however, that the Constitution is silent about whether the president has the exclusive power to *remove* appointees. Someone espousing a strict reading of the Constitution might therefore have to hold his nose and tolerate *congressional* removal of executive officers—the Constitution would not clearly forbid that. Of course, such a result would create shameless political gamesmanship and ultimately mayhem, with a president beholden to Congress for virtually every executive decision for fear of having her cabinet gutted. Many years ago, the Supreme Court reasonably construed the Appointments Clause as contemplating a reciprocal power to remove appointees (although it later found that Congress can constrain that power). Otherwise, the court reasoned, how could the president follow the Constitution's mandate that she take care that the laws be executed?[25]

The president's power to appoint and remove executive branch officers gained renewed importance under the Clinton and Trump administrations. After the Saturday Night Massacre, Congress decided that Nixon's attempts to stymie the special counsel reflected a serious threat to the integrity of government. Congress passed a statute that cut out the prosecutorial function from the president's job description in certain circumstances—most notably, if the president himself (as well as other high-level officials) was being investigated for possible violations of federal law. The Ethics in Government Act of 1978 lodged the power to appoint a special prosecutor (known for purposes of the statute as an independent counsel) in a panel of three federal judges. The independent counsel could only be removed by impeachment or by the attorney general for "substantial improprieties." In the case *Morrison v. Olson*, the Supreme Court found the statute constitutional—over a famous dissent by Justice Scalia on separation-of-powers grounds—even though the statute took quintessential constitutional powers (investigation and prosecution) away from the president.[26]

Perhaps in recognition of the statute's inherent flaws, Congress did not renew it. Instead, the DOJ passed internal rules that set forth certain terms and limitations for the appointment and removal of a prosecutor charged with investigating the president.[27] But rules are not the same as a statute. If a president wants to fire a special prosecutor (e.g., Robert Mueller) who is investigating him, he can probably do so—at least as a constitutional matter—under the Constitution's implied removal power. Thus, while President Trump dangled the threat of termination over Special Prosecutor Mueller and the deputy attorney general who appointed him, Rod Rosenstein, the very struggle for presidential accountability that ended Nixon's presidency was put on the table again.

Pardon Power

Now, a few words about the pardon power. The president's power to pardon those convicted of federal crimes theoretically functions to check potential abuses by other parts of the government. How? By relieving individuals of the full effects of a criminal judgment obtained through the judicial branch. In theory, it can also convey to Congress that a criminal law is unfair or has been used unfairly.[28]

The pardon power operates as a check on overzealous prosecutors too. Of course, federal prosecutors answer to the president. But in reality, they also function with a measure of independence from the president. This, once again, is not a rule found in the Constitution itself but a "best practices" standard for prosecutors. Otherwise, the federal system of criminal justice could devolve into one that hinges on the political predilections of the president who would be motivated to serve up justice to friends and come down hard on foes, despite the facts and the law.

A suggestion that the pardon power is affirmatively "absolute" is troubling, however. Article II, Section 2 of the US Constitution states that the president "shall have Power to Grant Reprieves and Pardons for Offences against the United States, except in Cases of Impeachment." A keen lawyer would ask: Where are the gray areas in this language? To be sure, the claim that the pardon power is unfettered relies on the term *shall*. In common language, *shall* is the equivalent of *mandatory*, suggesting that the power must go to the president alone.

But does that also mean the power is *unlimited* (in addition to suggesting that nobody else can exercise it)? Maybe not. The Constitution's use of *shall* in other places—such as Article I, Section 1's statement that "[a]ll legislative Powers herein shall be vested in a Congress of the United States"—has been riddled with holes. Kids are taught in school that the legislature makes laws. But as we've seen, so do federal agencies. And when federal agencies make laws, those laws function with the same power and authority that acts of Congress do. So we know that *shall* does not have one definitive meaning under the plain reading of the Constitution.

Historically, to be sure, presidents have widely exercised the pardon power without courts jumping in and telling them they violated the Constitution. In a 1925 case called *Ex parte Grossman*, the Supreme Court upheld President Calvin Coolidge's issuance of a pardon that reduced a man's sentence for violating a federal court's prohibition on the sale of alcohol. In 2017, President Trump pardoned former Arizona sheriff Joe Arpaio, who likewise violated a federal court injunction (which in lawyerspeak is simply a directive that someone do something or stop doing something). Does that mean the pardon power is absolute?

Not necessarily. In *Schick v. Reed* in 1974, the Supreme Court upheld the president's power to issue a pardon that reduced a death sentence to life in prison but added that "considerations of public policy and humanitarian impulses support an interpretation of that power . . . *which does not otherwise offend the Constitution*" (emphasis mine).[29] Under *Schick,* therefore, the same keen lawyer must ask whether a pardon offends some *other* provision in the Constitution. This is exactly the right next question. When it comes to laws, the Constitution is the boss of the boss. It is the boss of everyone who works for the federal government, including Congress. It is the boss of any legislation issues, which means that the Constitution trumps (no pun intended) a contrary law.

Again, the Constitution's packaging did not come with a bludgeon or an electric fence. It is merely a conduit for self-governance—the people's agreement to a set of rules that bind those who exercise power that ultimately resides in "We the People." The Constitution is the boss of the president too, to the extent that it reinforces the people's social contract for governance. The pardon power articulates no exception.

Commander in Chief

The Constitution sets up a micro struggle between Congress and the president when it comes to the power to control wars. It does not make clear who is the ultimate boss here. As a result, we've seen a quiet accumulation of power in the presidency.

Imagine that you do interior design. You are on a conference call with a customer who is looking for advice about renovating a kitchen. The company boss told you to work with Joe on the project. You and Joe were hired around the same time. You have respect for Joe and plan to deftly manage the client meeting by focusing on broad goals versus specifics. Once on the call, you learn for the first time that Joe has drafted a detailed kitchen renovation plan and forwarded it to the client in advance of the call. Everything from finishes to appliances to layout to pricing is already in the document, which the client accepts as the recommendation of the firm. On the call, your role is immediately marginalized because Joe has established himself as the lead.

Now put yourself in Joe's shoes, on a much larger scale. Imagine that you are the US president, and there is a brimming military crisis in a fictitious country rich with oil. The democratic president of that country has been toppled by a terrorist coup. Your own reelection is in six months, and you want to make a show of strength to convince voters that you are a strong leader. You order the US military to carry out air strikes in the hope that they will curtail the growth of the new terrorist regime. The strikes lead to hundreds of documented civilian deaths. You (like Joe) do not consult Congress at any point during the conflict.

As noted in chapter 2, Article I grants Congress the power to declare war. But Article II names the president the commander in chief of the armed forces. So who answers to whom—Congress or the president? When the president launches air strikes, is that an act of war that requires an advance congressional declaration? Or is it an executive decision to direct military operations within the meaning of Article II? Who controls war matters is, in other words, a classic chicken-and-egg problem. An act of war could be confined to something formal—such as what occurred after the bombing of Pearl Harbor to authorize America's entry into World War II. Alternatively, the Constitution could be read as treating Congress as having "declared" war whenever it approves ongoing funding for the armed forces, thereby leaving the president free to "execute" that declaration as she sees fit. The Constitution doesn't weigh in either way.[30]

For the most part, the Supreme Court has steered clear of this debate on the theory that it is a political question. The court has identified some claims of unconstitutional government activity so volatile and politically toxic that they should be left to the political branches. The idea is that the voters should rule on such issues, e.g., foreign affairs and the process for ratifying constitutional amendments.

Perhaps unsurprisingly, the political question doctrine's test is highly subjective. It is not grounded in constitutional text. And it has fluctuated over the years. It exists to give judges an out if there is something so politically thorny that they don't feel that it is their place—as unelected government officials—to touch it with a ten-foot pole. The conflict over the constitutional war powers is one of those things.[31]

Aware of the power struggle, Congress in 1973 passed a statute addressing two questions left open by the Constitution—first, what is an act of war that only Congress can trigger? Second, can the president use American troops on his own? The statute is called the War Powers Resolution, and it limited presidential power in response to the unpopular Vietnam War.[32] The president may introduce armed forces only pursuant to (1) a declaration of war, (2) a specific statute, or (3) a national emergency created by attack upon the United States. The law also requires that the president report to Congress and withdraw troops after sixty days if there's no formal authorization of war by Congress. But it hasn't been enforced.

The statute has been criticized as an unconstitutional constraint on the president's commander-in-chief power. Alternatively, it has been justified as a necessary check to address a constitutional gap that could otherwise edge the presidency toward monarchy. And without it, the argument goes, Congress's war powers under Article I would (if they haven't already) become null and void.[33]

As a practical matter, there is no cop on the block willing to enforce Article I in this regard. To make its power to declare war meaningful again, Congress might have to cut off funding to the military until the president complies with the Constitution and the War Powers Resolution. This won't happen, at least anytime soon. The power to wage a war is an area where the relative power of the presidency has steadily increased since the founding of America.

Treaty

Another area that creates a constitutional clash between Congress and the president is in the realm of foreign affairs. The Constitution gives the president the authority to make treaties, with the consent of two-thirds of the Senate. If a treaty conflicts with a statute, the Supreme Court has held, the most recent one controls.[34]

Although Congress ratifies treaties, the president can do a "treaty-lite" without Congress's buy-in. Presidents can negotiate what is called an executive agreement, which, like a treaty, is between the United States and a foreign country. There is no substantive distinction between the two—an executive agreement can accomplish precisely the same things as a treaty—but the former does not require Senate ratification. And "[n]ever in American history has the Supreme Court declared an executive agreement unconstitutional as usurping the Senate's treaty-approving function." President Franklin D. Roosevelt loaned Great Britain fifty naval destroyers during World War II—and recognized the Soviet Union for the first time—by executive agreement. In 1981, President Jimmy Carter struck an agreement with Iran to lift a freeze on Iranian assets in exchange for liberation of American hostages in Tehran.[35]

The only meaningful limits on the president's ability to negotiate what amount to treaties with foreign nations must be found elsewhere in the Constitution. A president could not agree, for example, to implement and enforce a ban on news that criticizes Syrian president Bashar al-Assad in exchange for an agreement to cease the commission of war crimes against his own citizens. Such a deal would violate the First Amendment, for starters.

At the end of the day, there is no king, but as construed by the Supreme Court, the US Constitution has tolerated some king-like powers inherent in the office of the president. Few Americans realize that many of these powers—including those surrounding foreign affairs—do not derive from an unambiguous reading of the plain language of the Constitution. It's of critical importance that Congress, and ultimately the voters, keep a close eye on the escalation of presidential powers under both Republican and Democratic presidents. Once in the toolbox, they are there to stay.

CHAPTER 4

The Courts: What Was That About Kings?

Article III, Section 1.

The **judicial Power** of the United States, shall be vested in one supreme Court, and in such inferior Courts as the Congress may from time to time ordain and establish. The Judges, both of the supreme and inferior Courts, **shall hold their Offices during good Behaviour,** and shall, at stated Times, receive for their Services, **a Compensation, which shall not be diminished** during their Continuance in Office.

Note, again, there's no definition of judicial power.

Jobs for life and no pay cuts; does this mean we're back to kings?

Section 2.

The judicial Power shall extend to all Cases . . . **arising under this Constitution, the Laws of the United States**, and Treaties made [and to controversies] . . . **between Citizens of different States**.

Here is one key to the federal courthouse door.

Here is another key to the courthouse door.

For all that the framers of the Constitution consciously rejected the idea of a monarchy, they still established an independent judicial branch and gave it a lot of power—making federal judges a bit like mini kings and queens. They also made it hard for the other branches (and impossible for voters) to fire them. This chapter talks about the power of the federal judiciary and how that power is kept in check by confining the kinds of matters that judges are able to consider in the first place.

But first, let's get *Marbury v. Madison* out on the table.[1] *Marbury* is considered by many to be the most important decision in constitutional law because the Supreme Court held in 1803 that American courts have the power to review actions by Congress and by the president in order to determine whether they comply with the Constitution. This outcome was not a given.

President John Adams won the election in 1796. He was a member of the Federalist Party. Toward the end of his administration, the Federalists in Congress created a number of judgeships to shore up their power. Adams filled one of those slots by appointing William Marbury as a justice of the peace, an appointment that required the secretary of state deliver a "commission" to Marbury. The delivery never happened.

When President Thomas Jefferson took over in March 1801, the new secretary of state—James Madison—refused to deliver the commission to Marbury. Marbury sued Madison, asking the Supreme Court to force Madison to turn it over under the judicial power to issue a writ of mandamus—a piece of paper that forces government officials to do their duties. Congress had given federal courts the power to issue writs of *mandamus* in the Judiciary Act of 1789, which created the lower federal courts too.[2]

The Supreme Court held that Marbury had a right to the commission but refused to issue the writ forcing Madison to turn it over, concluding that the statute giving courts that power was itself unconstitutional. Notably, the Constitution itself does *not* declare that federal courts have the authority to strike down unconstitutional laws enacted by Congress. The *Marbury* court came up with that rule, and the decision has stuck all these years. There would be nothing more concrete than respect for the rule of law to stop a renegade president from coming along and declaring that *Marbury* is wrong and that the president gets to interpret the Constitution however he sees fit. (Indeed, Trump's pick for acting attorney general during the volatile special prosecutor days of 2018, Matthew Whitaker, made this very argument.)[3]

Yet, with *Marbury*, the court established the federal judiciary as a strong and independent branch of the federal government. The Constitution was the supreme law of the land, it decided, and the judiciary was the final arbiter of what the Constitution means. *Marbury* is one reason why Supreme Court nominations have become so politically polarizing today: justices serve for life, and they refine the other branches' job descriptions—in addition to deciding how far the Constitution goes to protect individuals against an overbearing government.

The Keys to the Federal Courthouse Door

There are two more things you should understand about the judicial branch. The first is that before anybody can get before a court, she needs the keys to the courthouse door. There are two court systems in this country—state courts (each state has its own) and federal courts. For both of these, one key that is needed to get before a judge is a cause of action. As we've seen, Joe cannot sue Jane or help the government send Jane to jail for behavior that's not forbidden by some sort of law— whether that be the Constitution, a statute, a regulation, or judge-made common law (also known as case law). Giving someone the stink eye is rude, but it can't send someone to jail or even to court. To get before any judge, whether a federal or a state court judge, you need to have a cause of action.

For federal court, you need yet another key. State courts can hear virtually any kind of case. But federal courts' jurisdiction is limited. A plaintiff needs a dispute that raises a federal issue—like whether Congress had the power to make a particular law under the Commerce Clause, or whether an African American woman's federal boss violated the Civil Rights Act when he passed her over for a promotion. This is why the Constitution says that federal courts can hear cases "arising under" what amounts to federal law.[4]

Or, alternatively, for disputes that are local in nature (e.g., a slip and fall at a shopping mall), federal courts can hear the case if the parties are from different states. This is what lawyers and judges call diversity jurisdiction, and it is also clear from the Constitution's language.[5] The idea behind diversity jurisdiction is that, even though there isn't anything federal about a slip and fall at a mall (unless, of course, we are talking about the National Mall in Washington, DC, where the Smithsonian Institute and numerous federal buildings reside), federal courts are more likely to be fair to defendants from out of state than are elected state court judges. Imagine a slip and fall at a local hardware store in Plano, Texas. The person who fell is a multi-billionaire from Los Angeles who happened to be in town and swung by to pick up a book of matches. It is reasonable to presume that the local judge in the case will be biased in favor of the hardware store—particularly if that judge is elected and needs to make the neighbors happy if he wants to keep his job.

By contrast, federal judges—like other principal officers of the executive branch, such as the attorney general or secretary of state—are appointed by the president and confirmed with the advice and consent of the Senate. Moreover, the Constitution makes clear that they have jobs for life (absent impeachment) and cannot have their pay docked simply because they make decisions that are politically unpopular.

A few more basics about courts. Most of the time, parties file cases in the lowest-level courts, known as trial courts. Decisions from those courts can be appealed to a higher court, known as courts of appeals. From there, decisions can be appealed to a supreme court. Each state has its own trial, appeals, and supreme courts. So does the federal judicial system. Appeals to middle-level courts are "as of right"—if you lose the case in the lower court, you get to appeal no matter what. (Winners can't appeal just to rub it in.) The Supreme Court of the United States is an ultra appeals court for states, meaning parties can appeal *state* supreme court decisions to the *US* Supreme Court. In the federal system, appeals from the intermediate appellate courts—known as the US Circuit Courts of Appeals—also go to the US Supreme Court. The thing is, the US Supreme Court doesn't have to take any one case. The justices pick and choose what cases they want to take (and the court takes only about eighty a year). Appeals to that court are made by what's known as a petition for a *writ of certiorari*. Justices vote on whether to "grant cert" using various criteria, including things like whether there's a big split in the lower courts over an issue and whether the issue is urgent.[6]

One more thing to know about court structure: generally, people who are in state court can't get a federal court to review a state court decision except by a cert petition to the US Supreme Court. You can't leapfrog from one court system to another, in other words. With one exception: habeas corpus. Habeas is a topic that could find itself in several places in this book: under the chapter on Congress's powers, under the chapter on crimes under the Constitution, and here—in the chapter on courts' power, because it's a way of getting a judge to review an unlawful detention.

In Latin, *habeas corpus* means "you shall have the body."[7] The notion is that if the government has arbitrarily put you in jail, you can petition the courts to get out. Keep in mind that a habeas proceeding is separate from a direct appeal of your criminal case to higher courts in the ladder leading up to the US Supreme Court. It's a side-door channel to getting a warden to release you through a civil (versus criminal) proceeding.

Congress has passed statutes governing the process, and the Supreme Court has issued lots of decisions, making this area of law very complicated and difficult to navigate without an experienced lawyer. Bottom line: if you're in custody, you can seek habeas review if you meet a number of procedural hurdles, but you're unlikely to win release this way.

Additionally, few people realize that the Constitution does not create a federal judiciary other than the Supreme Court, and it does not specify how many Supreme Court justices there must be. In the Judiciary Act of 1789, immediately following ratification of the Constitution, Congress passed a law creating the lower federal courts. In theory, Congress could change its mind and eradicate all federal courts except for the Supreme Court with a statute, and change the composition of the Supreme Court to just one justice. As distinct from the other branches, then, the beauty—in theory—of the federal judiciary is that it cannot be influenced by power, money, or survival. The assumption instead is that judges on the federal bench will make decisions neutrally, apolitically, and legitimately. The reciprocal problem is that federal judges are not tethered to the real-time will of the people.

What is the sandbox for federal judges, then? Article III allows federal courts to resolve "Cases" and "Controversies," terms which are again undefined. The Supreme Court has filled in those blanks to say that the word *case* must mean something akin to what we see on *Judge Judy*—a discrete dispute involving distinct parties regarding events that occurred in the past. The rationale for this definition is that if courts are only empowered to make decisions as to individual parties, we should be less concerned that federal judges aren't elected. The parties get their day in court by showing up and arguing their case (plus the due process clause enshrines that right), and the decision does not broadly affect lots of people like legislation does. Courts are also bound by higher laws, which include statutes and the Constitution, and Congress can override court decisions that interpret statutes. Thus, judges cannot just make up rules out of thin air; by limiting the terms under which they function, courts' power is held in check even if federal judges aren't elected.

Under the "Cases" or "Controversies" requirement, therefore, people have to show standing in order to get into federal court. Standing means that, if we agree that the judges' role is to call balls and strikes as to discrete parties, then we want to make sure that calls for legislative action do *not* get before a court.

Imagine a plaintiff who tripped on a pothole in a sidewalk and broke her arm. She sues the city for damages, claiming that it was negligent in failing to repair the pothole; in other words, she wants a judge to say that a responsible city government that does its job would not allow a hazardous situation to continue until someone is hurt. The plaintiff walks into court with her broken arm and says, "Look at my broken arm! It hurts so I can't go to work, and the medical bills are not in my budget, and I cry all day in pain, which I wouldn't have to do if the stupid city fixed its potholes!" The court hears her story and—maybe with or maybe without the assistance of a jury—decides that the city was negligent and orders it to pay the plaintiff's doctor bills, give her money to make up for lost time at work, and give her more money to compensate for the "pain and suffering" it caused her (a difficult concept to quantify, to be sure, but that is how it goes).

A judge makes a decision that affects those particular parties but not necessarily the people who happen to be watching the proceedings in the courtroom or sitting on the jury. For other people—maybe someone whose car is damaged by running over a pothole three streets over—the judgment itself is not much help. He would have to file his own lawsuit against the city if he wants money to repair his car. He might get lucky and be assigned the same judge, who would presumably be inclined to rule in his favor. But if he is assigned a different judge, his lawyer will show the new judge the prior judge's decision involving the first person and say, "Me too!" He will basically tell the new judge that this case is just like the other one, so he should rule the same way. This is what judges and lawyers call judicial precedent or case law. Judges only resolve individual disputes, but their decisions can be used in later cases as a "me too."

For his part, the city's lawyer will say, "Not me," or "This situation is different." Maybe the second guy was drunk when he ran over the pothole, which had huge orange cones around it to make drivers aware it was a hazard. The city can say, "Don't follow that other decision here, Judge, because we did the best we could to warn Plaintiff Number Two, and he brought the accident on himself." This is what lawyers and judges call distinguishing cases.

Now imagine that a concerned citizen walks by the first pothole every day. He is aware of it and carefully steps around it. He pays his taxes and knows that eventually someone else will fall and get hurt. Can he sue to get a judgment directing the city to fix the pothole? Nope. He doesn't have a broken arm. He is like every one of the other hundreds or thousands of people who manage to walk around that pothole every day and don't have a particular dog in the pothole fight. The complaint about the city not repairing its infrastructure is a bigger one of broader appeal. The law of standing—which confines federal courts' power to cases and controversies—would not let that guy into court. His gripe is with the city council—the legislative branch of the city (but the same idea holds true at the federal level). He can lobby the city legislature to pass a law, say, requiring the city to fix potholes within fourteen days once they reach a certain circumference; but not go to court.

This question of standing came up with the court challenges to President Trump's first controversial executive order on immigration.

The broken-arm plaintiffs included people with family members who were barred from entering the United States who claimed to suffer from stress and anxiety as a result. But the problem with overly rigorous application of the broken-arm rule of standing is that what constitutes sufficient injury to distinguish the plaintiff from the rest of the population is inherently subjective.[8]

If you have followed this discussion so far, I hope you have some sense of why it is really about constitutional theory and why it is important. It is about constitutional theory because if the broken-arm plaintiff can't go to court, she must go to the legislature. Standing law is therefore about the separation of powers between the judicial and the legislative branches. If the legislature is dysfunctional (which many would agree has been the case at the federal level for a while and for a number of reasons), then problems of great importance simply won't get fixed even if the people want them fixed.

But the court system can also fail. Let's imagine a carpenter sues a restaurant owner for not paying a $10,000 invoice, and the restaurant owner ignores the court judgment directing that he pay up. The winner can go back to the judge. The judge can then direct another arm of government—the sheriff or the federal equivalent of a sheriff, a US marshal—to execute the judgment. This could literally mean marching into the restaurant and taking money out of the cash register and giving it to the carpenter. Again—without a cop on the block, or hidden speed cameras, the "rule of law" isn't worth the paper it's written on. One of the reasons why the American government is (or has been) revered around the world is that the rule of law matters here. Judges' decisions are enforced. We live in a society where one of the cultural norms and values is that we mostly obey judges' orders. If people stop obeying court orders and get away with it—particularly at the highest echelons of government—our democracy is in big trouble.

The Relative Power of the Courts

Courts are especially critical to the structure of government because macro questions regarding how much government is too much often wind up there. In 1896, for example, the Supreme Court upheld a Jim Crow law requiring segregated railroad cars in Louisiana. Homer Plessy, a free man of one-eighth African dissent, bought a first-class rail ticket and boarded a whites-only car in New Orleans. He was asked to vacate a seat and go to "the coach used for the race to which he belonged."[9] When he refused, he was arrested and fined.

In rejecting Mr. Plessy's constitutional claim under the Equal Protection Clause (more on that later), the court conceded that "[t]he object of the amendment was undoubtedly to enforce the absolute equality of the two races before the law." But with astonishing conviction, the court concluded that "[l]aws permitting, and even requiring, their separation in places where they are liable to be brought into contact *do not necessarily imply the inferiority of either race to the other*" (emphasis mine).[10] There was no constitutional right, in other words, to enforce a new social norm that would enable black people to mix with the white race—even if enforcement of that norm would effectively *lift* government bans on racial integration.

In 1954, the Supreme Court overruled the decision in Mr. Plessy's case in *Brown v. Board of Education*, which declared unconstitutional a Kansas law permitting segregated schools for black and white children. The court relied on the Equal Protection Clause that the *Plessy v. Ferguson* court rejected as means of enforcing "social" equality. "Segregation with the sanction of law," the *Brown* court wrote, "has a tendency to [retard] the educational and mental development of Negro children and to deprive them of some of the benefits they would receive in a racial[ly] integrated school system."[11]

There was substantial social resistance to *Brown*. An Arkansas governor called out the state's guard to prevent black students from entering a high school in 1957. A man named Medgar Evers sued to desegregate schools in Jackson, Mississippi, under *Brown*, and a member of a group called White Citizens' Council—which was formed to resist school integration—murdered him in 1963. That same year, an Alabama governor personally blocked an auditorium door to prevent black students from enrolling at the University of Alabama, and moved aside only when President John F. Kennedy intervened, ordering a general of the US National Guard—part of the military force's reserve—to allow the black students to enter.[12]

Five years after *Brown*, a Virginia judge charged Richard Perry Loving and Mildred Jones Jeter with a felony crime that made "marriages between a white person and a colored person . . . absolutely void."[13] The judge reasoned that "Almighty God created the races white, black, yellow, malay and red, and he placed them on separate continents. And but for the interference with his arrangement there would be no cause for such marriages. The fact that he separated the races shows that he did not intend for the races to mix."[14]

It was not until *Loving v. Virginia* in 1967 that the Supreme Court invalidated laws prohibiting interracial marriage (known as anti-miscegenation laws) on equal protection and other constitutional grounds. In markedly different prose, Chief Justice Earl Warren wrote that "[m]arriage is one of the 'basic civil rights of man,' fundamental to our very existence and survival," and that "[t]here is patently no legitimate overriding purpose independent of invidious racial discrimination which justifies this classification . . . designed to maintain White Supremacy."[15]

But was *Plessy* or *Brown* the better, truer construction of the *plain*-language *equal protection of the laws*? Courts have a lot of discretion to make this kind of decision. And in an age of tweets and memes, it is easy to gloss over the meaning of individual words. Think about it. A strict reading of *equal* might look to its application in 1868, when the Fourteenth Amendment containing the Equal Protection Clause was ratified after the Civil War. Presumably, the framers of the amendment believed that it had something to do with discrimination against African Americans by many southern states. So the clause can be fairly construed as ensuring that formerly enslaved persons receive equal protection of the law, that is, that laws cannot discriminate against them based on their race—or more accurately, that they had to be equally protected under the law.

What, then, does *protection* mean? In *Plessy*, the court appeared to construe the word—without explicitly saying so—to *not* include protection from social norms that forbid black people from riding in railcars with white people. The decision spawned the notion that "separate" can be "equal"—blacks can be legally required to sit in public transportation, eat in restaurants, and go to school in facilities that are separate from white people so long as they receive equivalent seats, food, educational materials, and teachers, etcetera.

Because neither *equal* nor *protection* are defined in the Constitution itself, we might look further to a dictionary definition of *equal* as meaning "the same measure, quantity, amount, or number as another."[16] Unless black children can attend *the very same* school as white children, the clause is violated. But equal can also mean "like," suggesting that—so long as the black children can attend a school that is like, i.e., similar to, a white school in terms of the facilities, teachers, materials, etcetera—the black school can be considered constitutionally the "same." A dictionary definition thus does not help us get to the plain meaning of the word *equal* under the Constitution.

Moreover, it's impossible to achieve *identical* equality when it comes to making sure that the government treats people equally across age, gender, race, socioeconomic status, and so forth. The government certainly cannot be expected to put everyone up in an LA mansion, or force those living in Beverly Hills to downsize to a one-bedroom condo so that everyone can be "equal." A critic would rightly call that socialism, which our capitalist democracy most certainly is not.

Interestingly, the same line of constitutional authority has been used to argue *for* the "right" to discriminate. In 1945, the Supreme Court heard a case in which a union of postal clerks claimed that a state law *prohibiting* racial discrimination in unions violated *their* property, liberty of contract, and social rights.[17] Although the court rejected the notion that there is an individual right to discriminate, the argument that the Constitution provides a right to discriminate has resurfaced several times over the decades since, with scant success, including, for example, in a suit challenging a federal requirement that hotels and restaurants serve all customers,[18] in a suit challenging a state law requiring a private club to admit women,[19] and in a suit by the Boy Scouts challenging a New Jersey law's ban on discrimination on the basis of sexual orientation.[20] Anti-minority animus is often packaged as religious liberty or another constitutional right much in the same way as those seeking to end discrimination used the Constitution to achieve what amounted—at least in part—to social objectives.[21]

A fair critique of "plainly" reading the Constitution, therefore, is that it gives judges *too much* power because they can reach decisions without disclosing their true rationale. This debate around originalist versus activist judges is, as I mentioned before, a central one among politicians and pundits discussing a president's Supreme Court nominee picks. It is not ivory-tower theory, but nuts-and-bolts politics. Understanding what it means is vital to being able to participate meaningfully in the discussion around federal judicial nominees.

PART II

Rights

This next part of the book discusses the other axis of constitutional analysis, which deals with individual rights. We already covered the axis that's about constitutional structure—the separation of powers and the respective authority and limitations of each of the three branches—which is important to ensuring that people keep what we call rights. This is because if we let any one branch accumulate too much power, that power can be used against individuals for arbitrary reasons.

But a constitutional right does *not* mean that people who are granted rights get special goodies from the government to the exclusion and/or detriment of other people. Constitutional rights are not a zero-sum game. Nobody *loses* constitutional rights by virtue of people gaining them. But we've become polarized over who gets rights and who doesn't. Ironically, the government's role is often left out of that fight.

If we instead think of rights as a way to stop government from being too overbearing, then it becomes clear that the *more* rights that are recognized, the *less* power that the government has overall. When government has more constraints, all people get more freedom from government bullying. Viewed this way, it's hard not to see some potential common ground between, say, gun-rights advocates and abortion-rights advocates. Both are saying, "Back off, government." One is saying, "Back off my gun collection." The other is saying, "Back off my body." In both situations, there are countervailing interests—extremely important ones involving life itself.

This part of the book walks through a number of rights that you might care a lot about: the right to freedom of speech and religion; the right to own handguns; the right to be free of government searches and seizures; the right not to be forced to say things to the government that could put you in jail; the right to be free of cruel and unusual punishment; the right not to be criminally tried over and over for the same thing (just because the government didn't win the first time); and the right to be treated equally by the government as a racial minority, a woman, an immigrant, or a gay individual.

Or put another way: this chapter is about *limiting the government's ability* to constrain speech, religion, and gun ownership; to snoop, coerce, punish, and otherwise abuse its police power; and to discriminate against certain people for the wrong reasons, i.e., reasons that are arbitrary, unfair, and in many cases, morally unjust. As we will see in the pages that follow, the juice really lies in how to balance the legitimate justifications for giving government power over certain aspects of individual's lives on one hand with the values that underlie the rules contained in the Bill of Rights on the other.

CHAPTER 5

Speech, Religion, and the First Amendment

Note that this says nothing about the separation of church and state.

But what about cities and states—can they restrict speech?

Do corporations "exercise" religion?

Does this just mean there can be no official "Church of the US," or does it do more to constrain government?

Is the press special when it comes to the First Amendment?

Amendment I [1791].

Congress shall make no law respecting an **establishment of religion**, or **prohibiting the free exercise thereof**; or **abridging the freedom of speech**, or of **the press**; or the right of the people peaceably to **assemble**, and to petition the Government for a redress of grievances.

Does *speech* include the ability to remain anonymous? What about symbolic conduct that involves no words?

What does the word *religion* even mean? Can someone just make one up and have it count?

Does *freedom of association* come from this language (because it's not expressed in the Constitution)?

The first thing to notice about the First Amendment is that, although relatively short, it's a whopper. One might reasonably expect that something so basic would be fairly easy to understand and apply. Yet if measured by the number of Supreme Court cases explaining what the language means, First Amendment law is massive. The court's decisions are complicated, multitiered, highly dependent on the particular facts before it, laden with squishy policy considerations, and even contradictory at times. Because nothing short of an algorithmic flowchart is needed for the law at a glance, even the best all-purpose lawyers can't answer many questions under the First Amendment without doing significant research first. Surely, then, the guy on the street has no meaningful idea about what the First Amendment is really doing for him. Which is all to say: What the heck is going on here?

Let's start with the text, which says that "Congress shall make no law." On its face, it restricts Congress—nobody else—from making certain kinds of laws. And "no law" suggests that it tolerates absolutely zero exceptions. Which laws? Those that do one of these six things:

- that are "respecting" an establishment of religion,
- that prohibit the free exercise of religion,
- that abridge the freedom of speech,
- that abridge the freedom of the press,
- that abridge the right of the people to peaceably assemble, and
- that abridge the right of the people to petition the government for a redress of grievances.

In short, Congress can't make laws that do any of the above. For our purposes, what is most important is that Congress can't *prohibit* free exercise of religion, *abridge* freedom of speech or the press, or make rules *respecting* an establishment of religion. (We don't have much space to discuss the others.)

Next question: What do the verbs mean? We all know what *prohibit* means; Congress can't forbid, outlaw, or disallow the free exercise of religion. Americans get to pray without the federal government telling them whether—or how—they can do it. But *abridge* appears to mean something slightly different—as in, "to diminish."[1] Congress can't prohibit the free exercise of religion, but it *can* probably abridge it based on these words alone.

The text of the First Amendment thus outlines two major areas that Congress must steer clear of—religion and speech. It also suggests that Congress must be especially careful when it comes to speech. If it can't abridge it, it surely can't prohibit it. According to the plain language, Congress can't even hamper speech. Or the press. Of course, the press speaks through the written word. So why did the framers of the First Amendment include an extra clause for the press? For emphasis? Or does the press get extra—or different—protections than other parties who speak? From the Supreme Court's perspective, the answer to this last question is: not really. It has generally held that the press should be treated like everyone else when it comes to the First Amendment—no better, and no worse.[2]

The word *respecting* is the broadest verb of all. It would seem to mean something like "regarding" or "related to"—as in, Congress can make no laws having anything to do with the establishment of religion, period. So Congress can't ban people from setting up a new religion and it can't stop people from adopting a religion from another part of the world, to be sure. But it also likely means that Congress cannot pass a law that makes one religion the official religion of the United States. This is where the concept of "separation of church and state" comes into play. It is not expressly stated in the Constitution but arguably follows from the explicit ban on Congress tinkering with establishing religion—whether by passing laws that officially favor one religion or by making it hard for certain religions to get a foothold in the United States.[3]

Keep in mind, though, that the term *religion* itself isn't defined in the First Amendment. Common sense equates religion with a belief in, and worship of, another power—one that believers treat as omniscient, omnipotent, or both. Christians call that power God. Muslims refer to Allah, and so on. But *religion* can also mean a pursuit of something you consider to be extremely important—as in, "going to the gym is my religion." It is unlikely that such a reading of the Constitution would fly at the Supreme Court.

But suppose someone believes that Mother Nature—untouched wilderness—is akin to a superhuman power. Suppose further that such belief is part of that person's religion—much like the land is considered sacred by many indigenous cultures. Would a federal law authorizing fracking violate the First Amendment's protections regarding religion? Lower courts have held that transcendental meditation triggers First Amendment concerns.[4] Even if some people view the very idea of Mother-Nature-as-religion as silly, who gets to decide if the Constitution cares about that particular religion? Are we comfortable with that decision resting with five (of nine) individuals who cannot be fired but who happen to be on the Supreme Court when the issue comes up for decision?

Note too that the text refers to the *free* exercise of religion and the *freedoms* of speech and the press. The text doesn't refer to plain old "exercise" of religion; it's the *free* exercise that is protected. As for speech and the press, the text assumes that such "freedoms" already exist—that their source is from somewhere other than the Constitution itself—but that the Constitution *preserves* them. What could that source be? This is a question with deep theoretical underpinnings that we can't cover here. But be aware that there are some scholars and jurists who believe that natural law was the backdrop for the framing of the Constitution.[5] Natural law is like a body of unwritten moral principles that we all intrinsically understand—things like freedom, liberty, tolerance, kindness, etcetera—should govern human behavior. But could the Constitution instead be construed with the values of a dictatorship in mind, so long as that's not banned by the clear language of the document? Most people would say no—at least publicly—which suggests that there is something to the basic idea of natural law. Regardless of one's philosophy of constitutional interpretation, it is hard to stomach the notion that the Constitution could be construed according to unwritten principles that are directly *antithetical* to natural law.

As part of our look at the First Amendment, let's also dip into its historical origins, which matter dearly to conservative judges and scholars who favor a plain reading of constitutional text. Up until 1694, the English press was tightly controlled. Nothing could be published without obtaining a government license first. It was also against the law to publicly criticize the government. To do so was considered "seditious" libel and people went to jail for it. The rationale was that the monarchy was above public critique. Even truthful speech—which could be particularly damaging—was punished.[6]

Against this backdrop, the Supreme Court stated in 1907 that "the main purpose of such constitutional provisions is to prevent all such *previous restraints* upon publications as had been practiced by other governments" (emphasis mine).[7] Both seditious libel laws and bans on criticizing the king restrained people from opening their mouths (or using their pens) to utter a certain something in the first place. They are different from, say, a ruling from a court that functions to *punish* speech that wasn't technically banned beforehand.

In that case from 1907, which was called *Patterson v. Colorado*, Colorado criminally charged a guy named Thomas M. Patterson with contempt for publishing articles and a cartoon that reflected poorly "on the motives and conduct of the supreme court of Colorado." The US Supreme Court refused to hear the case on the rationale that the First Amendment by its terms only constrains Congress—not the states (more on that later). Justice Oliver Wendell Holmes Jr. also laid out a narrow reading of the First Amendment, suggesting that even if the court did take the case, Patterson would lose. Why? Because he was not being prosecuted under a *preexisting* law banning "the rights of free speech and of a free press against hostile action by the United States," and, according to Justice Holmes, the First Amendment "do[es] not prevent the *subsequent* punishment of such as may be deemed contrary to the public welfare" (emphasis mine).[8]

As we will see, this cramped view of the First Amendment doesn't address many of the free speech issues that matter today. Moreover, it's complicated by the fact that in 1798—a mere seven years after the First Amendment was ratified—Congress passed the Alien and Sedition Acts, which prohibited public writings against the US government. The law also imposed fines and imprisonment on those who did, as happened to more than twenty Republican newspaper editors. (All very anti–First Amendment, no?) The "Alien" part of the law made it easier for the government to deport foreigners and harder for immigrants to vote. Many of the framers were on board with all this, and President John Adams signed it into law. The statute later expired, and the Supreme Court never got a chance to weigh in on its constitutionality. When it comes to the First Amendment, though, people who look to history for its definitive meaning may get a bit stuck, as the historical record reflects a tolerance for constraints on speech that undermine the plain language of the Constitution.[9]

Another factor to consider in construing the Constitution—one that more progressive jurists and scholars weigh heavily, i.e., the people in the so-called living Constitution camp—has to do with the purposes behind protecting speech and religion. The notion is that, in deciding whether the First Amendment protects against government intrusion into speech, judges should think about the goals of free speech, and tailor their decisions in individual cases to serve those goals (recall here the related concept of natural law). In addition to looking to history, judges use their own common sense and experience. Consider the words of Justice Louis Brandeis:

> Those who won our independence believed . . . that freedom
> to think as you will and to speak as you think are means in-
> dispensable to the discovery and spread of political truth; that
> without free speech and assembly discussion would be futile. . . .

[I]t is hazardous to discourage thought, hope and imagination; that fear breeds repression; that repression breeds hate; that hate menaces stable government; that the path of safety lies in the opportunity to discuss freely supposed grievances and proposed remedies; and that the fitting remedy for evil counsels is good ones.[10]

Justice Brandeis thus argued for free speech as tied to the ability to *think* freely, and the ability to think freely as tied to the avoidance of fear, repression, and tyranny. It doesn't get much more important than that: free speech is crucial to self-governance and democracy. This is particularly so when it comes to political speech that is critical of government, which the Supreme Court has deemed "the central meaning of the First Amendment."[11] Scholars have also justified free speech as linked to the discovery of truth, which is likewise important to self-governance; otherwise, people cast their votes based on emotion and false beliefs, which could unwittingly take them down a dangerous path to tyranny.[12]

So how well has the Supreme Court adhered to the plain language in the 228 years since the First Amendment's ratification? For starters, the court has not confined the First Amendment to Congress; the states are bound too.[13] Nor has the court read "no law" to mean zero laws—there are plenty of laws that restrict speech and religion, and for good reasons. It wouldn't work to allow protesters to shout down the president's State of the Union address such that nobody could hear what he has to say, for example. Most of the Constitution's provisions allow for moderate limits on rights. The question is, which limits are acceptable and which aren't—a question that comes down to balancing a bunch of important interests.[14]

The Constitution gives no explicit guidelines for this balancing act. Judges make them up. They make them up by looking to history, to be sure, but as we've seen, history isn't particularly helpful here. As a result, the factors that go on the other side of the balancing scale for the First Amendment—i.e., what interests does the government have in restraining speech and religion, and whether those outweigh the freedoms set forth in the text itself—are often subjective. They also waffle over time. As we've seen before, which side you're on depends mostly on which factors you care about most—not on some lofty view of the proper way to stay within the lines of the constitutional text.

The rest of this chapter has two major parts: speech and religion. Like the entirety of this book, it doesn't pretend to summarize the law comprehensively. Instead, it explains how the words of the First Amendment—which we've scrutinized with some care already—have mushroomed into a complex set of rules and exceptions and, in light of that, how we might think about our own individual rights under the First Amendment today.

Speech

Recall that the First Amendment forbids Congress from passing laws "abridging the freedom of speech." The Supreme Court has sliced and diced this language into a series of balancing tests and has applied those tests in ways that weight certain values more heavily than others. What kinds of things get the greatest protection?

For one, speech that is targeted *for its content* is super protected. We don't want government singling out certain people based on *what* they are saying, e.g., for supporting Republicans or Democrats. Congress could not pass a law stating that "anyone who speaks against the use of US military force in Syria shall be punished"—even if Congress had reason to believe that pro-Syrian rhetoric compromises national security. The idea is that the content of one's speech (and even worse for purposes of this example, the speaker's viewpoint) is inextricably tied with thought. If government controls the content of your speech—or your viewpoint—it ultimately controls your thinking too, and that's really scary. So Congress couldn't allow only pro-choice advocates to picket on the National Mall in Washington, DC, while banning anti-abortion protesters. But deciding whether a law is content-neutral can be difficult.

At first, the Supreme Court held that a law restricting speech is okay under the First Amendment so long as it applies to everyone equally.[15] Then came along a case challenging a law that banned adult movie theaters within one thousand feet of a residential zone, church, park, or school. The law was undeniably content-based—only theaters showing porn were covered. The court upheld the law, carving out an exception to the content-neutrality rule. Even though the law targeted certain content, it was constitutionally okay because, behind the scenes, the legislature had a valid concern over "secondary effects," i.e., that adult film theaters could harm communities by increasing crime and the like.

If you're thinking this is overly cute, you're right; if legislators could simply conjure up content-neutral justifications for squelching antiwar speech (e.g., by simply singing a few lines about national security) and get past go, we might as well throw the First Amendment out the window. Not to mention that an argument can be made that, in the movie theater case, the court itself created an exception to content neutrality based precisely on *content. Porn is bad, so it's okay to sideline speech just this once.*[16]

One last point on subject matter and viewpoint-based speech before we go on. As with many parts of the Constitution, even those things that get the greatest protection are not sacrosanct. Basically, the Supreme Court has set up a grading rubric. Certain things that we don't care so much about get graded on a pass/fail basis. In other words, so long as the government can show what's called a rational basis for a law restricting things that the court thinks aren't that important, it's good to go. (Setting the First Amendment aside, for the sake of example, a law that forces police officers to retire by age fifty gets rational basis review on the notion that we aren't too worried about the government picking on people because of their age.)[17]

For things that the Supreme Court has decided we care deeply about, like race, the standard is higher. It's like having to get all As in high school if you want to go to Harvard. There's nothing wrong with a B, but Harvard sets a higher bar. For content-based laws that restrict speech, that high bar is called strict scrutiny. The government has to have a really, really good reason for restricting that kind of speech. So, for example, the court has held that Congress could not pass a law making it a crime for people to lie about whether they received military honors.

There's also a medium-level bar, which the court has called intermediate scrutiny. Again, setting aside the First Amendment for example's sake, gender falls in this range. (Justice Ruth Bader Ginsburg argued for strict scrutiny on the basis of gender as a civil rights lawyer.) Of course, whether something passes one of these tests is pretty subjective. (And as an aside, it's one reason that the right to an abortion under *Roe v. Wade* is more complicated than meets the eye—the court started out attaching strict scrutiny to that right but watered it down to something more like intermediate scrutiny, without actually calling it that. More on these topics later in the book.)[18]

Recall the First Amendment framers' concern with the government putting *prior* restraints on speech. Well, that one is still a concern today: laws that stop speech from occurring in the first place are mostly no-nos and get strict scrutiny, the highest bar. The court has said there is "a heavy presumption against [the] constitutional validity" of such laws.[19] They don't get the benefit of any doubt. But here again, the court hasn't always been intellectually honest or consistent on toeing this line.

Consider its review of a court order forbidding protesters from speaking within thirty-six feet of an abortion clinic. It was a restraint on the time, place, and manner of speech, and one that was put in place *before* protesters showed up with their posters wanting to say their piece. A state court judge ruled it was okay anyway (remember the notion of balancing that threads throughout constitutional law), because it protected people's ability to enter and exit the facility. But the Supreme Court went further and said that the law wasn't a prior restraint in the first place, so strict scrutiny didn't apply—rational basis did. The court took this position even though the law made clear—in advance of anyone speaking—that people couldn't express their views within the thirty-six-foot buffer zone. The court reasoned that people could do it in other places, and the restraint didn't hinge on the content of what the protesters wanted to say, so it wasn't a constitutional problem.[20]

Bear in mind that the way case law works is that judges look at a prior court's decision on the facts of an old case and compare those facts to the facts of a new case. Then they decide if the new case is enough like the old case to reach the same conclusion. If it isn't, then the court needs to give reasons why the new case is different enough to justify a different conclusion.

So imagine a new case arises in which a law bans people's ability to advocate for animal rights in Finn Rock, Oregon, which is a big logging town. The town council decides that pro-animal advocacy hurts the timber industry, which the town relies on for its very survival. Under the basic test for what constitutes a prior restraint, this would appear to be a problem: the law tells people to shut up (or else) before they even open their mouths about the animals. Strict scrutiny?

But wait. The other Supreme Court case we just talked about concluded that a gag order within thirty-six feet of an abortion clinic was *not* a prior restraint. Is the ban on animal-rights advocacy more like that one or more like the case that held that banning porn in movie theaters *was* a prior restraint (but was nonetheless justified on public safety grounds)? Well, perhaps it depends on whether pro-animal advocates have another place to go, which is the criterion used by the Supreme Court to conclude that the ban on speech near an abortion clinic was *not* a prior restraint.

In our hypothetical, the ban is for the entire town of Finn Rock. Unlike in the abortion clinic case, people can't just step to thirty-seven (versus thirty-six) feet outside any building and legally argue on behalf of wildlife in Finn Rock. They have nowhere to go in Finn Rock under the law. So maybe it's more like a full-on prior restraint after all. Should the thirty-seventh foot make all the constitutional difference for purposes of the First Amendment? That seems arbitrary, no? Bottom line: things can get messy when the court makes little tweaks in applying the Constitution.

Prior restraints also get a bit tricky when it comes to some rather routine things that the government does. For one, the government is in charge of issuing licenses—to drive, to practice medicine, and so on. If you want to protest on the National Mall in Washington, DC, you need a license (i.e., a permit). The ban on the ability to speak without one is arguably a prior restraint on speech. But the court has held that if the government has a good reason for requiring a license, the law doesn't give the government much leeway in whether to issue a license (i.e., it can't be denied for the wrong reasons, like a person's political affiliation), and the government doesn't get to sit on your application for too long, it *can* require licenses to speak.[21] Again, it's about balancing. A reading of the First Amendment that required downtown Washington to operate as a big open mic for anyone to protest at any point and time wouldn't work.

In addition, the Supreme Court has (but only sometimes) held that the government can't condition government benefits on the basis of speech. It held that the government can't tell National Public Radio that it will give it federal funding only if it does not editorialize, for example. But it also upheld a law denying federal funding for family planning services unless clinics agreed to ban abortion counseling—a speech-based condition on the receipt of a government benefit. Somewhat bizarrely, the court reasoned in the second case that the government gets to make choices about what activities it should fund in the public interest—hardly a strong justification for its stark departure from prior cases limiting selective funding on free speech grounds.[22]

The court's analytical contradictions only underscore the debatable nature of the Constitution on both sides of the political spectrum. As Professor Erwin Chemerinsky tells it, "If the Court wishes to strike down a condition, it declares it to be an unconstitutional condition; if the Court wishes to uphold a condition, it declares that the government is making a permissible choice to subsidize some activities and not others."[23]

Another area of First Amendment law that people might want to know about has to do with vague laws. I say that people might want to know about it because it implicates all laws that penalize behavior—not just the ones that impact speech. If a person cannot tell whether a particular law bans a particular kind of speech or not, or whether it makes certain conduct criminal in the first instance, the law itself could be unconstitutional under the due process clause (which we will get to later).

Imagine a law prohibiting loitering. The law defines loitering as "being in a place for no apparent purpose." You're hanging out outside a Starbucks drinking coffee with a friend and get arrested under the no-loitering law. You had no way of knowing that the law meant that what *you* were doing was wrong. You are a rule follower. But under the language of this hypothetical law, it's impossible to know what counts as "no apparent purpose" and what doesn't. You were just socializing, after all! If the government is going to put you in jail for crossing a line—one that comes very close to the First Amendment right to peaceably assemble—that line had better be clear.[24] Otherwise, it's just not fair.

A law can also be too broad as a matter of the First Amendment. Think of a law that prohibits all live entertainment within one thousand feet of a school. The objective is to prohibit nude dancing, but the law wasn't crafted to only prohibit live nude dancing—it covers all live entertainment. A court might strike it down as too broad. Or consider a law that bans depictions of animal cruelty. In an opinion by Chief Justice John Roberts, the Supreme Court called the law overbroad because it could apply to *any* cruel conduct—not just illegal conduct—and thus potentially affect people's ability to publish hunting videos.[25]

For the most part, the court doesn't like to strike things down for being too broad and instead will just read laws in a way that makes them constitutional. This workaround comes awfully close to legislating from the judicial bench, to be sure. But courts can't be roundly condemned for being pragmatic. Imagine a law forbidding nude photographs of children: better that a court construe the law to only ban porn (even though it doesn't exactly say that), while allowing moms to snap pics of their babies in bathtubs, rather than throw the entire law out with the bathwater, so to speak.[26]

So far, we've talked about what the First Amendment has to say about the government prohibiting or punishing speech. But what about if the government tries to *compel* you to say something and you don't want to? Consider a public school rule requiring that kids salute the American flag. The Supreme Court has said it's not okay with that. Forcing someone to make a pledge is forcing that person to affirm a certain belief—which comes precariously close to mandating thoughts. Likewise, the court has said that the government can't force people to reveal their identities. So a ban on anonymous pamphlets is unconstitutional. Nor can the government force newspapers to give equal print space to competing political candidates. For that decision, the court relied on the First Amendment's reference to freedom of the press, but the idea is the same: the government can't force you to speak in a certain way.

Most recently, the Supreme Court issued a controversial First Amendment decision striking down public unions' requirement that workers pay them fees. The fees were used to support the unions' collective bargaining efforts—i.e., negotiations with the government to get better terms for the workers it employs. Not everyone wanted to pay the fees, but everyone benefited from the negotiations. The court sided with the "anti-fee" people because collective bargaining is about public policy, which is inevitably political, so the government can't force workers to participate in it.

The decision to strike down the fee requirement was controversial because the court did a 180-degree turnabout, overruling a 1977 case that had allowed unions to collect the fees so long as they weren't used for ideological causes.[27] This older decision recognized the beauty of a union: if you were stuck with having to gripe all by yourself, your employer wouldn't care—it would let you quit your job and just find someone else to do it rather than listen to your complaints. But if you complain along with a bunch of people, and you agree in advance to all walk out in the event that the employer refuses to negotiate, then you have some real leverage. The business cannot function without workers.

The court's later decision to ban mandatory union dues—regardless of what they are used for—made people upset, in part because it's very rare that the Supreme Court reverses itself, and for good reason. If the justices didn't feel bound to stick with precedents they didn't personally agree with, the law would be in constant flux and ultimately politicized, with the pendulum swinging back and forth on key issues every time the court's composition shifts. Regarding this particular case, critics contend that the 5–4 decision reflected the political motivations of a conservative majority, because fewer union dues generally translate into a smaller voice for Democratic (versus Republican) voters.

Now for a few lines regarding the types of speech that are *less* protected under the First Amendment: hate speech, obscenity, profanity, libel, campaign donations, speech by government employees, and commercial advertising. Bottom line: hateful or racist speech is protected under the First Amendment, with exceptions. Obscene or profane speech is not. The rest of the list falls on a spectrum of protected speech.

Let's start with hate speech, which can take a number of forms. The first is known as incitement. The question it raises is whether speech that tells other people to commit crimes is protected. A recent example could be the "Lock her up" chant that dominated many Trump campaign rallies and hinted at harsh punishment for unproven crimes by Hillary Clinton. There is an argument that incitement of illegal activity should never be protected because illegal activity is, well, illegal.[28]

The Supreme Court has mostly struck that balance in favor of First Amendment protections, however. From World War I to the present, the court has tried out a number of different approaches to this issue, all of which I won't bore you with here. Suffice it to say that during the Red Scare of the 1950s, when Senator Joseph McCarthy led efforts to out communists, there was more concern about the "revving-up-crime" side of the scale. But today, speech that urges people to break laws is protected unless it "is directed to inciting or producing imminent lawless action and is likely to incite or produce such action."[29] So a Ku Klux Klan rally that includes a film with racist and anti-Semitic speech, along with images of firearms, for example, may be protected. The court's prevailing First Amendment tests for hate speech also require that people who bring cases in court show that the speaker had a certain intent—which is hard to do—and the court hasn't defined what intent means here, so courts get lots of leeway.[30]

Hate speech can also take the form of insults. Imagine that a Jehovah's Witness denounces other religions at a rally and calls a listener "a damned Fascist." Or consider a hateful action such as a cross burning. The Supreme Court has mostly held that hate speech that hurts people's feelings is nevertheless protected—meaning the government cannot do anything about it. Cross burning can only be prohibited if it is done with an intent to threaten an individual or group with violence. So if a cross is burned in a field with nobody around, it's okay; if it's on somebody's front lawn, it's not.

The First Amendment's protection of verbal insults is a pretty interesting rule to keep in mind. Consider the push from progressives for so-called trigger warnings in advance of engaging in speech that may make certain people uncomfortable. Some people see this as a courtesy. Others consider it censorship. But say that a university sociology professor fails to let her students know that she is about to discuss homophobia in class. Certain students object to her launching into the topic with no warning, as they may have experienced homophobia and are emotionally triggered by the subject. If the university is public (i.e., government-run), the professors' "triggering" speech may be protected because laws regulating hate speech are only allowed if the speech is likely to produce a violent response from the audience. What this also means is that law enforcement officers have to be careful about overstepping First Amendment rights when they attempt to control an audience that's riled up by an angry speaker.[31]

At this point, let me pass along a lawyerly tip about how the doctrine we've discussed thus far actually plays out in court. Judges can choose from a menu of ideas—vagueness, overbreadth, or content-based prohibitions—to strike down a law (or not). All of these pieces of doctrine—derived from individual disputes that we call cases—intersect and interact with each other. Courts can pick which theories to apply. In doing so, judges can deliberately seize upon a theory that, if applied, leads to a certain result—and reject the one that, if applied, would lead to a different result. Judges on both ends of the political spectrum do this. It's called legal analysis, and it's one reason why law school—and lawyering—can be really hard.

Moving on. The Supreme Court has held that obscenity is not protected by the First Amendment, while profanity is, albeit with exceptions. The court's constitutional distaste for obscenity is a problem because it basically allows the government to decide what is morally acceptable. Sex is not the same as obscenity, according to the court; the difference occurs when sex "appeal[s] to the prurient interest." *Prurient* means "salacious" or "lustful," creating a big hole in the Supreme Court's foundational premise that the First Amendment protects people's thoughts from government interference. (Lustful thoughts are still thoughts.)

The court has also gotten itself into a mess when it comes to defining obscenity by creating a multifactor test that prompts more questions than it answers. It requires that courts determine when something is "patently offensive," when it appeals to "the prurient interest," and when it lacks "serious literary, artistic, political, or scientific value." Courts get to make these moralistic judgment calls. If you're thinking, *Wow*, then you're not alone. But if you're also thinking, *Wait a minute—what about the porn that is all over the Internet, accessible to toddlers? Isn't that lacking in value—at least so as to justify* some *limits?* The answer is that the court has allowed the government to prohibit obscene material or profane language over the telephone and broadcast media (ABC, NBC, CBS) and, to a lesser degree, over cable television. But not over the Internet.[32] (Some have argued that a conservative-leaning Supreme Court is increasingly using the First Amendment to justify fewer regulatory constraints on corporate America, period.)[33]

Let's talk next about defamation—also known as slander (if spoken) or libel (if written). Defamation is the making of a false claim about someone publicly. In 2018, failed Republican Senate candidate Judge Roy Moore filed numerous defamation suits against his critics—including comedian Sacha Baron Cohen, CBS Corporation, Showtime, and four women who accused him of sexual abuse when they were teenagers. Trump made headlines in 2018 for urging changes in libel laws that would make it easier for him to sue critics—not to mention file lawsuits against Stormy Daniels and others for defamation.[34] His presidency sparked a national conversation around whether stricter penalties should apply for publicly spreading false information about another person. In the #MeToo era, when many victims of sexual harassment are denounced as liars by some without a careful investigation into whether they are telling the truth, there is an especially good case to be made for allowing people to use the legal process to stop public bullying. But when does a defamation lawsuit itself become retaliatory? Can someone file a defamation lawsuit over the filing of a defamation lawsuit on the theory that the first suit contained lies that hurt someone's reputation? Courts have to draw lines all the time, and it isn't easy to anticipate a line that will work for the next fact pattern to come down the pike, and the next one, and the next.

For its part, the Supreme Court has created a layered framework for defamation, which hinges the scope of the First Amendment on factors like whether the plaintiff is a public official or running for office, whether the plaintiff is not in the government but is otherwise a public figure, whether the plaintiff is a private figure but talking about something the public is concerned about, or whether the plaintiff is a private individual and the speech being complained about is private too. I'm not going to belabor this list.

Just know that criticism against *public* officials and *public* figures is okay—that is, it's protected by the First Amendment unless the official can show that the speaker made the false statement with *actual malice*. This added factor is tough to show. (The plaintiff or prosecutor has to come up with evidence—documents or witnesses—that effectively shows the speaker's mind at the time of the statement and show that it was made in reckless disregard of the truth or that the speaker knew that the statement was false and not made by mistake or something else.) So while much is being bantered about over whether public figures (think President Trump) should tell the truth about other people, and whether the press is telling the truth about them (think Trump again), the law doesn't allow government actors to raise First Amendment claims as easily as regular people can.

Even though federal employees are entrusted with problems of immense political weight, if they speak about matters within the scope of their jobs, they *can* get fired—and there is nothing the First Amendment will do about it under current Supreme Court law.[35] This is why FBI agent Peter Strzok's texts criticizing then candidate Trump in the months leading up the 2016 presidential election was not protected by the First Amendment. He was on the job when he texted his colleague/girlfriend, so the Constitution didn't protect him. The court has also upheld a federal law called the Hatch Act, which prohibits government employees from taking "an active part in political management or political campaigns."[36] For other speech by government employees—speech that doesn't involve job-related or political topics—the government can take disciplinary action only if it can show that the speech interfered with the individual's job. So if a teacher is fired for sending a letter to an editor criticizing the school board, her termination would be unconstitutional, unless the government shows that it hurt her ability to teach math to seventh graders.[37]

A large area of First Amendment law that has special implications for our democratic process is campaign-related speech. We will discuss this more in chapter 10, but the idea is that by making donations to a campaign, people are engaging in political speech—the highest order of what's protected. We also know that *conduct* can constitute speech—think of wearing an arm band or desecrating a flag—and that even though conduct is not words, the government cannot regulate it without contending with the First Amendment. A campaign's spending decisions are also considered speech.[38] In fact, in a case called *Citizens United v. Federal Election Commission*, the Supreme Court held in a 5–4 decision that corporations possess First Amendment free speech rights.

You might be thinking, *Hold on a moment: corporations are legal fabrications!* They amount to a piece of paper filed with a secretary of state for the purpose of minimizing taxes and liability. A corporation is not a tangible *thing*. Today, corporations can be formed online with a few clicks and a credit card. They do not require physical buildings or employees to bring them into existence. Yet in *Citizens United*, the court held that the government cannot interfere with a *corporation's* speech—giving it the same constitutional protections as flesh-and-blood human beings get. "By suppressing the speech of manifold corporations," Justice Anthony Kennedy wrote for the majority, "the Government prevents their voices and viewpoints from reaching the public and advising voters on which persons or entities are hostile to their interests."[39]

Corporate America's free speech rights are protected in other ways. The Supreme Court has devised tests, for example, that distinguish between speech that proposes a commercial transaction, speech that occurs in an area that government traditionally regulates, and other kinds of speech. This grab bag of factors has produced an array of results for companies that run advertisements. For example, advertisements that contain information about illegal activities, or which are false and deceptive, can be prohibited or penalized without the government having to contend with the First Amendment. But complete bans on alcohol ads have been struck down even though they were justified by the societal benefits of encouraging people not to drink.[40] For tobacco advertising, the Supreme Court has only had problems with certain things—like an outdoor ban on ads for cigars and smokeless tobacco, and a prohibition on ads located lower than five feet above ground level in stores.[41]

I could go on with examples of First Amendment outcomes that, when strung together, seem pretty random. All told, the Supreme Court has concocted lots of nuanced distinctions from a pretty short paragraph of constitutional text.

Religion and the Establishment Clause

The First Amendment provides that "Congress shall make no law respecting an establishment of religion, or prohibiting the free exercise thereof." It's saying two things here: Congress can't mess with the *establishment* or with the *free exercise* of religion. These phrases are treated as two distinct branches of First Amendment law.[42] The government can violate one but not the other, or it can violate both at the same time. The creation of an official religion of the United States and a law requiring everyone to worship in accordance with that religion would violate both parts. If the government makes a law to facilitate the free exercise of religion—by providing religious ministers to soldiers during battle, for example—it could be criticized for "establishing" religion. If it refuses to do so on First Amendment Establishment Clause grounds, it could face "free exercise" challenges from soldiers stuck on foreign soil without access to ministers due to the government's decision to deploy them.

The primary test for determining whether the government has violated the Establishment Clause was set forth in 1971 in a case called *Lemon v. Kurtzman*.[43] Under that decision, the government cannot make a law whose primary purpose or effect is to advance, aid, or inhibit religion. The government also can't excessively entangle with religion. But what does all of that mean? Good question.

First, let's ask this: How helpful is history in guiding the court's application of the Establishment Clause today? The answer is, not much. The nation was less religiously diverse in 1791 than in 2019. As Justice William Brennan Jr. explained: "[O]ur forefathers . . . knew differences chiefly among Protestant sects. Today the nation is far more heterogeneous religiously, including as it does substantial minorities not only of Catholics and Jews but as well of those who worship according to no version of the Bible and those who worship no God at all."[44] There were no public schools in 1791, so the First Amendment cases arising around questions like whether public schools can require students to recite the Pledge of Allegiance aren't really helped by looking back in time.

Think for a moment about how these issues come before the Supreme Court. The government does something and a person responds by saying, "You can't do that because it violates my right to freely exercise my religion." So can someone facing a misdemeanor charge for possessing marijuana get off by claiming that his use of cannabis was part of a religious sacrament? The problem with no for an answer is the text of the First Amendment itself: "*no law* . . . prohibiting the free exercise thereof" is okay (emphasis mine). On one hand, a law banning pot is a law prohibiting the exercise of a religion that incorporates the use of that substance. On the other hand, there are problems with the answer yes. An entirely faithful approach to the plain language would allow people to simply play the "religion card" any time they're charged with violating a law. Arrested for shoplifting? Speeding? Abusing an animal? Concoct a story about how your religion requires that you have meat for dinner once a week, which you cannot afford. Or how you could not obey traffic laws and reach your church service on time. Or how the Bible itself contains stories of animal sacrifice and your religion incorporates similar rituals that are sacred to you even though secular people might consider them abusive.

Well, the Supreme Court has resolved this conundrum by allowing the judiciary to consider whether a person's religious views are "sincerely held." The test is not true or false. In one case, the leaders of a religion called I Am promised to cure diseases in exchange for money. They collected more than $3 million based on false promises and were prosecuted for mail fraud. The Supreme Court held that the jury could not be asked to decide whether the defendants' curative claims were actually true because "[h]eresy trials are foreign to our Constitution."[45] But the line between sincerity and truth is hard to draw. It's difficult to measure sincerity. Some people are great liars, while others are infallibly honest but nervously seem like they are lying when telling the truth. What about the person whose religion does not teach what he claims as a personal religious belief? In one case, a man quit his job because it was contrary to his personal religious beliefs as a Jehovah's Witness. He lost his unemployment benefits and sued. The religion itself did not object to the job, but the court considered that fact irrelevant, reasoning that "the guarantee of free exercise clause is not limited to beliefs which are shared by all of the members of the religious sect."[46]

Assuming that the Supreme Court was able to settle on a definition of religion for the Establishment Clause, how much interference by the government is tolerable? We know by now that the Bill of Rights is not an impenetrable bulwark. Some infringements on constitutional rights eke through if the government's reasons are good enough. When it comes to religion, the justices aren't in agreement on how much is too much. The big battleground has to do with whether government can tango with religion *at all*. Some scholars and judges believe that "[t]he First Amendment has erected a wall between church and state . . . that must be kept high and impregnable."[47] We can call this the strict approach. The theory is that when the two mix, certain religious beliefs—the ones that government hasn't adopted in one way or another—become vulnerable, so no mix whatsoever is the only feasible option.

This argument hits home personally. I was raised Catholic and attended strict Catholic schools through eighth grade. In first grade, we had a full mass every lunch hour of every day in preparation for our first Holy Communion. There were a few kids who weren't Catholic, and they would sit while we stood, sit while we knelt, and sit while we went to the altar to practice accepting the Eucharist. If the school were the government, and Catholicism were the official religion, the people who adhered to other religious beliefs would be sidelined. I'm speaking metaphorically, but hopefully you get the idea.

But if the government's approach to separation were too strict, silly things would happen. It would be a problem, for example, if the government refused to provide police or fire assistance to churches on the theory that it would be an unconstitutional entanglement with the Establishment Clause. We might draw the line at favoritism—government can't rush to a mosque faster than it rushes to a Catholic church, for example. The problem with "favoritism" is the definition. Consider a case in which the Ku Klux Klan wanted to erect a huge cross in a park across from the Ohio Statehouse. The state said no. The KKK argued that the state violated its right to freely exercise religion. The government argued that allowing the cross would violate the Establishment Clause. How to break the impasse? The court sided with the Klan, reasoning that a reasonable person wouldn't view the cross as an endorsement of the KKK by the government. "Where the government's operation of a public forum has the effect of endorsing religion, even if the governmental actor neither intends nor actively encourages that result, the Establishment Clause is violated."[48] The Klan cross scenario didn't qualify as favoritism.

Here again, the problem with the Supreme Court's middle-ground approach to the Establishment Clause is that it gives judges lots of power to subjectively determine what is and is not an endorsement of religion. Certainly, African Americans seeing a Klan cross on public grounds would feel unwelcome—we could point to that as at least one reason to consider restricting the Klan's access to that particular space for the exercise of their religious beliefs.

A third camp of scholars and judges argue that the Supreme Court should not use a strict approach or a favoritism approach to the Establishment Clause but, rather, that it should interpret the First Amendment to allow religion in government. In other words, the "accommodation" approach goes, *Let's be practical here; religion, society, and government intersect. So long as government doesn't literally create a national church, or coerce people to participate in one religion over another, or give lots of money or other tangible benefits to one religion to the exclusion of others, we're fine.* The benefit of this approach is that it draws clearer lines and leaves less discretion for individual judges to make subjective determinations of constitutional importance. The downside is that the Establishment Clause doesn't do much work under this approach—if the government is going to mess around with religion, it's not going to do it in such blatant ways. And the subtle ones make an impact.[49]

So imagine a county courthouse with a nativity display, a Christmas tree, and a menorah on the front lawn. A "strict" view of the Establishment Clause would find the display unconstitutional because government should reject all entanglement with religion. The "favoritism" approach might be okay with one Christian symbol—the nativity or the tree, but not both—because such double-dipping tends to favor one religion over another. The "accommodation" approach would allow this scene because surely government is neither establishing its own official religion nor coercing anyone to be Christian or Jewish. In a 5–4 decision, the Supreme Court found the courthouse tableau unconstitutional, but the justices' reasoning ran the gamut of the various approaches to Establishment Clause cases.[50]

In most cases, the court applies a three-part test set forth in the *Lemon* decision I mentioned earlier, looking to whether a problematic law has a nonreligious reason behind it; whether it has a principal effect of helping or hurting religion; and whether it fosters government entanglement with religion. You can see by reading this list how each justice's theories regarding how best to read the Establishment Clause will inevitably inform the court-made rules he or she develops under it. How cases are decided turns on subjective answers to unanswerable questions like: When is a religion helped or hurt? How much government entanglement in religion is too much entanglement? And is there a secular purpose behind the law—and if so, does that make government entanglement with religion okay?

To see how all this ambiguity might play out in a particular Establishment Clause case, consider a law requiring the posting of the Ten Commandments on the wall of a public school classroom. It's hard to imagine a nonreligious purpose for the law. But what about requiring a mandatory period of silence? Meditation has scientifically proven benefits to overall health and well-being. Or a law requiring that public schools teach creation science alongside evolution? You can try your hand at applying the three-part test to each scenario. It turns out that, in all three cases, the Supreme Court found the laws unconstitutional.[51] There are many others. Too many to cover here.

Religion and the Free Exercise Clause

Our last topic under the First Amendment is the Free Exercise Clause: "Congress shall make no law . . . prohibiting the free exercise [of religion]." Now, "free exercise" might be read as protecting all conduct relating to religious beliefs. But that's not how the Supreme Court sees it. Freedom to believe is pretty much sacrosanct—the government cannot punish or constrain individuals' ability to hold particular religious beliefs.[52]

But how often does it happen that people in the United States are punished for *believing* the teachings of one religion over another? Post–September 11, there were valid arguments to be made that Muslims in America lost freedoms because they were Muslim. Over the past few years, hate crimes against American Muslims have "soared to their highest levels since the aftermath of the Sept. 11, 2011 attacks," as similar concerns thread through public discourse around President Trump's ban on immigrants from certain countries.[53] But the practical reality is that, if government is going to regulate religion, it is probably going to do it by regulating conduct—not beliefs.

So, what has the Supreme Court said about regulating religious conduct? Consider polygamy. Certain Mormon men claim that their religion requires them to have multiple wives. Yet the Supreme Court upheld a law forbidding the practice.[54] The court also upheld federal laws mandating Social Security numbers and payment of Social Security taxes—including by Amish people who claimed that the requirements violated their religious beliefs.[55] But the court struck down laws denying unemployment benefits to people who quit their jobs for religious reasons.[56] Where does the court draw the line?

Here's the overarching problem: If the court draws the line too far in favor of the free exercise of religion, people can point to religion as an excuse for getting away with all kinds of stuff that general laws forbid. If the court draws it too far in favor of government regulation of religion, then the government can infringe upon religion so long as it comes up with a reason that's neutral.

At the end of the day, the Supreme Court has basically held that a law that is neutral on its face (i.e., not expressly about religion) and applicable to everyone gets the lowest grading rubric: it is okay so long as there's a rational basis for it. For those laws, any government excuse that is rational will do. Thus, a law forbidding the consumption of the hallucinogen peyote was held to be constitutional, even though its use was required by some Native American religions, because it applied to everybody equally. But the Supreme Court struck down a law that prohibited ritual sacrifice of animals because it was directed at a particular religious group.

In 1993, Congress tried to override the Supreme Court's "neutral on its face" standard by passing a law that imposed a strict scrutiny rubric any time courts had a case under the Free Exercise Clause. That law—the Religious Freedom Restoration Act of 1993 (RFRA)—was struck down as unconstitutional, at least as it applies to state and local governments. For now, RFRA still applies to the federal government. (The big fallout from the lingering effect of RFRA was the Supreme Court's decision in *Burwell v. Hobby Lobby*, which applied the statute—not the Constitution, mind you—to relieve certain closely held corporations from having to comply with Obamacare's requirement that they provide birth control coverage to employees.)

First Amendment law is an enigma. Because it protects individuals' freedom of thought, it is perhaps the most important provision of the Constitution when it comes to ensuring that we live in a truly free society. But by the same token, it can be used as a means of pushing political agendas that are more traditionally conservative in nature—by keeping religiously oriented "crisis pregnancy centers" from having to provide women with abortion-related information, for example. A conservative-leaning Supreme Court struck down that law, despite previously upholding one that required doctors performing abortions to provide other kinds of information to patients—such as facts about adoption services. A disgruntled Justice Stephen Breyer quipped that the decision was wrong: "After all, the rule of law embodies evenhandedness, and 'what is sauce for the goose is normally sauce for the gander.'"[57]

CHAPTER 6

Guns and the Second Amendment

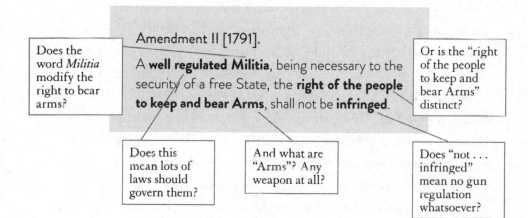

Does the word *Militia* modify the right to bear arms?

Or is the "right of the people to keep and bear Arms" distinct?

Amendment II [1791].

A **well regulated Militia**, being necessary to the security of a free State, the **right of the people to keep and bear Arms**, shall not be **infringed**.

Does this mean lots of laws should govern them?

And what are "Arms"? Any weapon at all?

Does "not . . . infringed" mean no gun regulation whatsoever?

Every few weeks another brutal mass shooting renews the ongoing national debate about the regulation of gun ownership in America. And, like many issues of constitutional importance, the heated discussion often gets the law wrong. We can't address the issue of gun regulation if we don't understand the Second Amendment.

Look up at the text of the Second Amendment. To me, all controversy over the meaning of this text comes down to commas. Yes, commas. In the last chapter, we spent a lot of time with the language of the First Amendment. The people who wrote that language also wrote the Second Amendment. They could have phrased the Second Amendment in much the same way as they did the First Amendment. Imagine, for example, that the Second Amendment stated, "Congress shall make no law abridging the right of the people to keep and bear Arms." Then it would be much clearer: no laws abridging the right to gun ownership. Of course, *abridging* is itself a flabby word, as we've seen. But even if that word were used here, it wouldn't mean that zero laws infringing upon gun ownership are constitutional. Some would be okay, so long as there was a good reason for them. Most people would say public safety is one such reason.

But the Second Amendment doesn't say that. It doesn't say that Congress can't abridge gun rights. To be sure, unlike the First Amendment, it expressly refers to "the right" to bear arms. *Right* sticks out. But what does it mean by "right"? And where does this "right" come from? The question is a bit like the source of the term *freedom*, which is expressly named in the First Amendment. I've mentioned how some people view concepts such as freedom as deriving from natural law—some set of generalized, unwritten rules regarding the moral order of humanity. Guns probably don't qualify as part of that order (and they need not, because the Second Amendment doesn't speak of freedoms, it speaks of a right).

But back to commas. By any account, the Second Amendment's statement that "[a] well regulated Militia . . . shall not be infringed" preserves the states' ability to raise militias because militias were necessary to the security of a free state. Remember that the framers of the Constitution had just made it through a bloody revolutionary war. They wanted independence from England, and were acutely aware of the Brits' temptation to march back into the colonies and take over. Moreover, in 1791, when the Second Amendment was ratified, the federal government was not the powerhouse it is today. At this early phase in the nation's history, there was deep concern that it not accumulate too much power in relation to the states. Composed of regular civilians who could be called up to fight on behalf of a state in an emergency, militias were crucial to maintaining young America's hard-fought independence.[1]

The rub around commas is that, on one hand, we could interpret the phrase "the right of the people to keep and bear Arms" as having a completely separate meaning from the words that precede it. It is bookended by commas—one preceding the phrase and the one after it. And those commas are important. One argument goes like this: There is an individual right to bear arms, and also a right for states to raise militias. They are two separate things linked together in one amendment by a few commas. Militias need arms to function, of course, and we aren't taking anything away from them. But the words *bear arms* should be pulled out of the rest of the text. What these words mean is that—even without militias—individuals can constitutionally possess weapons to protect themselves against various possible threats, including those posed by their own government.

The other hand is that the Second Amendment has another possible meaning. It contains no words that distinguish between the militia clause and the right-to-bear-arms clause or otherwise suggest that they should be read as freestanding mandates rather than as linked to the objective of maintaining state militias. It doesn't say, for example, that a well-regulated Militia, being necessary to the security of a free State, *is one reason why* the right of the people to keep and bear Arms shall not be infringed. The "is one reason why" is missing. It is thus equally reasonable to read the plain language of the Second Amendment as only about militias, full stop. Under this reading, *all* the language in the Second Amendment modifies the first clause. In other words, states' ability to maintain militias *that bear arms* are necessary to the maintenance of the states' own security. After all, without weapons, a militia is hardly worth anything. If the framers were worried about limiting the ability of the new federal government's ability to deprive states of their traditional ability to protect themselves, it is reasonable that they would make it abundantly clear that the newly formed federal government couldn't get around the militia requirement by banning the states' use of weapons.

Note that *weapons* is my word here—not the Constitution's. The Constitution refers to *arms*, or armaments. In 1791, this mostly meant handguns or rifles that had to be reloaded before each shot. Some version of so-called repeating arms—the closest thing to modern-day assault weapons that fire multiple rounds with the pull of a trigger—was reportedly invented around 1779 and available in the colonies, but it was expensive. People could also make their own repeating arms, but it was uncommon.[2] Someone who adheres to a plain-reading approach to constitutional interpretation might stop there and confine the reach of the Second Amendment to what the framers understood to be arms. Semiautomatic machine guns of the modern day would not count (and that makes some logical sense, as people don't need semiautomatic weapons to protect themselves in their homes).

Ironically, a conservative majority of the Supreme Court rejected the argument "that only those arms in existence in the 18th century are protected by the Second Amendment."[3] Given what we know about constitutional interpretation by this point in the book, it's hard to discern the line at which historical practice should dictate modern thinking around the Constitution and when it should not. Somewhat conveniently, the court picks and chooses when history binds it and when it does not. At a bare minimum, this issue makes clear that there is no single, abiding, unambiguous reading of the plain language of the Second Amendment. Other factors must—and do—come into play, and they are not clear from the text itself.

A final term that is worth exploring—and also undefined—is the Second Amendment's "well regulated" requirement for militias. Today, when we think of regulation, we think of laws restricting private behavior. But with the use of *well regulated* in the Second Amendment, the framers perhaps meant that it was okay for states to train private people over long periods of peacetime so that they could be called up for duty as needed on a moment's notice.

As Alexander Hamilton explained in Federalist No. 29, "A tolerable expertness in military movements is a business that requires time and practice. It is not a day, or even a week, that will suffice for the attainment of it."[4]

Today, when we think of a militia, the National Guard comes to mind. It's a reserve military force composed of people from every state who aren't soldiers or military personnel. They mostly carry on with their lives and have regular jobs unless they are called to duty. Its motto and theme song "Always Ready, Always There!" sounds like a hangover from an understanding of *well regulated* as meaning "well prepared and ready." Without preparation, a militia can't do what it's supposed to do.

So the plain language and the history of the Second Amendment suggest, for sure, that militias were to be protected and that militias can use arms. Or at least that particular use of arms cannot be "infringed" upon. In common language, *infringed* means "restricted," "limited," "curbed," or "checked." But as we know from the First Amendment discussion, this doesn't mean that militia members can park armored trucks on their front lawns and terrify the neighbors without the government being able to say a peep about it. Restrictions abound when it comes to constitutional rights. The question is how many are too many.

That said, the Second Amendment is a constitutional topic that is subject to a lot of misunderstanding—at least when it comes to the governing law. So let's dispel a few legal myths about gun "rights" in America. And remember, by rights we mean the ability to walk into court and force the government to withdraw or stop enforcing a law that somehow limits an individual's ability to "bear arms." This is assuming, of course, that we start from the premise that the clause separated by two commas creates a stand-alone right that is not tied to the needs of a militia. As we will see, this is one assumption around which the Supreme Court has flip-flopped, and its gyrations culminated in the now-famous decision that recognized a constitutional right to own a handgun for self-protection in one's home.

Myth #1: The Supreme Court has long been clear that people have a constitutional right to carry firearms. Like much paraphrased law, this is an overstatement. As we've discussed, the Second Amendment itself talks about two things: "[a] well regulated Militia" and "the right of people to keep and bear Arms." Back in the day, American revolutionaries wanted to make sure brethren settlers could grab their muskets and join the military establishment in a crisis (or fight against it).[5] In 1939, the Supreme Court held that the Second Amendment clearly safeguards the possession of firearms for purposes of serving in a militia, and "must be interpreted and applied with that end in view." That was the law for decades. In upholding a federal law banning sawed-off shotguns, the court noted that such weapons were not used by militias at the time the Bill of Rights was ratified—a classic originalist argument. The majority opinion went even further into the annals of history to justify the conclusion that the constitutional right to bear arms is *confined to militias.* The court explained: "The signification attributed to the term Militia appears from debates in the Convention, the history and legislation of Colonies and States, and the writings of approved commentators."[6]

In 2008, the Supreme Court reiterated in *District of Columbia v. Heller* that the Second Amendment says "yeah, sure" to armed militias. But crucially, it added that the amendment also protects an individual's right to use "arms" in self-defense. In the constitutional law world, this was a big deal. In a 5–4 decision, the court struck down a law regulating guns that had nothing to do with militia service. So the old case was overruled to the extent that the prior court had read the various clauses of the Second Amendment together (option two, previously discussed), and the current court instead held that they should be read as separate and distinct (option one, previously discussed).

Writing for the majority, Justice Antonin Scalia concluded that "[t]he former [Militia clause] does not limit the latter grammatically, but rather announces a purpose." He then declared that purpose to be "defensive." The thirty-two-year-old law at issue in *Heller* banned the possession of handguns in the District of Columbia, so in its simplest formulation, the court's decision meant that you can keep a pistol under your pillow to defend yourself—i.e., to protect yourself and your family against intruders.[7]

Note that this was a big deal not just because it declared the right to bear arms a stand-alone individual right to force the government to restrict its limitations on gun ownership. It was also a big deal because the court blew up its long-standing precedent that the Second Amendment was about protecting gun possession in connection with militias—as well as all the subsequent cases and laws that were based on that holding. As we've seen before, when the Supreme Court ignores what its forebearers did, it can wreak havoc on lots of things. Given that few, if any, cases coming before the court in the late twentieth to early twenty-first century are cut-and-dried under the language of the Constitution, there is an argument to be made against this kind of second-guessing, period.

One problem with it is that it makes the court appear political and not neutrally tethered to the law and the facts. When the Supreme Court is perceived as politicized—whether rightly or not—its legitimacy falters and people lose faith in the integrity of the judicial system as a whole. This is not to say that it's wrong to overrule precedent in all cases. Infamously, the court held in *Plessy v. Ferguson* (discussed earlier in the book) that "separate but equal" treatment of racially segregated African Americans was constitutional. That's an example of a constitutionally based decision by the Supreme Court that was dead wrong, and the court rightly overruled *Plessy* in *Brown v. Board of Education*.[8] But in my humble opinion, if the court is to turn precedent on its head, it should probably do so unanimously—or not at all.

Note too that allowing DC to regulate handguns (the opposite of what the Supreme Court said in *Heller*) would also be justified on "feder-alism" grounds. Recall that federalism is shorthand for the dividing line between state and federal power. The notion is that one way to confine the power of the federal government is to guard the power of the states. The DC handgun ban was a local law supported by local residents re-garding how they wanted to solve problems inherent in living and work-ing in their own community. In dissent, Justice Breyer argued that "the District's decision represents the kind of empirically based judgment that legislatures, not courts, are best suited to make." He also argued that a reasonableness test should be applied to gun bans—something like the lowest level of scrutiny (again, it's known as rational basis) that the court applies to other kinds of rights protected under the Constitution. The majority struck down the handgun ban without showing its hand as to what level of scrutiny—strict, intermediate, or rational basis—should apply in future gun cases.[9]

Myth #2: Arms necessarily include handguns, rifles, and semiautomatic weapons. This one is also off, as I previously indicated. *Arms* is not de-fined in the Second Amendment itself, but would anyone seriously ar-gue that it means your neighbor can store plutonium in his garage and make a nuclear bomb to protect his family? Of course not. What the Supreme Court specifically found in *Heller* was that handguns can be kept and used in the home for self-defense. The court then laid out a bunch of factors that may be important in deciding if something else constitutes "arms" under the Second Amendment—including whether a weapon is one that musket-bearing settlers would have commonly used, and whether it is "dangerous and unusual." The court also carved areas where the right *can* be limited—such as for mentally ill persons and fel-ons, or in and around schools and government buildings.[10] (The justices don't even want cameras in their courtroom, let alone machine guns.)

Myth #3: Gun ownership is a Second Amendment issue, period. This one gets us into the wonky world of separation-of-powers theory, but it's of vital importance. These days, the Supreme Court is the branch of government that's basically drawing the lines on gun use. But should it? Our state and federal legislators make rules too—and we elected them. When a matter is enshrined in a Supreme Court decision that interprets the Constitution, it's very hard to change—even by Congress. Thus, we might think twice about making gun safety first and foremost about the Second Amendment. Of course, this argument could overstate the point, in that we can't have legislatures overriding the Constitution all the time. If the Second Amendment says "x," legislators must abide by that, and it's the Supreme Court's job to say so. But as we've seen, constitutional provisions don't always say "x" in unambiguous prose, and the Second Amendment is one of those provisions.

Keep in mind that, while bans on gun ownership have been struck down as unconstitutional, stand-your-ground laws exist in a number of states, which protect people from criminal prosecution if they injure or kill someone in perceived self-defense rather than retreating. To be clear: these laws give immunity to people who use violence in alleged self-defense even if they could have protected themselves by retreating. In many cases, the only witness who was in a position to argue against the self-defense claim is dead. If this is the will of the public, enacted through the legislature, should courts get involved?

Critics point to the multifold increase in self-defense claims following enactment of such laws as evidence that they encourage violence.[11] Some also argue that the defense is more effective when used by whites to justify violence against blacks than vice versa. Laws passed electorally are not set in stone—the Constitution is the law of the land, and voters cannot agree to bypass it by, for example, voting to exclude black people from lunch counters. Those days are over. But the tension between respecting the will of the people through legislatures and restricting the will of the people through constitutional interpretation is intense—and resolving that tension puts an extraordinary amount of power in the hands of nine individuals on the US Supreme Court.

Myth #4: The Second Amendment right to bear arms is sacrosanct, so any limits on it are unconstitutional. Wrong. Regardless of which side of the political aisle you are on, this is incorrect. Lots of constitutional rights have limits. In *Heller* itself, Justice Scalia wrote: "Like most rights, the right secured by the Second Amendment is not unlimited. . . . [T]hrough the 19th-century cases, commentators and courts routinely explained that the right was not a right to keep and carry any weapon whatsoever in any manner whatsoever and for whatever purpose."[12] This part of the *Heller* holding might come as a surprise to many of you who might have gleaned through popular culture that the Second Amendment is impenetrable.

Think about the First Amendment's right to free speech, which we just discussed. It's pretty foundational to American sensibilities. But we treat government restrictions on religious and political speech differently than we do "speech" via child pornography or threats to the US president. It's all about balancing—we balance the good things about free speech with the bad things about free speech, and we make a call—we draw a line (often through the Supreme Court).

When it comes to gun violence, we might all agree that the line can be drawn at nuclear weapons in the home. Some might draw it at automatic weapons. Or semiautomatic weapons with bump stocks. Or at mandatory background checks or safety training or post-purchase cooling-off periods. The question comes down to this: Does the Second Amendment right to self-defense outweigh the heightened dangers of increasingly lethal guns? US assault rifles were engineered by Germans in World War II, when commanders realized they needed more powerful battlefield weapons. Compared to "standard" guns, they are harder for law enforcement to counteract, they increase the risk of hurting and killing bystanders, and they inflict greater damage on human flesh. If the shooter who killed twenty small children at Sandy Hook Elementary School hadn't had to stop and reload, nine more youngsters might not have managed to escape the carnage.[13]

The question for us all is not whether to draw the line—the Supreme Court has already answered that as a "yes" many times over—but where. The government cannot take away all guns. That is clear and undisputed. But the government is not constitutionally forbidden from restricting guns either. That is clear and—at the Supreme Court—also undisputed.

CHAPTER 7

Crime and the Fourth, Fifth, Sixth, and Eighth Amendments

Amendment IV [1791].

The right of the people to be secure in their persons, houses, papers, and effects, against **unreasonable searches and seizures**, shall not be violated, and **no Warrants shall issue, but upon probable cause**, supported by Oath or affirmation, and particularly describing the place to be searched, and the persons or things to be seized.

The ban on unreasonable searches and seizures is one place where the notion of "privacy" appears in the Constitution. The word itself is nowhere.

Courts cannot issue arrest or search warrants without a sworn statement justifying them.

Amendment V [1791].

No person . . . shall be **compelled in any criminal case to be a witness against himself**.

This is where the notion of "pleading the Fifth" comes from.

Amendment VI [1791].

In all criminal prosecutions, the accused shall enjoy the **right to a speedy and public trial, by an impartial jury** of the State and district wherein the crime shall have been committed . . . and to be informed of the nature and cause of the accusation; to **be confronted with the witnesses against him; to have compulsory process for obtaining witnesses in his favor, and to have the Assistance of Counsel** for his defence.

The Sixth Amendment has rules aimed at making sure criminal trials are fair.

Amendment VIII [1791].

This is where the death penalty debate plays out.

Excessive bail shall not be required, nor excessive fines imposed, **nor cruel and unusual punishments inflicted**.

This chapter is about crime under the Constitution. The framers of the Bill of Rights cared a lot about fairness to criminal defendants (and justice for victims), as demonstrated by the fact that four—yes, four—amendments to the Constitution address the topic. But it's not just the people who wind up prosecuted for crimes who will find protections in the Constitution. It's anybody who lives in America and doesn't want the government peering into his or her personal business.

The Constitution draws some very clear red lines here. It won't let the government knock down your door and rifle through your stuff willy-nilly. Nor does it let judges give the go-ahead for that kind of thing (by issuing a warrant) without having a certain kind of evidence first. It won't let the government trump up charges against a political dissident and throw her in jail indefinitely. The Constitution contains language that won't let the government torture prisoners into confessing to stuff they didn't do, or force people to make statements that could land them in jail, and so on. Only government—not regular people—can "press" charges. Nonetheless, there are times when the government forces reluctant witnesses to take part in a prosecution against their will.

As you know by this point, when the Constitution says "thou shalt not" do something, it needs consequences. There are bad cops, bad prosecutors, and bad judges. And cops, prosecutors, and judges who make mistakes. By affording individuals specific rights in the Fourth, Fifth, Sixth, and Eighth Amendments to the Constitution, the framers put tools in each of our individual backpacks of rights, which we can take out to stop the government from doing something it isn't supposed to do.

How are these tools employed? Sometimes we can sue for money damages. Sometimes the evidence won't be available to the prosecution—i.e., a defendant can file a motion asking the judge to throw out a case or to ban the government from presenting certain evidence to a jury on the theory that, for example, the Fourth Amendment was violated when the government searched the accused's iPhone and found incriminating documents. (The Supreme Court held in 2014 that the police *usually* need a warrant to search data stored on a cell phone.)[1] Sometimes the government violates your privacy and, even though they can't use the information in a trial against you, there's nothing else that can be done.

It's not unusual to read these days about how some cops cross the line and abuse people whom they pulled over for minor offenses, particularly if the suspect is African American. There are countless stories in the annals of American history about juries convicting innocent people as well. So obviously, the Constitution doesn't protect everyone all the time; in each case, the Constitution works only if—at a minimum—the person whose rights were harmed went to court and demanded that the Constitution be enforced. As we've seen thus far, in construing the Constitution, judges often do some wild things—both for and against individual parties—that don't necessarily seem obvious from the constitutional text itself. This is what I call legal gray areas. Things are rarely clear-cut under the Constitution.

But keep in mind that rulings under the Constitution can serve another function, in addition to making someone whole or stopping bad behavior before it gets worse. Decisions in individual cases create new rules—nuanced, fact-based threads delineating what behavior is acceptable and what is not—that guide the government's actions going forward. Consider a recent ruling by the Court of Appeals for the Ninth

Circuit over the summer of 2018, which held that a Mexican mom could sue a US Border Patrol agent who killed her son through a border fence in Nogales, Arizona. The court held that the officer—who shot the sixteen-year-old multiple times, mostly in the back—violated the Fourth Amendment's ban on unreasonable searches and seizures. As a practical matter, all the court held was that the agent couldn't get the entire lawsuit thrown out. The mom still might lose the case later in the litigation. But this threshold ruling alone will likely change how border patrol agents brandish their firearms going forward.

Bear in mind though that it's really hard to sue a law enforcement officer for violating the Constitution. To get money damages, a person needs to show that the officer should have known that what he was doing was constitutionally wrong. The behavior has to be something that was clearly illegal, and the wronged individual must show that a reasonable officer would know it was illegal. Look again at the text of the Fourth Amendment—it doesn't say much. As we've discussed, most of what constitutional law means is set forth in cases. Each case represents a different story involving different parties and different facts.

Does this mean, then, that in the face of a constitutional lawsuit, an officer can simply say, "This *exact* thing never happened before, so I'm off the hook"? Not quite. Judges make the call as to whether—even if no court has exactly decided that a particular search of a car was illegal, for example—it still might have been obvious *enough*. If a hypothetical "reasonable officer" would *not* have known that a particular act is unconstitutional—if instead a reasonable officer could *not* have foreseen how a court would rule—the officer generally gets immunity. He can't be sued for what he did, period.[2]

In the case I just mentioned, even though the victim was a Mexican citizen standing on Mexican soil, the court held that any reasonable officer should have known that shooting and killing a person through the border fence is unlawful under the Constitution. Think about this. The court was not saying that the officer could be charged with *murder* by the Mexican government (good luck extraditing him). The question was whether, by shooting a Mexican citizen who was standing on Mexican soil, an officer on US soil could be charged with violating the *US Constitution*. The victim was Mexican and in Mexico at the time. But the Fourth Amendment forbids unreasonable seizures, the court reasoned, and taking (i.e., "seizing") a life with bullets counts—even if those bullets land in Mexico.[3]

The counterargument is that police officers can't do their jobs if they are afraid that well-meaning actions—even well-meaning mistakes—could bankrupt them in litigation later. If we expect law enforcement officers to read the minds of future courts in order to stay out of trouble with the Constitution, then they might not act. Officers won't do what it takes to do the job of law enforcement if it means a parade of lawsuits. So again, it's about balance: balancing enforcement of the Constitution's requirements on one side of the scale (because without enforcement, the document means nothing), and balancing on the other side the public policy implications of holding officers accountable for actions that, in hindsight, are unconstitutional.

Fourth Amendment

Three undefined words in the Fourth Amendment especially matter: *unreasonable*, *search*, and *seizure*. In 1791, the framers were worried about British soldiers searching through a family's home for no legitimate reason. Back in England, the monarch had access to such a thing as a "general warrant." He could snoop as he pleased. The Fourth Amendment grew out of the framers' concern "that indiscriminate searches and seizures conducted under the authority of 'general warrants' were . . . immediate evils" to be avoided by, first, "protecting the basic right to be free from unreasonable searches and seizures" and, second, "requiring that warrants be particular and supported by probable cause."[4]

The Constitution's warrant requirement means that a search has to be cleared by a judge or a magistrate (a sort of "lay" judge) in advance. The framers didn't want the government to be able to do a search just to see if there is something they can find. That's why they have to show a judge that there's probable cause in the first place.[5]

What does the ban on unreasonable searches and seizures mean today? Back then, documents were kept in homes and private offices. They were written on parchment. There were no duplicates. Things were simpler. Nonetheless, to understand what *search* means, we still might begin with the meaning of the plain text. To "search" means to hunt or look for something. A woman drops an earring at an outdoor barbecue. She searches for it through the grass. We likewise understand the idea of a police officer searching a car or a home office. A person in uniform opens up a glove compartment or file cabinet to find a stash of drugs or an "aha!" document that shifts the storyline of a particular case.

What if the government takes someone's Facebook data and learns that he donated money to an organization that helps Syrian refugees? The government then connects that data with other data it purchased from a data broker by applying a sophisticated algorithm. Based on the new information gleaned from that process, the government decides that the guy has a higher-than-average likelihood of becoming a terrorist. It knows that the man plans to be at a protest on the National Mall in Washington, DC, next month, and decides to keep an eye on him. Is the government's use of publicly available data to create *new data* about somebody—a very detailed portrait of that person's job, personal history, business, friends, financial history, purchasing preferences, reading materials, interests, and beliefs—a "search"? The Supreme Court hasn't answered this question.[6]

A few more takeaways about the Fourth Amendment. The first is that the court has expanded the definition of *search* to include "when the government violates a subjective expectation of privacy that society recognizes as reasonable."[7] Let's stop for a moment to unpack the logic of this. The question is whether a reasonable person would expect that whatever the government probed would be kept private. There are two parts to this inquiry: whether the individual's actual, subjective expectation was that a space would be private and whether society in general would expect it to be private. For the second part, the court looks to a hypothetical "reasonable person" for answers about what the Fourth Amendment covers. If a reasonable person would expect privacy, then the government's probe constitutes a search, and the Fourth Amendment applies. Applying this test, the Supreme Court has held that a person has a reasonable expectation of privacy in a hotel room and in old-fashioned phone booths (if you can find one).[8] But beware: there's a reduced expectation of privacy in your car.[9]

The "reasonable expectation of privacy" part, though, is running into trouble with modern technology. Long ago, the Supreme Court declared that "[w]hat a person knowingly exposes to the public, even in his home or office, is not a subject of Fourth Amendment protection."[10] Thus, there is no reasonable expectation of privacy in abandoned property, like garbage left out for collection, or in the movements of an automobile on public thoroughfares, because it is available for members of the public to view. There is no reasonable expectation of privacy in one's voice or handwriting. Or in smells that can be picked up by a drug-sniffing dog during a routine traffic stop. (Although the same dog picking up marijuana from your front porch is performing a Fourth Amendment search of your house—courts are *very* vigilant about protecting the core sphere of privacy that is your home.) In short, if you make something public, you walk away from any Fourth Amendment protections. They are yours to lose, and if you choose to lose them, the Supreme Court won't stop you or let you put that genie back in the bottle later.[11]

Relatedly, the Supreme Court has held that the Fourth Amendment does not prohibit the government from obtaining information revealed to a third party. It's like telling someone a secret and saying "don't tell anyone"—anything you share with a third party cannot be expected to remain private. So the court has found that there's no Fourth Amendment ban on the use of information obtained through government informants. It also found no reasonable expectation of privacy in phone numbers dialed because callers "voluntarily convey [] numerical information to the phone company." Providing tax documents to an accountant or records to a bank also relinquishes Fourth Amendment protections. One court has decided that there is a reasonable expectation of privacy in emails (but to date no other court has agreed).[12]

So far, we've talked about homes (get high Fourth Amendment protection) and cars (less so). What about cyberspace? With each click of a mouse and swipe on a phone, we turn over bits and pieces of information about ourselves to third parties. Are we giving up Fourth Amendment protections to that information? A CNN reporter bluntly described a typical person's cyber-data trail back in 2012:

> Google has every e-mail you ever sent or received on Gmail. It has every search you ever made, the contents of every chat you ever had over Google Talk. It holds a record of every telephone conversation you had using Google Voice, it knows every Google Alert you've set up. It has your Google Calendar with all content going back as far as you've used it, including everything you've done every day since then. It knows your contact list with all the information you may have included about yourself and the people you know. It has your Picasa pictures, your news page configuration, indicating what topics you're most interested in. And so on.

If you ever used Google while logged in to your account to search for a person, a symptom, a medical side effect, a political idea; if you ever gossiped using one of Google's services, all of this is on Google's servers. And thanks to the magic of Google's algorithms, it is easy to sift through the information because Google search works like a charm. Google can even track searches on your computer when you're not logged in for up to six months.

Facebook has even more interesting stuff: your pictures, your comments, your likes, your friends, your un-friends.[13]

Under the reasonable expectation of privacy test, the Fourth Amendment protects none of this stuff because we give it away voluntarily. Of course, we really have no choice—unless we go off the grid and live in a cave somewhere.

The Supreme Court knows it needs to figure out what to do about this loophole in the law because Congress isn't regulating how our data trail can be used by the government or by the private sector. Technology is moving so fast, and the Constitution just isn't keeping up. The court recently pulled back on the rule that if you tell a "third party," you waive your Fourth Amendment rights. Although by signing up for a plan with Verizon and AT&T people consent to sharing location data, the court found that getting that data requires a warrant.[14]

The next takeaway is a big-picture one. The Supreme Court has identified an underlying goal of the Fourth Amendment that is broader than stopping government searches. It has recognized that "[t]he overriding function of the Fourth Amendment is to protect personal privacy and dignity against unwarranted intrusion by the State."[15] In a case called *Mapp v. Ohio*, the court went so far as to characterize the Fourth Amendment as establishing a "*right* to privacy, no less important than any other right carefully and particularly reserved to the people" (emphasis mine).[16] I raise this point because an actual right to privacy is nowhere expressed in the Constitution, and it's a major legal component of hot-button issues like abortion. Privacy is one of the "soft" norms that we've talked about before—values that are intrinsic in a good life and a society marked by individual freedom and liberty but are not spelled out as a constitutional rule that can be enforced through clear terms.

The final point about the Fourth Amendment is the warrant requirement. The idea here is that each search or seizure should be cleared in advance by a judge. To get a warrant, the government must produce documents or a sworn statement by an FBI agent or someone else that there is a certain level of suspicion of criminal activity by the person who is about to be searched. That level is known as probable cause, which varies slightly depending on whether we are talking about a search or an arrest. Probable cause to arrest means that there was a crime committed and that person likely committed the crime, while probable cause to search means it is likely that evidence of a crime is located in a specific area.

There are a lot of exceptions to the warrant requirement—none of which, again, are spelled out in the Constitution—particularly when it comes to searches of cars. A Supreme Court case, *Carroll v. United States*, created the vehicle exception, which permits police to search a car without a warrant as long as there is probable cause. Police can also detain people on the street without a warrant and can search and seize things in an emergency, on the rationale that there's no time to get before a judge. We won't go into details here, but know that you *do* have rights if you are pulled over; cops cannot search your car for zero reason. (And if you are arrested, you get *Miranda* warnings—telling you your rights—which the Supreme Court mandated in a case applying the Fifth and Sixth Amendments. If the cops don't do that, prosecutors can't use your statements against you at trial.)[17] But the bar to searching your car is not as high as the Fourth Amendment's plain language might otherwise suggest.

The warrant requirement was in the news in 2018 with the search of former Trump lawyer Michael Cohen's home and office as well as the government's surveillance of Trump campaign foreign policy adviser Carter Page. People debated whether those searches were politically motivated, based on fake information, or otherwise improper. Missing from these debates was a discussion of the basic law governing how these searches came about. Both were done pursuant to warrants, which were signed off on by Article III judges who were required under the Constitution to satisfy themselves that the government produced sufficient evidence of probable cause to search. (Page's warrant implicated a statute called the Foreign Intelligence Surveillance Act—or FISA—as well, but the idea is the same.)[18]

Because judges cannot issue warrants based on speculation and political motivations, and judges take their jobs seriously, it's just wrong—and hazardous—to politicize that process, as many people have done recently, including members of Congress. We want federal judges to remain independent of political attacks and factual distortions. It keeps the process fair for everyone. And although judges can make mistakes, and judicial procedures are oftentimes flawed, we should not be seriously wringing our hands about the federal judiciary these days. Judges are bound by a lot of rules, including that they have to apply the law and the facts of the cases before them. The facts can only come into that calculus if certain standards are followed. This is not the case with politicians—they can consider whatever comes across their desks or on their computers, regardless of how reliable or unreliable the information is. This is a big distinction between judges and politicians, and one that preserves the integrity of our judicial system.

Fifth Amendment

Now imagine someone is arrested for speeding. The police officer runs a search of the person's record and finds that there are three outstanding warrants for the guy's arrest—two robberies and an assault. The officer puts the suspect in the back of his cruiser, gets behind the steering wheel, and says, "I see you have a record a mile long. We can do this the easy way or the hard way. I'll take your confession right now, and you won't get beat up in jail. Or you can pretend that you are innocent, and face the consequences. You choose."

If the suspect complies and confesses to the robberies and assault, it could go one of two ways for him. The suspect could go to jail—even though the police officer got him to confess by threatening him with physical violence. That threat violated the suspect's Fifth Amendment right not to incriminate himself. The Fifth Amendment embodies the notion that we don't want the government to be able to bully people into admitting to things they did or didn't do if the penalty is jail—and remember, that's the big difference between a civil case and a criminal one. A civil case can't land someone in jail. But because the suspect didn't pull out the Fifth Amendment tool from his backpack of individual rights under my hypothetical, the Constitution would remain unenforced. The cop would get away with it, and future cops might get away with it too.

The other way it could go is that the suspect gets a lawyer who reads the confession and hears from her client that the confession was coerced with a threat. First off, the lawyer would call the government and tell the prosecutor that this is a bunch of BS. But let's assume the government won't budge. When the suspect is later brought before a court by the government on formal charges of robbery or assault (via a piece of paper called either an information or an indictment, the latter being something that is issued by a grand jury), the defense lawyer would enter a plea of not guilty. If the government takes the case to trial anyway, and endeavors to introduce the confession into evidence, the defense lawyer would then move to exclude it because it was obtained in violation of the Fifth Amendment (something known by lawyers and judges as the exclusionary rule, which also applies to unlawful searches and seizures under the Fourth Amendment, as well as the failure to give *Miranda* warnings). The tool would come out of the backpack. The judge would likely grant that motion. The government would then have to either drop the case or come up with better evidence of the suspect's crimes. If the case is dropped, the guy walks free.

A few additional notes about "pleading the Fifth." Technically, this issue comes up when someone is brought before a grand jury or at trial to testify about her knowledge regarding a crime. When a question is asked that, if answered, would get the witness in criminal trouble, she can refuse to answer it unless she gets immunity. If she gets immunity (from being prosecuted for related crimes or from having her testimony used against her later), she *can* be compelled to testify. At this juncture, the question becomes: What's the penalty for not talking to a grand jury— i.e., what's the equivalent of the threatened violence in my speeding hypothetical? The answer is contempt.

This topic has come up with Special Counsel Robert Mueller's probe of Russian interference in the election; if President Trump receives a grand jury subpoena and refuses to testify, then what? Well, the matter would go before a judge. Either the witness would move to quash or kill the subpoena altogether or, in my hypothetical, if she refuses to answer, the government would file a motion asking the judge to hold the witness in contempt until she testifies. This can literally mean going to jail (it happened to a woman named Susan McDougal in the Whitewater investigation by Independent Counsel Kenneth Starr, on which I worked). In both instances—whether on a motion to quash or a motion for a contempt order—the judge would be deciding whether the Fifth

Amendment "tool" applies to protect the witness from having to say things that hurt her.

Note that pleading the Fifth is generally done on a question-by-question basis. Answering "What's your name?" is not an issue that could incriminate a witness. Answering "Did you pull the trigger of the gun?" is one that would. So the Fifth is not a blanket protection. (For Trump, it's a bit different, as there is an argument that he gets blanket protection on separation-of-powers grounds, because he's the head of the executive branch, but for regular people, that argument does not apply.) Some people criticize the very notion of pleading the Fifth as some sort of cop-out. But it's in the Constitution for a reason: to protect individuals from being unfairly bullied by the government through the criminal justice system.

The notion that a person can plead the Fifth just to avoid answering uncomfortable questions—even if there is no criminal liability for doing so—is also a bit dodgy. Most people won't do it "just for the heck of it" because it looks really bad. It looks like a person has something to hide. It also turns out that the Fifth Amendment privilege only kicks in if you actually do have stuff to hide.[19]

So imagine that you are a witness in a grand jury trial who was an accountant for a defendant who is charged with tax fraud (yes, I'm referring to the 2018 trial of former Trump campaign chair Paul Manafort in the Eastern District of Virginia; a number of those people who testified initially pled the Fifth). Your invocation of the Fifth Amendment privilege gets to a judge, either by your motion to quash a subpoena or via a government's motion for an order holding you in contempt for refusing to testify (either side, in other words, can bring the issue before a judge). You will need to tell the judge that your claim is legitimate, meaning you will have to show your cards (privately to the judge) as to what you would say, if forced, that will get you in trouble. If you are fibbing, the judge won't let you plead the Fifth. He will deny your motion or grant the government's, and you could go to jail until you agree to testify. Again, if compelled to testify after pleading the Fifth, by contrast, the government will often give you immunity from prosecution later, so your statements cannot be used against you. In that event, you can't get away with refusing to testify anymore—there is no legal danger in your doing so.

Sixth Amendment

If the Fifth and Fourth Amendments are about events prior to a criminal trial, then the Sixth Amendment covers the trial itself. Here's what goes in the accused's backpack for that process: a speedy trial, a fair jury, an attorney if the accused person wants one, and the chance to confront people who are accusing that person of a crime.

Let's tease this list apart. *Speedy* means that the government can't leave you in jail for months or years while it actually gets around to proving in a jury trial that you did what it says you allegedly did wrong. Imagine that you are not guilty of any crime but a crooked cop arrests you, and a crooked prosecutor charges you, and they know they can't convict you. But they want the community to think they "got the man" responsible for, say, a brutal murder that has gone unsolved and is making the public restless. So they catch you and lock you up. They secretly plan to throw away the key and never actually go to trial—but they tell you they're just backlogged and will get around to proving why they have the right to put you in jail at some point soon. The Constitution says, Get on with it. Most judges allow both sides of a case to take the time at trial that the judge believes they need, at least—but not unlimited time. At some point, the government needs to either prove its case against you or let you go home.

That said, the practical reality is that lots of people are incarcerated— often for long periods of time—waiting for trial. They can lose their jobs and their homes in the interim—all the while being "innocent until proven guilty." (That phrase is about the government's burden of proving crimes—it's not itself a right in the Constitution.) Generally, poor people and their families are more likely to suffer these kinds of harms than are people who have the money to make bail.[20]

As for the jury, it has to be impartial. This means that the government can't put a murder victim's entire extended family in the jury box and expect them to fairly hear the evidence against the alleged murderer. And it can't have people in the jury box who think all murderers should be executed, or something else along such prejudicial lines. That's not fair either. The lawyers and the judges will go through a Q and A process called *voir dire*—which derives from the French language and today means "to see, to say"—to find out whether the jurors are biased or whether they can fairly consider the evidence in a neutral fashion. Of course, as one can imagine, this process is more of an art than a science. How often do you think the question "Do you all promise to be fair and impartial?" will actually produce an accurate response? I mean, who is going to say no to that (except as an excuse to go home)? Most lawyers realize that they need to be more strategic in asking subtle questions that get at this issue in other ways. (Note that some cases get tried before a judge—not a jury—even in criminal cases. They're called bench trials, and for those, judges need to be impartial too.)

However, just because someone in the jury pool is a mom, or a Republican, or African American, or wealthy, etcetera, doesn't mean that she will stereotypically go one way or another on the ultimate issues in the case. Juries are funny things. When you think about it, they are exquisitely democratic. They are arguably the most democratic institution we have these days, because regular people get to decide matters of immense importance. Think about a jury trial of a member of Congress accused of insider trading; if the jury convicts, the message is clear to all elected leaders that this kind of thing is not going to fly. Juries are made of regular people with their own unique experiences. We know from our own personal, day-to-day relationships that people—even those close to us—can surprise us. For attorneys and judges, juries are no different.

A few final points about the Sixth Amendment. The Constitution says that the government can't have "secret" witnesses lodge accusations against you. You generally get to probe those folks face-to-face (or your lawyer does), or their testimony stays out of the trial against you. Again, it's all about fairness. The Constitution also says that you get to force the accuser to come to court and air their grievance against you before a neutral decision-maker.

Finally, if the accused wants his own attorney, the government can't say no, and if he can't afford one, the government must pay for one. This is important, because it means the government can't ambush someone by leaving them defenseless at trial. Lawyering is not easy. Anyone who tells you the opposite is lying. It can't be done well without a law degree. In 1963, the Supreme Court extended the right to a free lawyer to state prosecutions. Sadly, as a practical matter, in many states the right is a fiction because there just aren't enough public defenders to go around. Moreover, it's not clear *when* the right to free counsel attaches. Does a person immediately get a *free* lawyer after he is arrested and receives his Miranda warnings (i.e., the right to remain silent speech)? (No.)[21] How about for an appeal of a death penalty sentence? (No again, although some state constitutions provide for a lawyer post-conviction.)[22]

The Supreme Court has stated that a defendant gets a lawyer "at or after the time that judicial proceedings have been initiated against him, whether by formal charge, preliminary hearing, indictment, information or arraignment"—but that doesn't mean a paid one. A good defense lawyer can cost upward of a hundred thousand dollars to try a murder case. The constitutional right to have a lawyer at your criminal trial is one that benefits rich people more than poor people, to be sure. It's not just the lawyers' time, but the time of experts, investigators, jury specialists, audiovisual specialists—on and on—that can suck up a lot of money. Under an ideal budget, the defense team conducts a mock trial of the entire case before a mock jury to work out any kinks. Imagine the cost of paying people to act as jurors, prosecutors, and everything else. Bottom line is that it's good to have access to a lot of money if you are accused of a crime.[23]

Eighth Amendment

Finally, the Eighth Amendment. It's something that every American should know about for one key reason: we have a death penalty in the United States. This is a big deal, for the obvious reason that taking a life is morally problematic and pretty much the most severe kind of punishment imaginable. That's all assuming that punishment is a valid end game in a criminal justice system—some argue that rehabilitation should be a goal as well.[24] Be that as it may, the other reason that the death penalty is a huge deal has to do with government power. It's the government that is taking a life here, and it's often taking the life of an American citizen for reasons that have nothing to do with, say, national security (unlike soldiers who kill enemies or civilians on a foreign battle-field, for example).

As we've just discussed, the Constitution contains rules limiting the government's ability to act arbitrarily and unfairly when it comes to in-vestigating and prosecuting crimes. But people in charge of these things get them wrong—both deliberately and mistakenly. And when they get it wrong, it can only be fixed if an individual is willing and able to bring a claim before a court. The tool has to come out of the backpack for that process to work. So, in addition to lots of other arguments against the death penalty, the question to keep in mind for present purposes is one that we've been talking about throughout this book: How much power should we allow the government to have over our individual lives, liberty, and property (among other things) before it becomes too much? And it's really no answer to make the death penalty other people's problem, on the assumption that "it can never happen to me." Lightning strikes innocent people too. Even though most of us will escape the death penalty, we can't escape government power, so we have to be careful about how much of it accumulates. It can be used against our interests in other ways—a fait accompli before we are even aware of it.

First, a few Eighth Amendment basics. The Constitution bars "cruel and unusual punishment" of people held in jail or in prison. But what is "cruel"? What is "unusual"? Should courts confine themselves to what was uncommon and considered cruel in 1791? To be sure, the phrase bans medieval practices like torture, burning at the stake, and crucifixion. But even here, it gets tricky. We saw this with the debate over waterboarding of suspected terrorists during the George W. Bush administration. Is simulated drowning torture? Most modern Americans would think so. But the famous "torture memos" out of the DOJ under George W. Bush concluded no—nothing is torture if it doesn't produce near-organ failure. A suspect might feel that he's drowning and therefore confess in sheer terror for his life. But so long as the procedure stops short of actually killing him, the government's official analysis went, it's totally fine.[25]

Bush ultimately agreed that waterboarding is not acceptable, as have presidents after him. It might come as a surprise to some people, however, that prisoners in the United States *can* be physically beaten by prison officials without necessarily violating the US Constitution. Guards can also take physical violence too far for the Eighth Amendment, of course. But remember: if there is no consequence when that happens—if the prisoner can't persuade a court to honor his Eighth Amendment tool in his constitutional backpack—the bad behavior will continue. Excessive-force claims under the Eighth Amendment also require that an inmate prove that physical force went beyond what was needed to maintain order. Prisoners are shackled and forced to move in certain ways and to certain places every day. When does maintaining order cease to become maintaining order and move into cruel-and-unusual land? Again, you won't find the answer in the Constitution's text.

In 1992, the Supreme Court considered what it means by "excessive" force in a case involving a handcuffed and shackled inmate who was beaten in plain view of a supervisor. The court rejected the government's argument that no Eighth Amendment violation occurred unless the prisoner showed "significant injury." A minor injury sufficed. Still, it held that the prisoner must show that the force was used "maliciously and sadistically to cause harm," rather than "in a good faith effort to maintain or restore discipline." As one can imagine, it's very hard for prisoners—often without a lawyer and without access to prison records and other information in the government's possession that might help prove their claims—to show that a guard didn't use force for disciplinary reasons but instead acted out of malice or sadism. The government will always make the argument that force was justified. The cards are stacked against prisoners. But the counterargument is that, if it were easy to bring lawsuits against prisons over how prisoners are treated, prisons would not be able to function. Correctional officers would be so tied to acting "with kid gloves" that they wouldn't be able to maintain discipline, and prison resources would be overly invested in litigation.[26]

Violence in prisons isn't the only place the Eighth Amendment's ban on cruel and unusual punishment shows up. It is often raised to rectify harsh conditions of confinement and has been extended to ban things like vermin-infested prisons that lack toilets. The standard that prisoners have to satisfy is one of "deliberate indifference"—words that are nowhere in the Constitution, unsurprisingly. Deliberate indifference is a standard that's hard to meet because it requires proof that prison officials knew about a problem *and* that they deliberately chose to do nothing. Showing that rats are in prison cells is not enough. An inmate must show that prison officials knew about the rats and deliberately chose to do nothing. This kind of showing requires the plaintiff to come up with evidence that essentially climbs into the brain of another person, which is always hard to do.[27]

Keep in mind, moreover, that for prisoners to bring claims in court, they first must "exhaust their administrative remedies." What this means is that there are a lot of procedural hoops that they must go through within the prison's bureaucracy before they can even attempt to get before a judge. They have to complain first to the prison, and that complaint process includes filing—on time—whatever internal prison appeals are required. And they have to dot their i's and cross their t's when they do these things. If they don't, they can't be heard in court— even if their claims are legitimate.

The rationale here is that, if prisoners have to run things by the warden first, maybe prisons will do the right thing and fix problems without having to bother the courts with the dispute. As with any balancing test, however, the rub is that the prison's procedural hoops can't be so complicated that it's virtually impossible for prisoners to meet them. The Supreme Court has held that—for constitutional claims, at least—the hoops have to actually facilitate a resolution of the prisoner's complaint.[28] As a practical matter, the hoops can be complicated even for novice lawyers—let alone inmates, who may lack even a high school diploma—and the law doesn't care much.

Now for the death penalty. Except for a brief period in the 1970s, the Supreme Court has not considered death to be cruel and unusual punishment under the Eighth Amendment. This should come as no surprise, because we all know that it's legal to execute people in the United States—in thirty-three states, to be more precise, and by the federal government. More than 1,490 people have been legally executed since 1976.[29] By this point in the book, this fact of life in America might raise some new questions in readers' minds. How is it that killing someone isn't at least kind of "cruel"? And "unusual," in that it doesn't happen every day in America and it doesn't happen at all in most countries around the world?

In 1972, the Supreme Court held in a case called *Furman v. Georgia* that the death penalty is not cruel or unusual but that it was being implemented in really awful ways. Burning and bludgeoning had stopped in the early nineteenth century, but the way executions were going down in 1972 was considered "freakish and wanton" (in the words of concurring Justice Stewart, who noted that the imposition of the death penalty is cruel and unusual in the same way that being struck by lightning is cruel and unusual).[30] The court accordingly told states to clean up their acts and change the way they killed people so as to comply with four criteria: the manner of execution can't be degrading to human dignity, it can't be arbitrary, it can't be rejected throughout society, and it can't be unnecessary. Here again, these standards do not exist in the text of the Eighth Amendment itself.

In 1976, the Supreme Court looked again at how the government was killing prisoners in America under *Furman*'s criteria and signed off on death penalty statutes that had been enacted by thirty-five states. Since then, the court's scrutiny of executions under the Eighth Amendment has focused on the "how" instead of on the "whether." The "how" has included firing squads, the gas chamber, hangings, lethal injections, and electrocutions. Electrocutions mostly fell out of favor at some point on the rationale that lethal injection is more humane. But there have been many instances in which inmates suffer horribly due to ineffective drugs. Does one botched execution condemn the entire practice as cruel and unusual? Part of the problem now is that drug manufacturers are refusing to sell the particular chemicals that go into the cocktail used on death row, so states have to consider other options—which may or may not work. If they don't work properly, the execution can become ugly and mean.[31]

A few other things to keep in mind when considering whether, on balance, the way we execute people in this country is constitutional or, even if it is constitutional, worth doing as a policy matter. Since 1976, 144 people have been released from death row on grounds of innocence—that's 10 percent of the total number sentenced to death.[32] If we assume that some people aren't making it all the way to proving innocence through the appeal process—which is an entirely fair assumption given what we know about how hard and expensive it is to prove things in court, particularly without a lawyer—it means that the government has killed, and will likely continue to kill, innocent people.

Statistics show that the death penalty process is very expensive for taxpayers (with death row costing more per year than life in prison), and that it doesn't really deter people from committing offenses that carry the death penalty.[33] They also suggest that geography (southern versus northern states), race, gender, and the ability to afford a lawyer (i.e., wealth) all come into play regarding whether someone is executed by the government—rather than the heinousness of the actual crime relative to other crimes. (In this connection, the death penalty has triggered other constitutional problems, primarily under the Equal Protection Clauses, but so far the Supreme Court has rejected them.)[34]

"Eye for an eye" retribution is on the other side of the scale, to be sure. Some people will say that certain crimes are so awful that we must have execution as an option, and even if a few stray people get killed by mistake, and even if people of color are disproportionately executed, it's too bad, but making sure we are harsh on really awful crimes is too important to give up. But even on that metric, the statistics don't line up. Really scary criminals sit in jail for life. Others have been executed for being entangled in a murder they didn't actually commit. Statistics show, moreover, that a majority of Americans don't care whether a politician opposes the death penalty. There isn't strong public support *for* it. And internationally, the United States trails only five countries in the number of executions from 2007 to 2012: China, Iran, Saudi Arabia, Pakistan, and Yemen.[35]

CHAPTER 8

Liberty and Equality: Fifth and Fourteenth Amendments

Liberty has come to mean more than freedom from incarceration.

Amendment V [1791].

No person shall be . . . deprived of life, **liberty**, or property, without **due process of law**.

There are two due process clauses; this one applies to the federal government.

Amendment XIV [1868].

No State shall make or enforce any law which shall abridge **the privileges or immunities of citizens of the United States**; nor shall any State deprive any person of **life, liberty, or property, without due process of law**; nor deny to any person within its jurisdiction the **equal protection of the laws**.

What's a *privilege* or an *immunity?*

This one applies to the states.

This is where many of our civil rights come from.

For the purposes of this discussion, think of "liberty" as a person's ability to live life without too much government interference. Liberty is connected to fairness and some version of equality. The Declaration of Independence states that "[w]e hold these truths to be self-evident, that all men are created equal, that they are endowed by their Creator, with certain unalienable Rights, and that among these are Life, Liberty and the pursuit of Happiness." But the Declaration of Independence doesn't bind government. You can't put it in your backpack to pull out in court one day if the government goes too far in stomping on your rights. Those rights are—if anywhere—in another document: the Constitution.[1]

Many people take for granted that the Constitution ensures "blessings of liberty," whatever that might mean to a particular individual. Although undefined, it turns out that the words *equal* and *liberty* do appear in the Constitution. But their meaning has fluctuated significantly since the beginning of the republic. Today, arguments for securing equality of outcomes for all people in American society may be associated with the political left, or even with socialism. Nonetheless, across the political spectrum, there are many things we all freely do, and which we all take as a given, that are not expressed in the Constitution. We wouldn't want those rights taken away—whether we happen to be Republicans, Democrats, socialists, or even anarchists.

As residents of one state, for example, we can drive into a neighboring state without that state's troopers harassing us at the border just because we are "foreign" state citizens. We freely sign contracts for employment, for home ownership, for purchasing goods—all without arbitrary restrictions by federal, state, or local governments. (Imagine, by contrast, if only people who earned $100,000 or more per year had the privilege of entering into contracts.) We get to decide whether—and whom—to marry without government weigh-in, whether to have children, how to raise those children, and what jobs or careers we choose to have. Imagine if all of this were dictated by the government.

There is a lot to discuss here. This chapter focuses on four primary themes: race, gender, sexual orientation, and immigration. It asks: How far can the government go in imposing restrictions on men just because they are men? (Of course, in real life this comes up mostly with discrimination against women, but not exclusively.) On African Americans? On gays and lesbians? What about immigrants—do they get rights too? Or can the government do what it pleases with them (like arbitrarily separate mothers from their children at the border and put them into separate prisons, with no plan or viable means of reuniting them)?

Remember that the Constitution cares about the scope of government power. So, we need to be cautious in framing issues of equality and fairness under the Constitution as about giving people "special treatment." Liberty is about containing the government's ability to exercise authority over how we live our lives. If we put more gas in the government's power tank, regardless of who is immediately affected, our own rights necessarily become diminished.

Let's review the two constitutional provisions that come into play here. First are the due process clauses—one in the Fifth Amendment, which binds the federal government, and one in the Fourteenth Amendment, which binds the states. Bear in mind that neither binds private behavior. The basic idea is that the government can't take away your life, liberty, or property without some kind of process (a hearing at which you get to say your side of the story). The government has the authority to execute you—to take your life—but only if you get a trial first. It can take away your liberty too, but only with a trial (or a plea, whereby you agree to go to jail). The government can't take your property without a hearing either. For each of these, you get two basic things: notice of what you allegedly did wrong, and an opportunity to be heard on why you believe the government is wrong to take whatever it's taking away.

The concept of due process traces back to King John's Magna Carta, which was a peace treaty struck in 1215 between the king and a group of rebellious barons who had grievances against him. In the Magna Carta, the king made a series of promises to his subjects, including that "[n]o free man will be seized or imprisoned, or stripped of his rights or possessions, or outlawed or exiled, . . . nor will we proceed with force against him, or send others to do so, except by the lawful judgement of his equals or by the law of the land." The Magna Carta is important because it established the principle that everybody—including the king—is bound by the rule of law. It's a mantra that remains critically important to this day, as President Trump pushes back on virtually any force that seeks to hold him accountable for his actions while president (albeit they did so to a lesser degree).

The Constitution only says that a person gets "process" if the clauses are triggered. It doesn't define what that process must be. If life or liberty is in question, the process is a full-blown jury trial. Trials are constrained by detailed rules of evidence, which are designed to ensure that juries aren't making decisions based on lying witnesses or falsified documents and the like. They are managed by a neutral decision-maker—a judge—who is not allowed to talk privately to either side about the case. That would be unfair. Both sides get to be represented by attorneys if they want, and the losing party gets to appeal to a higher court. The jury trial is the "gold standard" for process. All the details for ensuring a fair trial—a neutral judge, the ability to cross-examine witnesses, the ability to have your own lawyer, etcetera—are part of the cluster of elements that make up the gold standard for "process."

The government does many things that affect a person's liberty or property in ways that are less drastic than execution or imprisonment, however. Liberty has been construed to include the ability to choose a profession, for example.[2] So if the government wants to take away a doctor's medical license, the doctor gets a hearing because the Constitution says so. There are many additional federal, state, and local laws that overlap with or supplement the Constitution's protection of due process. Those might cover the doctor too. But for our purposes, the question is what does the "boss of all bosses" say about what the government can and cannot do to individual liberty—i.e., the Constitution.

Property has also been expanded to mean more than just physical objects. The Supreme Court has construed welfare benefits as property.[3] If a person qualifies for benefits under the law, the government can't strip those benefits arbitrarily; due process requires a hearing. Some people might think this goes too far, on the theory that welfare benefits are perks at taxpayers' expense—not a constitutional right. That's a fair argument, but it misses the mark. Here again, the question for the Constitution is whether the government has the power to act arbitrarily in ways that impact people's life, liberty, and property. If the government is going to authorize the receipt of welfare benefits, which it doesn't have to do, it can't then arbitrarily pick and choose who gets them among people who are otherwise equally qualified under the welfare laws. It can't only give benefits to white people, for example, despite the equal qualifications of certain people of color.

As a practical matter, hearings that comply with the Constitution can run the gamut, from a desk decision based strictly on paperwork (yes, that's a hearing), to a judicial-type proceeding that allows a party to present witnesses and documents. The more procedures an agency must follow, the more expensive a hearing gets, so the Supreme Court uses a balancing test to determine how much procedure is necessary in light of the liberty or property interests at stake. Denials of welfare benefits get more process than denials of disability benefits, for example, although the reasons for the Supreme Court's distinction here are sketchy.[4]

Although seemingly lofty, the due process clauses can impact everyday life. Imagine that your daughter gets suspended from the University of Maryland because she allegedly cheated on a law school exam. Because a law degree is obtained in pursuit of a profession, there is a constitutional liberty interest at stake for her. The University of Maryland is an arm of the state, so the Fourteenth Amendment's due process clause applies. She gets a hearing. Suppose you want to hire the best lawyer in the area for that hearing. The lawyer might want to present a parade of witnesses to testify that your daughter is an honest and trustworthy person, and maybe additional witnesses who were present during the exam to testify that they didn't see her cheat. Maybe the lawyer will also want to present an expert witness to explain the latest research regarding best practices for exam administration, so she can argue to the dean that the school's testing procedures are part of the problem here.

Under the balancing test for due process, your daughter might get none of those things. She might get nothing more than the opportunity to draft a letter to the dean giving her side of the story, on the rationale that the other things are just too expensive and cumbersome for the school to administer regularly. Or a court might find that more process is warranted because only a few students a month find themselves in this position, so the school can reasonably accommodate the hassle of additional procedures. If all of this happened at Georgetown University, your daughter would get no process at all unless the school decided unilaterally to give it; Georgetown is a private university, so the due process clause doesn't apply.

The meaning of due process has been expanded beyond mandated hearings. The idea behind what's known as substantive due process is that certain rights—although not expressed in the Constitution itself—are so central to the concept of liberty that the government cannot get at them regardless of what procedures it uses. Substantive due process includes things like the right to work, the right to marry, and the right to decide how to raise your own children. When these rights are at stake, the government can't interfere with them unless it has a very good reason to. *Roe v. Wade*—which legalized abortion on the theory that women have the right to make choices about their bodies without the government telling them they can't—is grounded on substantive due process. Like the right to marry and the right to refuse medical treatment, the right to an abortion is not spelled out in the Constitution. But if the Supreme Court were to do away with the concept of substantive due process, a number of other rights that we take for granted could later go with it. This is a wrinkle that is rarely discussed when the topic of abortion rights comes around, but it's very important for people to understand if they are committed to unraveling *Roe*.

The other provision that is important for liberty and equality is the Equal Protection Clause, which provides that no state may deny any person within its jurisdiction "equal protection of the laws." Note here that this language says nothing about the *federal* government treating people equally under the law. Nor is there a separate amendment for that purpose, unlike for due process. In an important case decided in 1872, the court fixed this disconnect on both ends by holding that the due process clauses apply the First through Eighth Amendments to the states and the federal government alike.

An equal protection challenge to a law has three steps. The first is that a law has to draw a distinction based on a personal trait. Requiring a person to be twenty-one years old in order to purchase alcohol, for example, is discrimination on the basis of age. The second is that the government's distinction-drawing must be for a good enough reason. The first step really matters for the second one. If the distinction—or "classification"—is one that we don't want the government drawing distinctions around, then the government has to have a really good reason for it. Race is like that, and it gets "strict scrutiny." Age discrimination is less of a hot-button issue and enhancing public safety is a good reason for a no-teen-drinking rule. You get the point.[5]

There are a couple of nuances that you might find interesting. Imagine a law that says, "Nobody under the age of twenty-one can purchase alcohol." But what if the law is written in language that is totally neutral but unfairly affects a certain group of people anyway? Take gender, for instance. What if the same law stated that only people who are five-foot-ten and weigh more than 150 pounds can purchase alcohol? A small percentage of women as compared to men meet this criteria. This law discriminates against women because it's harder for them to purchase alcohol—they need tall friends to do it for them. But the Supreme Court has essentially said too bad. Unless it's shown that the *purpose* behind the law was to discriminate against women in this hypothetical, there is no equal-protection case. As we've seen, when standards require proof of motive or intent, we're climbing into minds again, and it becomes very hard for plaintiffs to win their cases.

Additionally, how does the court decide what grading rubric to use: strict, intermediate, or rational basis scrutiny? Well, as a first cut, it comes down to how a person is born. If the government is discriminating based on immutable characteristics that a person has no control over—like race, gender, what part of the country or world he came from, and whether his parents are married or divorced—then something more than rational basis applies. Race gets strict scrutiny. Gender gets intermediate.[6]

So assume that we've identified a class that gets protected (step one) and decided what grading rubric applies (step two). The third step in the equal-protection analysis is that, whatever level of scrutiny is applied, a court must decide whether the government's reasons for the law are good enough to satisfy the test. Sometimes, the answer seems like a slam dunk. In 1942, the Supreme Court applied strict scrutiny to strike down a law that required surgical sterilization of people convicted of three or more crimes involving "moral turpitude." The court found that the law was about the right to procreate.[7] If you want to have babies, the law basically said, the government will stop you from achieving that goal because public safety requires that your genetic material be taken out of the gene pool. Not okay.

Note that, on the other end of the spectrum, it's almost impossible for the government to fail rational basis review. So long as the state can concoct a rational excuse for a law, it will stand—which means that if something gets rational basis review, the plaintiffs are almost sure to lose their case. New York's law prohibiting physician-assisted suicide was upheld on rational basis review, for example, because it applied equally to everyone; there was no group being singled out. Across all three classifications, the government is more likely to win if it can say the law is about protecting things like safety and public health.[8]

Race

Race may be one of the most important and divisive issues in American life today, and so—full disclosure—this section may contain more than a usual amount of summarizing important cases. Here goes:

Prior to the Fourteenth Amendment, the Supreme Court upheld the constitutionality of slavery. In 1793, Congress enacted the Fugitive Slave Act requiring that captured slaves be returned to their "owners." Pennsylvania then passed a law outlawing the use of violence to return slaves. The Supreme Court struck down the Pennsylvania law in 1842, citing "the complete right and title of ownership in their slaves, as property, in every state in the Union into which they might escape from the state where they were held in servitude." The court based its ruling on language in Article IV of the Constitution requiring "a person held in service or labor" who escapes to another state to "be delivered up on claim of the party to whom such service or labour may be due." The original Constitution required that abhorrent result, but the language was overridden by the Thirteenth Amendment's slavery ban.[9]

In 1819, Congress admitted Missouri into the United States as a slave state and Maine as a free state. The legislation was known as the Missouri Compromise because it was designed to retain the existing balance of power between the North and the South. Part of the deal was that slavery would also be prohibited north of the 36°31' parallel, which was an unorganized territory known as the Great Plains. In a famous case called *Dred Scott v. Sandford*, the Supreme Court declared the Missouri Compromise unconstitutional because enslaved people were *property*, not citizens. The government couldn't force people who moved to the Great Plains to give up property that happened to be in the form of human beings.

The case involved a man who was taken by his owner to a free state. When the owner died, the man sued the administrator of the estate, seeking his freedom in the free state of Illinois. The court applied an originalist, history-based approach to the case, concluding—horrifically—that at the time the Constitution was ratified, slaves (and even their freed descendants) were considered "a subordinate and inferior class of beings, who had been subjugated to the dominant race, and whether emancipated or not, yet remained subject to their authority and had no rights or privileges but such as those who held the power and the Government might choose to grant them."[10] The Fourteenth Amendment did away with the *Dred Scott* decision by mandating that all persons "born or naturalized in the United States . . . are citizens of the United States and of the State wherein they reside."

After the Civil War, every southern state passed Jim Crow laws that separated people by race in a wide range of contexts, including public accommodations, transportation, and schools. Private violence against African Americans was rampant too (3,446 blacks were lynched in the United States from 1882 to 1951).[11] In 1875, Congress passed the first Civil Rights Act, which banned discrimination in private places of accommodation like inns and theaters. But the Supreme Court struck the statute down in 1883, concluding that the Fourteenth Amendment applies only to *government* action and that Congress cannot regulate private conduct.[12] (In 1968, the court ruled that Congress could prohibit discrimination by private parties under the Thirteenth Amendment instead.)[13]

We already talked about *Plessy v. Ferguson*, the case in which the Supreme Court in 1896 upheld laws that mandated separation of blacks and whites so long as their respective facilities would be "separate, but equal."[14] And of course, in 1954, the Supreme Court issued *Brown v. Board of Education*. In hindsight, it's amazing that *Brown*—the case that challenged public schools with stark differences on the basis of race—actually came to pass. (South Carolina, for example, had a 1:28 teacher-student ratio for whites and a 1:47 ratio for blacks.) The court heard the case during the 1952 to 1953 term but couldn't agree on a decision, and punted it to the following year. Yet in the interim year, Chief Justice Fred Vinson died of a heart attack. President Dwight D. Eisenhower appointed Earl Warren as the new chief justice. He convinced the other justices to unanimously rule that separate but equal in public schooling was unconstitutional.[15] Note that the *Brown* decision was decidedly not originalist. Warren's opinion reflected compassion and humanity, and redefined black people as equal human beings rather than an inferior race.[16]

Supporters of segregation hated *Brown*, condemning it "as clear abuse of the judicial power."[17] Ninety-six southern congressmen issued a declaration that the case "climaxes a trend in the Federal judiciary undertaking to legislate in derogation of the authority of Congress." The southern congressmen's attack on *Brown* encouraged states to defy the authority of the Supreme Court.[18] Facing a stalemate, the Little Rock school system asked the court for authority to halt its integration plan. In a rare opinion signed by all nine justices, the court said no: "The constitutional rights of respondents are not to be sacrificed or yielded to the violence and disorder which have followed upon the actions of the Governor and the Legislature."[19]

In response, states began closing schools rather than integrating them, and doing other things to get around *Brown*, like integrating only one school per year, so it would take decades to desegregate all schools. The Supreme Court hit back in 1964, declaring it unconstitutional for school systems to close rather than desegregate, and struck down other attempts to bypass *Brown*, including laws that allowed students a "choice" of schools, effectively keeping all the white kids together.[20]

This gamesmanship only ended when Congress stepped up to the plate, enacting the Civil Rights Act of 1964, which prohibited discrimination by schools receiving federal funds. This legislation was followed by the Elementary and Secondary Education Act of 1965, which appropriated billions in funding for schools.[21] With money in the mix, states finally began to fall in line. For the first time, the Civil Rights Act of 1964 also banned *private* racial discrimination that occurs with no government involvement. The statute covered racial discrimination in voting, in places of public accommodation such as hotels and restaurants, in public facilities, in public education, in publicly financed programs, and in employment. More legislation was passed, including the Voting Rights Act of 1965, the Age Discrimination in Employment Act of 1967, the Fair Housing Act of 1968, and the Age Discrimination Act of 1975. Because it had already discarded the Fourteenth Amendment as a means of constraining private—versus governmental—behavior, the Supreme Court looked to other constitutional provisions like the Commerce Clause to uphold these laws.[22]

Despite *Brown*, racial segregation in schools has increased since the 1980s. In 2016, the US Government Accountability Office reported that from 2000 to 2014, the percentage of high-poverty schools with 75 to 100 percent black and Hispanic students increased, while the number of minority students attending low-poverty, mostly white schools dropped.[23] Although there are many possible explanations for this, the court's approach to the Fourteenth Amendment is certainly one of them. As much as the Supreme Court pushed the country toward racial integration with *Brown*, it went backward in cases that didn't involve laws that expressly discriminate on the basis of race. If a law is only subtly discriminatory, with effects on racial minorities that don't spring from the plain language, it's extremely hard to do anything about it under the Equal Protection Clause.[24]

As I mentioned previously, there are two ways to show in court that the government made an unlawful distinction based on a suspect criterion such as race. Option one is available if a law uses language that discriminates against racial minorities—like laws mandating separate but equal schools for African American kids. Option two applies when a law is written in neutral prose but impacts race when it's put into effect. The problem with option two is that, in order to win a case challenging a law's impact, a plaintiff also has to show that the lawmakers *intended* to discriminate against black people.[25] Not only is intent hard to prove, but in this day and age most people who draft legislation know to avoid drawing blatant distinctions based on race or national origin, so option two is often the only one available anymore.

The only time the Supreme Court upheld a classification under option one was in connection with the government's internment of 110,000 Japanese Americans during World War II. These Americans were taken from their homes and put in concentration camps to live in horse stalls and behind barbed wire—all on grounds of national security. The court upheld regulations imposing a curfew on "all persons of Japanese ancestry"—an unequivocal distinction on the basis of race—on the rationale that they "were defense measures for the avowed purpose of safeguarding the military area in question, at a time of threatened air raids and invasion by the Japanese forces." (In its recent decision upholding President Trump's travel ban, *Trump v. Hawaii*, the Supreme Court finally condemned that case.)[26]

The other big issue with respect to option one is in the area of affirmative action—the use of race to remedy past discrimination, enhance diversity, and foster positive role models for minority communities in college admissions, faculty hiring, contract awards, and the like. The Supreme Court has held that these justifications are *not* sufficient to satisfy strict scrutiny of review of racial quotas (meaning the setting aside of a specific number of seats for minority students)—"No can do" to such affirmative action. However, colleges and universities can have a compelling interest in a diverse community, which justifies using race as *one* of many factors that can be used in admissions determinations. The court later held, in addition, that it's legally acceptable for universities to consider an applicant's race or ethnicity in admissions decisions when "no workable race-neutral alternatives would produce the educational benefits of diversity." What might those race-neutral characteristics be? Things bearing on socioeconomic status—like median family income, adult educational attainment, home ownership rates, the number of single-parent households, and the percentage of non-native English speakers.[27]

Gender

As I mentioned already, gender classifications get what's called intermediate scrutiny. What that means is that legislators need a better reason than what comes off the top of their heads in order to pass laws that treat women differently from men because they are women (and vice versa). But the intermediate bar is lower than strict scrutiny, so in the eyes of the Supreme Court, gender discrimination is more tolerable under the Constitution than discrimination on the basis of race or national origin.

Prior to 1971, the Supreme Court upheld numerous laws discriminating against women, including laws forbidding women from becoming attorneys and laws automatically exempting women from jury service on the theory that a "woman is still regarded as the center of the home and family life."[28] The court explained in 1872 that "[t]he paramount destiny and mission of women are to fulfill the noble and benign offices of wife and mother. This is the law of the creator."[29] Women couldn't vote until 1920. They were excluded from the Fifteenth Amendment, which was ratified in 1869 and granted that right to black men (although, as with desegregation, that right was frustrated by things like literacy tests that made it all but impossible for formerly enslaved men to vote).[30]

In 1971, the Supreme Court struck down a gender-based law for the first time. The law expressly preferred males over females for purposes of determining who would administer an estate. Applying rational basis review, the court concluded that gender had no bearing on the ability to do that job.[31]

It was not until 1976 that the court came up with its intermediate scrutiny standard, however. The case involved an Oklahoma law that allowed women (but not men) to buy alcohol at age eighteen, the idea being that men drive drunk more often than women. Because it was justified by public safety, the law would have clearly passed rational basis review. But under intermediate scrutiny, the court held "classifications by gender must serve important governmental objectives and must be substantially related to those objectives." Traffic safety was an important government objective, but gender discrimination was *not* substantially related to that objective. Of course, what's "important" and what's "substantially related" are subjective questions that judges ultimately answer.[32]

In a particularly famous case, the Supreme Court applied intermediate scrutiny to find in 1996 that the exclusion of women from military academies was unconstitutional. The court reasoned that the male-only policy of the Virginia Military Institute was based on gender stereotypes regarding "the different talents, capacities, or preferences of males and females." Federal military academies had integrated women with no problems, so Virginia was left with nary a leg to stand on.[33] But since then, the results have been mixed around the constitutionality of gender stereotypes. In 1979, for example, the court upheld a law that effectively gave hiring preference to veterans, 98 percent of whom were male.[34] As with racial classifications, a law that doesn't *expressly* make distinctions on the basis of gender is hard to challenge.

Abortion

While abortion may be one of our hottest button issues, to understand its legal precedents, consider a 1923 case called *Meyer v. Nebraska*, in which a teacher was tried and convicted for the crime of reading a German Bible to a fourth grader. The state of Nebraska had passed a law banning the teaching of anything other than the English language before the eighth grade. Reversing the teacher's conviction, the Supreme Court wrote that "[t]he salutary purpose of the statute is clear. The Legislature had seen the baneful effects of permitting foreigners, who had taken residence in this country, to rear and educate their children in the language of their native land. The result of that conviction was found to be inimical to our own safety."[35]

In slapping Nebraska's overbearing hand, the court construed the word *liberty* in the due process clause as meaning more than just a hearing before government takes something as precious as liberty away. Mr. Meyer, after all, got a trial. As a matter of constitutional procedure, he could fairly go to jail. The court held that liberty captures something deeper. Liberty "denotes not merely freedom from bodily restraint but also the right to the individual to contract, to engage in any of the common occupations of life, to acquire useful knowledge, to marry, establish a home and bring up children, [and] to worship God according to the dictates of his own conscience."[36]

How did this lead to *Roe*? Much like Nebraska could not jail people on the government's belief that "the English language should be and become the mother tongue of all children reared in this state," *Roe* held that the liberty of a free person means that the government cannot send a woman to jail for making a personal decision about ending a pregnancy on the rationale that the government thinks the decision is categorically wrong. Conservative scholars and judges today take issue with whether the *Meyer/Roe* notion of substantive due process—the idea that government cannot take away certain rights, whether it affords a hearing or not, without a really good reason, which I mentioned earlier—is constitutionally legitimate.[37] After all, the right to make decisions about your child's education is not laid out in the Constitution. But like the Bible, or a poem, there are lots of things about our working Constitution that fall in this "implied" category that we would not want to do away with—regardless of our own political or ideological beliefs.

In 1992, a so-called plurality* of the Supreme Court in *Planned Parenthood v. Casey* upheld *Roe* but took a huge bite out of it. For the first time, the court identified a government interest that can tip the scale against abortion, that is, the "profound respect for the life of the unborn" at any stage of pregnancy. Thus, the state can attempt to "persuade [pregnant women] to choose childbirth over abortion" and make it "more difficult or more expensive" to get an abortion so long as it's not *too* hard. The court called this the undue burden standard, and it's the reason why states today can lawfully put restrictions on abortions—such as parental consent requirements and mandatory counseling or waiting periods—even if those requirements make it very hard for women (especially poor women) to reasonably exercise their constitutional right to choose an abortion.[38]

This is of critical importance to today's abortion debate. It means that courts can balance the right to an abortion with something else—something that belongs to the state—which is an interest in a fetus. And an argument can be made that the interest in potential life distinguishes abortion from the facts of *Meyer*.

However, even if one agrees that a fetus is a manifestation of human life, that does not necessarily justify the *government's* unlimited ability to

---

* No one opinion got the agreement of a majority of the justices, although a majority did agree on the case's basic outcome.

constrain a woman's pregnancy. A woman's life is a life too, and the government should care about it. And what does "an undue burden" mean? In *Casey* itself, the Supreme Court approved a law imposing a twenty-four-hour waiting period, which is a serious problem for women in rural areas who have to drive hours or even days to get to a facility that performs abortions. States wanting to make abortion illegal can keep trying new things to make it difficult to get an abortion—but not *too* difficult so as to violate *Casey*. The only way to know if something is too difficult for the Constitution is to litigate it all the way up to the Supreme Court.[39]

Sexual Orientation

The Supreme Court has issued a number of decisions in favor of equal rights for gays and lesbians—without coming down one way or another on whether sexual orientation itself warrants a higher level of constitutional scrutiny. In 1996, the court declared unconstitutional a Colorado voter initiative that would have repealed all laws protecting homosexuals from discrimination. (Recall that legislatures can pass laws that overlap with the Constitution.) In the majority opinion, Justice Anthony Kennedy suggested that discrimination on that basis is inherently wrong, and questioned whether there was a good enough reason for the law under any level of scrutiny. In dissent, Justice Antonin Scalia wrote an opinion arguing that sexual morality is justification enough for anti-gay laws.

Justice Kennedy also wrote both of the decisions that culminated in a constitutional right to gay marriage. In 2013, the Supreme Court struck down federal—but not state—laws that interpreted the word *marriage* as only opposite-sex unions. In his opinion, Kennedy suggested that laws discriminating against homosexuals should get some sort of heightened rational basis scrutiny if they were motivated by hate. But he did not firmly establish that sexual orientation is a category that gets strict (the highest) or even intermediate (medium) scrutiny.

Then, in 2015, Justice Kennedy wrote the opinion in a case that identified a constitutional right to marriage for gays and lesbians. Here again, Kennedy reached his conclusion without finding that gays and lesbians are a class that the Constitution especially cares about. He combined the due process right to liberty with equal protection. Because the laws burdened homosexual couples' liberty interest in marriage under the due process clause for *discriminatory* reasons, the Equal Protection Clause was violated. "No union is more profound than marriage, for it embodies the highest ideals of love, fidelity, devotion, sacrifice, and family," he wrote. The dissenters frowned upon the use of substantive due process as a concept at all (recall that it is derided by conservatives as quintessential activist judging). Chief Justice John Roberts reasoned in his dissenting opinion that preservation of the traditional definition of marriage was a sufficient basis to pass rational basis review.[40]

A few closing points on gay and lesbian rights under the Constitution. The court's decision to identify a right to gay marriage in the Constitution fastened on the institution of marriage—not on being gay. On the one hand, it was a progressive decision because it brought gays and lesbians into the official marriage tent, so to speak; the government now has to treat their marriages like anybody else's. But because it didn't create a new *category of people* for which discriminatory laws get a higher level of scrutiny, the decision is a ticket for that train only. The next case involving gay and lesbian rights—say, a state law permitting people to refuse to participate in same-sex wedding ceremonies—would not automatically get heightened scrutiny just because it targets homosexuals. The court would have to get at the issue in some other way.

In the case involving a Colorado baker's refusal to make a wedding cake for a gay couple, for example, the issue was framed around the *baker's* First Amendment right to freedom of expression—not around discrimination against gay men. What many people don't realize about that case is that the baker didn't actually "win" the core dispute. The court decided that the state-level agency that had first heard the couple's complaint had displayed hostility to the religious beliefs of the baker. The court thought that decision was unfair and sent it back for a do-over at the state level, passing the buck to Colorado (for now).[41]

Immigration

Given the widespread anti-immigration sentiment in America today, it might surprise people that discrimination against noncitizens who are legally in the United States—sometimes called aliens—gets strict (the highest level) scrutiny. The Supreme Court's rationale has been that aliens are a "discrete and insular minority for whom heightened judicial solicitude is appropriate." They cannot vote; they have no political clout, and are therefore highly vulnerable and unable to do anything about it through the electoral process. They need extra help from the courts to make sure that they aren't being subjected to abuse or arbitrary action by the political branches of government. Even for *undocumented* aliens, therefore, the Equal Protection Clause offers protections.[42]

Let's lay out some other constitutional basics regarding the power to regulate immigration and naturalization. Article I, Section 8 of the Constitution grants Congress the power to establish a "uniform Rule of Naturalization," which means that states can't grant citizenship. Early on, the Supreme Court wrestled with whether this means that only Congress can deny people admission into the United States or remove noncitizens. Starting in 1889, the court made a few pronouncements on this topic that still apply today. First, it held that the admission of aliens is not a right but a privilege, and that the United States can prescribe the terms of admission. Second, it concluded that "[t]he exclusion of aliens is a fundamental act of sovereignty . . . inherent in the executive power to control the foreign affairs of the nation," so it belongs to the *president*. Third, and a bit weirdly, the court reasoned that when Congress legislates procedures regarding who gets to come into the country, it isn't just *legislating*—it's implementing an inherent *executive* power. Fourth, it held that courts can't review decisions to exclude aliens unless *Congress* specifically says they can—also weird, because Article III of the Constitution gives federal courts the power to hear "cases."[43]

How did we get from broad presidential power over immigration to a *strict scrutiny* standard for aliens under the Equal Protection Clause? The answer is that, under the Equal Protection Clause, the issue isn't whether the rules governing admission, naturalization, and deportation are okay. The issue is whether it's okay that *other* kinds of laws—state and local—treat aliens differently once they are in the country. Consider an Arizona law requiring that 80 percent of all employees be voters or native-born citizens, for example. The Supreme Court struck it down on equal protection grounds in 1915.[44]

There are a few exceptions to the strict scrutiny lens for people who are not United States citizens or nationals, which distinguishes the law regarding government discrimination against noncitizens from the law regarding, say, government discrimination against people of color. First, when it comes to the political process, states can call the shots, and rational basis review applies. So a state can deny noncitizens the right to vote, to hold political office, or to serve on juries. Second, Congress and the president can discriminate against noncitizens in ways that the states cannot because together they wield a lot of power under the Constitution to control immigration. Noncitizens can be categorically denied federal Medicaid benefits, for example.[45]

But as I mentioned, strict scrutiny generally applies to noncitizens when it comes to a small category of benefits once they are in the country. States can deny noncitizens things like food stamps and Medicaid, but they can't deny undocumented persons—who are in this country illegally—a free public education, or make them pay for it. In 1982, the Supreme Court rejected Texas's argument that such a law is justified in order to reserve government benefits for citizens—a rationale that would have surely passed rational basis review. A majority of the court was sympathetic to alien children, who are not to blame for being in this country.[46] This point of view is significant in today's political climate; with the ideological shifts on the Supreme Court, the arguments put forth by Texas might prompt a different outcome if the issue were revisited.

CHAPTER 9

What Does the Constitution Say About the States?

Article IV [1787].

Section 1.

Full Faith and Credit shall be given in each State to the public Acts, Records, and judicial Proceedings of every other State.

These are both about making sure states play nice with each other.

Section 2.

The Citizens of each State shall be entitled to all **Privileges and Immunities of Citizens in the several States**.

This "guarantee" seems important. But is it?

Section 4.

The United States shall **guarantee to every State in this Union a Republican Form of Government**.

Amendment X [1791].

The powers not delegated to the United States by the Constitution, nor prohibited by it to the States, **are reserved to the States respectively**, or to the people.

This is about not allowing the federal government to have too much power.

This chapter is about federalism, which again is a wonky name for the power struggle between the federal government on the one hand and the states on the other. (Indian tribes are also sovereigns in their own right, but different laws apply to them.) Dealing with laws from different government entities is nothing new in day-to-day life. We complete at least two tax returns—one for the IRS, and one for our state of residence. When we move from one state to another, it means getting a new driver's license and new tags for the car. Speed limits change, too, during road trips between states. Some states have different rules about when and where we can purchase alcohol. But we use a single currency—the US dollar—regardless of where we are in the United States, and things like whether highway reststops have wheelchair accessibility do not change from state to state. Federal laws mandate that, among other things.

But can the federal government simply gobble up regulation of anything and everything? By holding back on certain matters, is it just being "nice" to the states? Or are there are certain things that only the states can do, and what are those things?

The framers realized they had two options here. They knew that the British government was centralized in London with a monarch at the helm. Local governments existed, but they mostly got to do what the king—and today, Parliament—decided they could do.[1] The other option was one that the colonies had tried under the Articles of Confederation, which basically amounted to an agreement between "mini sovereigns"— the states—over how to band together and fight the Revolutionary War. In a confederation, state governments are strong and the central government is weak, or largely nonexistent. The central government only gets to do what the states tell it to do, and if the states don't like what they see, they have the power to ignore what the federal government is doing. The downside is that lots of sovereign states mean nonuniformity and conflict. This handy chart lays out the pros and cons of a strong national government versus a confederation of states.[2]

	Strong national government	Confederation of states
Advantages	Laws may be applied uniformly to all	Laws may be made to suit individual needs of the states
	Efforts seldom duplicate or contradict themselves	Tyranny can be avoided more easily because power is disbursed
	Fast and efficient decision-making	Government is closer to the people
Disadvantages	Concentration of power can lead to tyranny	State governments are susceptible to quarrels, creating rifts that destabilize the nation as a whole
	If the country is large, a distant central government can lose control	Subgovernments may lack the resources that a central government has
	Central officials may not always understand the needs of their citizens	

After the Revolutionary War, a national convention was called in May 1787 to revise the Articles of Confederation. The central government had no power to tax anybody, and it could not pay its war debts. The big question was whether the states should remain pure sovereigns.

Rather than amend the document they had, a decision was made to scrap the confederation and create a constitution—a compromise that kept some power in the states but enhanced the power of the federal government.

Federalism, therefore, is all about the *vertical* division of labor between the federal government and the states and local governments (all being sovereigns), while the separation of powers deals with the *horizontal* division of power between the president, Congress, and the federal judiciary. In this chapter, we will walk through two of the places where the Constitution addresses the federal government's relationship with the states: Article IV and the Tenth Amendment.

Article IV

Article IV of the Constitution has three things in it that matter here. It says that states must give "Full Faith and Credit" to each other, meaning that states have to respect the "public Acts, Records, and judicial Proceedings of every other state." So a legal document issued in Nebraska is good in Colorado and in every other state of the union. This is why marriage licenses and birth certificates issued in New York must be honored in California. Same thing with death and divorce decrees. A deadbeat parent who owes child support can't simply run off to another state and dodge a court order—the order follows him; courts in other states must honor it. If the dad flees to Virginia by car with his Maryland driver's license, Virginia must respect his legal right to drive on Virginia roadways because Maryland issued him the license.

The words *privileges* and *immunities* also appear in Article IV, Section 2 to prevent states from discriminating against out-of-staters in other ways. (There is similar language in the Fourteenth Amendment, but the Supreme Court has largely gutted it of meaning.)[3] In an influential opinion, a federal trial court (which is much lower than the Supreme Court) asked in 1823, "What are the privileges and immunities of citizens in the several states?" According to that court, the clause covers "those privileges and immunities which are, in their nature, fundamental; which belong, of right, to the citizens of all free governments," including many things we take for granted, such as:

- "Protection by the government." So, if you're robbed while on vacation in Florida, the Florida police can't refuse to help you just because you hail from New Jersey.
- "[T]he enjoyment of life and liberty, with the right to acquire and possess property of every kind, and to pursue and obtain happiness and safety." Florida can't pass a law banning you from purchasing property in Florida just because you live in New Jersey either.
- "The right of a citizen of one state to pass through, or to reside in any other state." The Supreme Court once struck down a Nevada statute that taxed people who left the state.
- "[T]o institute and maintain actions of any kind in the courts of the states." If a drunk driver rear-ends you and totals your car while you are in Florida and you decide to sue the guy, the Florida courts can't turn you away simply because you're not a Florida resident. And so on.[4]

That said, the Supreme Court hasn't been all that clear about what privileges and immunities really are. The clause has mostly come up in two contexts: fundamental rights and economic activities. Regarding the fundamental rights category, the Supreme Court has held, for example, that a state can't refuse to allow abortions for out-of-staters. But for matters that are not considered "fundamental"—like the ability to copy and inspect a state's public records—the court has allowed states to discriminate against nonresidents. Virginians can get Virginia public records, but if Virginia says no to Marylanders, it's fine with the Privileges and Immunities Clause. Regarding the second category, economic activities include things like giving preference for government jobs to people in state (not okay), and imposing higher fees for hunting licenses (okay because it's not a fundamental right or an important economic activity).[5]

All that said, when I teach first-year law students, I find it both amazing and unsurprising how little general thought goes into the source and meaning of such basic American freedoms as being able to drive into the next state without being stopped and harassed just because you don't live in that state. The Privileges and Immunities Clause does that for us. And happily, for most of American history, states have generally respected the Constitution's mandate that they respect each other. If that mutual consideration were ever to fall apart, the question would become whether a cop on the block exists to make sure that the troublemaking states comply. It's hard to ponder how that would work without the use of federal force or, worse, another civil war. So the Privileges and Immunities Clause is no small thing.

Last up for Article IV is the guarantee that each state gets a "Republican Form of Government." In simple terms, a republican government is one in which the people choose their own representatives—as distinct from a monarchy or a dictatorship, whereby one person or a small cadre of people control the entire government. In the United States, a monarch, dictatorship, or military rule would be unconstitutional. Elections are the only way of doing business.

It's not clear in the Constitution, however, whether there are consequences if states violate the Republican-form-of-government rule. The key case on this arose in 1849. Back then, Rhode Island was the only state still without its own constitution. Rhode Island was governed by a charter King Charles II granted in 1663. A state constitutional convention was held in 1841, and a new constitution ratified. Unhappy about losing power, the existing Rhode Island legislature passed a law prohibiting the constitution from going into effect and making it a crime to vote in the new election. A few people voted anyway, and a sheriff broke into the house of one election commissioner to find out who "illegally" participated in the election. The commissioner sued the sheriff for trespass and argued that, by ignoring the new constitution, the Rhode Island government had violated the Constitution's Republican Form of Government Clause. The Supreme Court refused to hear the case on the rationale that it wasn't properly within its constitutional sandbox—the debate was for the political process to fix. Since then, the clause has never been enforced.[6]

Tenth Amendment

The Tenth Amendment basically states that the only power the federal government gets is what's in the Constitution's text. "The powers not delegated to the United States by the Constitution, nor prohibited by it to the States, are reserved to the States respectively, or to the people." Thus, any *leftover* government power—once the federal government gets its share—goes to the states.

There was a debate among the framers of the Tenth Amendment over whether the language of the first clause should include the word *expressly* to indicate that any powers not *expressly* delegated to the federal government must stay with the states. Including this single word would have dramatically narrowed the Supreme Court's ability to read implied federal powers or anything else into the text of the Constitution. As we now know, the word *expressly* didn't make it into the ratified text.

In an important case called *McCulloch v. Maryland*, Chief Justice John Marshall—one of the founders of the Constitution as a delegate to the Virginia Ratifying Convention in 1788—rejected the argument that Congress can't do anything that's not expressly authorized in the Constitution's text. That case involved Congress's creation of a national bank in a statute that stated that the bank could not be *taxed* by the individual states. The states didn't like that. Maryland tried to tax the national bank, which had opened a branch in Baltimore. The head of the Baltimore branch of the national bank refused to pay its tax bill. Maryland sued, arguing that the Constitution didn't specifically authorize Congress to charter a national bank, and that power could not be implied. The Supreme Court disagreed, concluding, "[T]he powers given to the government imply the ordinary means of execution."[7]

Without implied powers, the Constitution would have required dozens—if not hundreds—of amendments to address its many ambiguities and holes. If those holes went to the states for filling, we would have a patchwork of laws that vary from state to state—a difficult thing to manage in a national and global economy. There are some things that need uniform rules.

So, what's the point of the Tenth Amendment if Congress can exercise all kinds of implied powers anyway? The Supreme Court has shifted back and forth since the nineteenth century over the question of whether to turn the Tenth Amendment into a tool for striking down federal laws. Sometimes the court has upheld federal laws so long as Congress acts within the scope of its authority. But sometimes the Supreme Court has treated the Tenth Amendment as a separate limit on Congress's power. I won't belabor the specifics of how the court has toggled back and forth over what to do with the Tenth Amendment other than to bookmark it as yet another example of the problem with pigeon-holing judges as either activist or text-based. All judges construe ambiguity and have different views on how to do that.[8]

The Supreme Court's approach to the Tenth Amendment finally gave the text some teeth in 1992, when New York challenged a federal statute requiring states to safely dispose of radioactive waters generated within their borders. If the states succeeded in getting rid of the waste—

said the law—they would get federal money; if they pawned their waste off on a neighboring state, that state could charge them money for it. The thorniest part of the statute had to do with a provision stating that if states failed to get rid of their waste by a certain date, they'd be forced to "take title" to the waste itself. What that meant is that people harmed by the waste could sue the state—versus the manufacturers or other private polluters who were responsible for the waste in the first place—for damages flowing from the radioactivity.

The Supreme Court found the "take title" part unconstitutional because it was a congressional ultimatum: *"either do as we say with the waste or it becomes your property, states, along with the litigation fallout from it."* The court accused Congress of forcing the states to adopt a federal law as if it were the states' own law—and thus to make them do the dirty work of Congress. Writing for the majority, Justice Sandra Day O'Connor explained that "[t]he Federal Government may not compel the States to enact or administer a federal regulatory program."[9]

The "dirty work" rationale played out again in 1997, when the court struck down the Brady Handgun Violence Prevention Act, which mandated federal background checks on firearm purchasers and imposed a five-day waiting period before people could buy them. The bill was named after former presidential press secretary James Brady, who was shot and sustained brain damage when a man named John Hinckley Jr. attempted to assassinate President Ronald Reagan in 1981. In that case, the court split 5–4, with Justice Scalia writing the majority opinion invalidating the law based on the Tenth Amendment, among other reasons. By requiring state officials to conduct background checks, he reasoned, Congress was again conscripting state officials—here, police officers—to do its bidding by getting them to "enforce" the statute as if they were part of the federal executive branch. The problem with this view is that the language of the Tenth Amendment certainly means that

Congress can exercise the powers *it already has* and under Article I, it has the power to pass legislation. Under the Commerce Clause, that power is broad and can implicate legislation that binds the states.[10]

Since that case, what has become of the Tenth Amendment is odd: Congress can't make states do stuff to implement federal law, but it can prohibit states from doing something that's harmful—it can ban states from sharing personal information that people turn over to the department of motor vehicles while getting a driver's license, for example.

Enter the Affordable Care Act. It required states to cover a certain percentage of low-income people within its Medicaid programs if they wanted to get *any* federal money for Medicaid whatsoever. (Medicaid is health care for low-income people; Medicare is for the elderly. Both were in place long before Obamacare came on the scene.) *Expand your programs*, in other words, *or you get nada*, said the statute.

In the opinion upholding the gist of the statute, Chief Justice Roberts declared this aspect "a gun to the head of the states" and thus unconstitutional under the Tenth Amendment.[11] Given that there are so few Supreme Court cases actually striking down laws under the Tenth Amendment, this one is important because it found the violation in how Congress gave money to the states. It said that Congress can't condition federal funding on certain behavior by the states. Remember—the radioactive waste and gun control laws weren't about money; they were about making the states do something "governmental" (like clean up radioactive waste and conduct background checks). If the Tenth Amendment turns into a squeeze on Congress's power to spend money, it could go a long way toward decreasing the federal legislature's power relative to the power of the states, while at the same time *increasing* the power of the Supreme Court—an unelected branch of government—to blow up federal legislative programs that, in theory, are reflective of the will of the voting populace. Now that's a bit ironic, no?

PART III

Why Care?

As nightfall does not come all at once, neither does
oppression. In both instances, there is a twilight when
everything remains seemingly unchanged.[*]

At this point in the book, I hope it's no overstatement to say that the
rights and freedoms provided by the Constitution are like winning the
lottery. But as with a lottery ticket, we need to cash in that windfall for
the piece of paper to retain its value. And that means voting.

This final part reviews how the electoral and legislative processes
were meant to work and how they work today. It then outlines some
warning signs that the "twilight" of democracy may be near. You know
the fable. If a frog is suddenly thrust into boiling water, it will jump out.
But if it's put into warm water that's brought slowly to a boil, it won't
notice it is in danger. It gets cooked to death.

The final chapter offers ideas for how to keep the precious frog alive.

---

[*] William O. Douglas, "A September 10, 1976, letter to the Young Lawyers
Section of the Washington State Bar Association," *The Douglas Letters: Se-
lections from the Private Papers of Justice William O. Douglas*, eds. Melvin I.
Urofsky and Philip E. Urofsky (Adler & Adler, 1987), 162.

CHAPTER 10

Why It Matters How Politicians Get Hired and Fired

You may know all this already, but here's a quick recap of how politicians get their jobs.

To elect presidents, primary elections and caucuses are held. They produce conventions at which the political parties select presidential nominees. Every four years in November, Americans cast their votes for president. But those votes don't determine who wins; the Electoral College does.[1]

The Electoral College is not a place, but a process, which consists of three parts: the first is the selection of 538 electors, the second are the meetings in state capitals at which electors (i.e., senior party officials) cast their ballots, and the third is the actual vote counting. The winner of the presidency has to receive a majority, currently 270, of the electoral votes.

Each state is allotted a number of electors that corresponds to the numbers of senators and members of the House of Representatives that they have in Congress (the US Census determines the latter). The candidates have their own slates of electors in each state, which are mostly selected from leadership positions within their parties. For most states, if one candidate wins the popular vote, all of her electors get to vote in the Electoral College.

Next, the electors meet in December in their respective states, where they vote for president and vice president on separate ballots. Although there's nothing in the Constitution requiring electors to cast votes according to the popular vote of their states, some state laws require that electors "pledge" to do so—and may even impose penalties or disqualify electors if they don't follow through. Electors rarely vote against the popular vote of their states. The votes are counted in a joint session of Congress on January 6. If a majority doesn't happen—i.e., if there's a tie or a three-way division among electors, leaving no one with a majority—the House of Representatives picks the president and the Senate chooses the vice president.[2]

Why have an Electoral College instead of a straightforward national popular vote system for picking presidents? There are many reasons. As the Supreme Court has stated, the framers "did not want the election of the President to be left to the people." Alexander Hamilton explained in Federalist No. 68: "This process of election affords a moral certainty, that the office of president, will seldom fall to the lot of any man, who is not in an eminent degree endowed with the requisite qualifications."[3] The confidence of this hopeful statement makes one think twice; it's the structure that counts.

The framers also didn't want big states drowning out smaller states in presidential elections. In theory, the process also allows party leaders to act as a check on an electorate that could otherwise act irrationally. Under the original constitutional framework, electors couldn't specify whom they wanted for president and vice president. This led to weird results in the 1796 election, which produced a president and vice president (John Adams and Thomas Jefferson) from different political parties. Jefferson spent his vice presidential term preparing to run against his boss, Adams. Jefferson won the 1800 election, but almost lost it to Aaron Burr because the electors put both men's names on their ballots on the assumption that Jefferson would automatically be president and Burr would be vice president. But by doing it this way, the electors inadvertently created a tie for president. That tie went to the House of Representatives. With the ratification of the Twelfth Amendment in

1804, the position of vice president became a separately elected office and no longer went to the runner-up in the presidential election.[4]

It is precisely because the Electoral College "evens out" the relative influence of states that we've had elections in which the losing candidate won the popular vote—Al Gore in 2000, John Kerry in 2004, and Hillary Clinton in 2016. This oddity has occurred five times in the nation's history, and it's why some people would rather do away with the Electoral College altogether. They argue that the process overrepresents people in rural states and operates to suppress voter turnout because people assume their votes don't really matter.[5]

Of course, the Senate is even more unreflective of the relative populations of the states. Despite their vastly disparate populations, for example, California (approximately 39.7 million people) and Wyoming (approximately 573,000 people) each get the same number of senators: only two.[6] Senators serve six-year terms. Every two years, one-third of the Senate is up for reelection. Candidates must meet various state requirements in order to get on the ballot (such as petitioning for signatures by a minimum number of registered voters).

Initially, the Constitution had state legislatures picking senators. In 1913, the Seventeenth Amendment was passed, which requires the election of senators by popular vote. In most states, the person who gets a plurality (versus a majority) of votes wins. So, in a three-way race, the candidate with the highest percentage of votes goes to the Senate.

Members of the House of Representatives only serve two-year terms. In 1911, Congress passed a law fixing the House at 435 members.[7] States divvy up that number based on their relative populations. Each state is then subdivided into congressional districts of equal population, with one member per district. California is the largest, with fifty-three representatives, while Alaska, Delaware, Montana, North Dakota, South Dakota, Vermont, and Wyoming each have one. The process for electing House members is the same as for the Senate, although only eligible voters residing in a particular congressional district can vote for that district's candidates (not all eligible voters in the state).

Although straightforward on paper, the legislative process has morphed over the past few decades. The on-paper process is as follows.[8] A representative sponsors a bill, which is assigned to a committee for further consideration. There are about forty legislative committees and more than a hundred subcommittees across both chambers of Congress, and each is responsible for a certain subject matter (e.g., armed services, appropriations, energy and natural resources, and so on).[9] Committees function as mini legislatures and allow members to develop specialized expertise in a particular topic and make recommendations to the House or Senate on things like potential legislation. They also conduct oversight of the executive branch and investigations of alleged problems, wrongdoing, and other issues.

Not all committees can actually work on making laws. But most can make recommendations on funding—called authorizations or appropriations—for new or existing legislative programs. Budget committees set overall budgets, and appropriations committees decide how much money to give to certain federal agencies and programs within those agencies. "Select" or "special" committees are often the ones that do investigations or study certain issues that cut across more than one permanent or standing committee. There are also joint committees with people from both the House and the Senate. Subcommittees take on smaller tasks within the umbrella of a full committee. They can also hold hearings.

A "conference" committee is a committee that gets together to hash out differences between House and Senate versions of the same bill. Conference committees are usually bipartisan, meaning there are members from both political parties. Because both chambers of Congress (the House and the Senate) must pass an identical version of a bill for it to become law, conference committees make compromises so that both chambers can vote yes on a single bill.

If "reported"—meaning passed—by a House committee, the bill is put on a calendar to be voted on, debated, or amended by the full House. If the bill passes by simple majority (218 of 435), the bill moves to the Senate, where it's assigned to another committee in that chamber. If "reported" there, the bill is again debated and voted on. If the Senate makes changes, the bill returns to the House for a vote on those changes. Conversely, a bill can start in the Senate and go to the House for consideration. Once a bill passes through both chambers, it goes to both the House and Senate for final approval. The president has ten days to either veto the final bill, do nothing, or sign it into law. Sometimes, the president will sign a bill and add a "signing statement," which is basically a commentary about the law, e.g., "I'll sign but the law is probably unconstitutional."[10] Of course, Congress can also override a veto.

The Polarization of Political Parties

Once a bill is introduced in Congress, the procedural maneuvering that takes place in order for it to become law is extremely complex. People like Senator Mitch McConnell (Republican, Kentucky) and Representative Nancy Pelosi (Democrat, California) are experts in manipulating or influencing the process of moving or stopping legislation, judicial and Cabinet nominees (in the Senate), and appropriations. It's a skill that takes years to master. But the rules of the game have quietly changed during our lifetimes, making it much harder for bipartisan deal-making. As a result, the party in a congressional majority—and its respective constituents—may have much more power than in years past, and the voters whose House and Senate representatives are in a congressional minority are all but sidelined in what is supposed to be a fair and functioning democracy in America.

Keep in mind that the rules for how Congress does its business are not set out expressly in the Constitution. Technically, the process is governed by Article I, Section 5, which states that "[e]ach House may determine the Rules of its Proceedings, punish its Members for disorderly Behaviour, and, with the Concurrence of two thirds, expel a Member." House rules can be changed by simple majority—primarily by the party in power while it's in power. Senate rules are harder to change. But if a majority of individual representatives are willing to throw out those norms for political gain, there is no Constitution cop on the block to stop them. And because much of the arcane procedural maneuvering occurs outside of the public eye (most people don't really care to follow it), America has no idea that it's happening—let alone how it ultimately affects people's lives.

Consider the Senate's confirmation of Justice Brett Kavanaugh to the Supreme Court. The Constitution has very little to say about the confirmation process, other than to state that the president "shall nominate, and by and with the Advice and Consent of the Senate, shall appoint . . . Judges of the Supreme Court." Nothing requires the nominee to turn over documents, or meet individually with senators, or candidly answer questions regarding hypothetical cases. The criteria for confirmation are personal to each senator—although much wrangling occurs behind the scenes. Publicly, they consider things like legal qualifications, character, diversity on the court, and judicial philosophy.

Yet historically, Congress has adhered to a number of norms that foster fairness and bipartisanship in the process. Even for the most divisive confirmation in recent history—that of Clarence Thomas—Democrats did not resort to the filibuster, despite the fact that the final tally of opposition votes would have been more than enough to defeat a so-called cloture motion to end debate (more on this later). After four days, the Senate agreed to reschedule the vote to allow the Judiciary Committee to hold public hearings on law professor Anita Hill's sexual harassment allegations. This was done by unanimous bipartisan consent.[11]

By contrast, Senate Majority Leader McConnell refused even to consider President Barack Obama's nominee, full stop, on a gamble that his party would take the presidency in the next election. Later, Republicans declined to disclose Kavanaugh's complete records to the full Senate and dumped forty-two thousand documents on Democrats the eve of the hearings, making a thorough bipartisan review of the candidate's record impossible. Although numerous witnesses publicly testified during the Thomas hearings, the supplemental FBI background check for Kavanaugh was conducted out of the public eye and in a truncated manner.[12]

How did we get to this winner-takes-all style of politics? Well, we have former House Speaker Newt Gingrich (Republican, Georgia) to thank for ushering in an era of congressional obstructionism with the Republican takeover of the House of Representatives in 1994. This was by design because Democrats had controlled the House since 1954. As Representative Steny Hoyer (Democrat, Maryland) explained, Gingrich's thinking was that, so long as the parties continue to cooperatively pass legislation, Democrats "get to say they solved the problem and had a bipartisan bill," leaving "no incentive for the American people to change leadership."

Brass-knuckle tactics thus became the new normal, like refusing to raise the debt ceiling or to authorize disaster relief funding (including in the aftermath of the Oklahoma City bombing) unless President Bill Clinton agreed to Republican tax or spending cuts. In 1996, Gingrich led an unprecedented twenty-one-day shutdown of the federal government, halting vital programs for everyday Americans—such as new health services for veterans and visa applications—all to gain leverage over spending on social services programs. The ultimate blow to bipartisanship was the impeachment of Clinton over his sexual relations with an intern (an effort Gingrich led while engaged in his own extramarital affair).

As Speaker of the House, Gingrich also gave his own office the power to appoint important committee chairmanships, term-limited those chairs, and shortened the congressional workweek to three days. Today, the bulk of members' time goes to fund-raising or campaigning— instead of engaging with each other personally through the legislative process. The Speaker and his party leadership have near-total control over what comes to the House floor, which means they can screen out any bills that go against the majority party's wishes. The minority party can't move things forward, period. The party in power often negotiates bills by "ping-ponging—rather than going through a conference com- mittee, it bounces a bill between the two houses."[13]

Because bills can still be filibustered in the Senate, the minority power has more influence there than in the House.[14] Filibustering (a term that stems from the Dutch word for "pirate") keeps debate going on a bill in order to extract concessions and even stop it from passing. Historically, filibustering was used relatively sparingly out of respect for congressional colleagues and deference to the bipartisan process. (South Carolina's J. Strom Thurmond holds the record for the longest speech, which lasted twenty-four hours and eighteen minutes in a filibuster over the Civil Rights Act of 1964.)

As of 1975, moreover, the Senate could close debate—or achieve cloture—by a supermajority of sixty votes. The majority party usu- ally had to account for the demands of the minority in order to move a controversial bill to a vote. That meant compromise. Yet in November 2013, President Obama's executive branch and judicial appointments languished in a divided Congress due to Republican filibusters. In re- sponse, Senate Democrats changed the rules to require a simple majority to stop filibusters of executive branch nominations and federal judge- ships other than for the Supreme Court. Later, with the nomination of Neil Gorsuch to the Supreme Court, McConnell extended the so-called nuclear option—i.e., the majority vote requirement for cloture—to the process for confirming Supreme Court nominees. This maneuver effectively secured one-party rule over the "advice and consent" component of presidential nominations. Debates on legislation may still require a supermajority vote for cloture to go forward.

Legislation overcomes these barriers in a couple of ways. One is when the majority has sixty votes. The other is by special budget bills, called reconciliation. Reconciliation is one of the minority party's few remaining weapons of defense. In the Congressional Budget and Impoundment Act of 1974, Congress created a budget reconciliation process that allows for expedited consideration of legislation involving taxes, spending, and the debt limit.[15] These types of bills can be passed by a simple majority, with Senate debate confined to twenty hours. Although amendments can be added later, they are considered with scant debate—a process called *vote-a-rama*. The use of budget reconciliation to pass laws can only happen three times a year.

Although, officially, the reconciliation process can't increase deficits or pass legislation that has no bearing on the budget, it has been used to implement major policy initiatives. President George W. Bush's massive tax-cut bills were passed via reconciliation, for example—with no chance of passage under the normal sixty-vote rule for cloture.[16] A reconciliation bill was used in 2010 to get part of the Affordable Care Act passed. In 2017, a Republican-controlled Senate also used a reconciliation bill to pass tax legislation gutting the individual mandate that was the cornerstone of Obamacare (effective for 2019). In both instances, the so-called Byrd Rule—which limited the use of reconciliation bills to fiscal issues—was ignored.[17]

Congress also makes appropriations, which are discretionary decisions over how much money various parts of the federal government get to spend each year. Appropriations amount to more than a trillion dollars annually, so it's a big deal in Congress—and a source of tremendous power. By prioritizing certain spending, Congress controls federal programs. A Republican president typically wants to push more money into defense, for example, while a Democrat wants more spending on, say, the environment or education. Because appropriations decisions are made annually, they can be implemented quickly—which often leaves federal agencies scrambling to shift course.

Prior to 1995, appropriations committees in both houses "operated in [a] relatively bipartisan way." Today, appropriations bills take longer to get through Congress—if they get through at all. Rather than funding the federal government, appropriations became a way of stymieing a political opponent in the White House. As Professor Charles Tiefer explains, "[W]hen the House changed to majority Republican after the 2010 election, it adopted a radical stance of not wanting to pass appropriations without receiving, in return, major changes in policy from [President] Obama."[18]

This procedural outmaneuvering is bad for democracy. Good decision-making occurs through collaboration, deliberation, and expertise—not bullying. But these days, voters whose representatives happen to be in the minority party are left out in the cold. And when the minority party becomes the majority party, there's little incentive to return to bipartisanship and consensus building over the sharp tools of its predecessors.[19] The loser in this high-stakes gamesmanship is the American public—not individual members of Congress. Without a functioning Congress, voters have little say in how their government operates. Ideally, we should all seek out candidates who reject a winner-take-all approach in favor of bipartisanship and fair process to the US Congress.[20]

Money in Politics

Let's again lay out a few basics—this time, about federal campaign and election laws, which made headlines in 2018. The hush money payment made by Donald Trump's personal lawyer to adult film star Stormy Daniels in the run-up to the 2016 presidential election violated federal campaign laws. The lawyer, Michael Cohen, admitted under oath that he made the payment "in coordination with and at the direction of a candidate for federal office" and DOJ prosecutors confirmed that account in a court filing. President Trump suggested that violations of federal campaign finance law aren't really crimes.[21] What do those laws do?

In short, federal laws regulate money in politics. To guide the discussion that follows, consider this illustration:

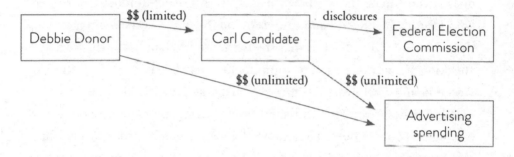

Imagine Carl Candidate, a candidate for federal office. He wants to win a seat in Congress. In order to win, he needs to spend a lot of money on advertising. Under the Supreme Court's interpretation of the First Amendment, Carl can spend a virtually unlimited amount on advertising, because political ads are protected speech. Carl raises a war chest of money for his election. His campaign is careful to disclose a bunch of information to the federal agency charged with overseeing campaigns and elections—the Federal Election Commission (FEC)—because federal law requires it. The information he must disclose includes lists of donors and lists of the expenditures his campaign made.

Next, imagine Debbie Donor. Debbie is a billionaire. Many years ago, Congress became concerned that if people like Debbie are allowed to give an unlimited amount of money to Carl, he could become "corrupted"—meaning that Carl might agree to a quid pro quo: "You (Debbie) give me money so I can win this election, and once I'm in office, I'll use my power to do favors for you or your political causes." Congress accordingly constrained that type of exchange by statute. As a result, Debbie cannot give an unlimited amount of money to Carl. Nor can other types of entities, such as unions. Corporations can't give money to Carl at all. Nor can foreigners.

But Debbie (or her corporation, Debbie's Donuts, Inc.) *can* run her *own* ads that aim to influence the campaign in Carl's favor, so long as she doesn't coordinate those ads with Carl. In fact, the Supreme Court has held that it's Debbie's—*and Debbie's Donuts, Inc.'s*—First Amendment right to do so.[22] The trick is that she has to do it all on her own, without checking in with Carl's campaign about what kinds of ads he thinks would be most helpful. Of course, Debbie is aware of Carl's public views and his policy platform, and she knows lots of information about his opponents. So she doesn't really need Carl's input in order to help his campaign. But it's not the effect of her ad campaign that matters under the law—it's whether she coordinated her ads with Carl or not.

The federal campaign and election laws contain lots of technicalities, but the bottom line is this: it's perfectly legal for anyone to *spend* an unlimited amount of money on campaigns and elections—in fact, the First Amendment protects that right—so long as the spending isn't done in coordination with a candidate. As a consequence, instead of donating to candidates who get to decide how to spend money to get themselves elected, the big bucks now go toward the airwaves and Internet—spent on ads benefitting that candidate. So long as those ads aren't coordinated with a candidate, they are fair game and legally unlimited. All of this has led to a surge of *outside* spending on campaigns and elections. This is the big problem with our campaign finance system: outside spending has skyrocketed, and there is no accountability whatsoever for it.

Federal law does regulate money spent directly on campaigns and elections in two primary ways: (1) by limiting the amount of money that individuals can contribute to federal campaigns (again, corporations can't contribute anything to candidates, so they do it through political action committees [PACs] and other mechanisms, which I'll discuss soon); and (2) by requiring that campaigns and entities that advocate on behalf of campaigns make a bunch of disclosures to the FEC. Thus, a person who wants to run for office only has to think about two things when it comes to campaign finance: managing direct contributions (which today are capped at $2,800 per person for an individual candidate) and making disclosures to the FEC.

Spurred by President Theodore Roosevelt, the first statute to ban corporate contributions for political purposes dates back to 1907 (it was called the Tillman Act). Today's law is known as the Federal Election Campaign Act of 1971, or FECA. Passed under the Nixon administration, FECA was amended in 1974 to create the FEC. In 2002, Congress passed a statute known as the Bipartisan Campaign Reform Act (BCRA), which the Supreme Court later deemed unconstitutional to a degree that has far-reaching implications for regular Americans. Prior to the BCRA, only money spent on "express" advocacy—ads that expressly or clearly oppose a particular electoral outcome (e.g., "Vote for John!")— had to be disclosed to the government. So corporations started running ads that focused only on issues—even though everyone knew they were really about a candidate. The BCRA dealt with those work-arounds, which were known as "sham issue ads," in addition to something called the "soft money loophole," which I'll talk about later.[23]

Obviously, by passing these laws, Congress took the position that the laws matter. But how do they? Some people argue that federal campaign and election laws are good, and some argue that they're bad. Polling shows that most Americans believe the commonsense notion that money buys political favors.[24] The bigger the bank check, the argument goes, the more influence a donor can have on lawmaking, which is unfair to regular people. Again, it's the classic quid pro quo: "I'll pay to have you elected, so long as once you are in office, you do my personal bidding." The voter without a huge bank account gets marginalized in the process. Under federal law, foreigners and foreign entities cannot donate or spend money in our elections. But through loopholes and dark money (which I'll explain), we don't know how much foreign influence is occurring anyway. Think about the implications: Do we really want anonymous foreign powers running campaign ads in the United States? Really?

The argument on the other side of the debate is that candidates need a lot of money these days in order for their voices to be heard. Voters and corporations have their own points of view that deserve to be heard too. One way to get those views heard is by allowing voters and corporations to financially support the election of candidates who will legislate in ways that are consistent with their points of view. Limits on contributions and expenditures are bad because they restrict those voices.

These arguments only go so far, however. Remember that federal campaign laws also require disclosures to the FEC. FECA's reporting requirements make candidates' donors transparent (if they give over $200), so that voters know who is lining those candidates' pockets—and therefore how they might be influenced once in office. The desire to influence an election through money is not undermined by laws requiring transparency.

To be sure, this is a relatively simplistic portrait of federal campaign and election laws, but the point is extremely salient: In a democracy, do we want our own votes to make the difference in what laws are passed and how they are enforced? Or are we okay with the strongest political influence coming from wealthy people, big corporations, and foreigners (in that we don't know the sources of the money that's being spent)? Regardless of political party, it's fair to assume that most people would opt for the former—we have real needs and concerns in our everyday lives, and we want our elected leaders to care about them. Health care, education, housing, food security, environmental health and sustainability, public safety—the list goes on and on.

Now let's clear up some terminology. When donations are made directly to a campaign or a candidate, it's called *hard money*. Under federal law, you can give money to candidates, political parties, and other entities, but the law substantially restricts how much individuals and organizations can contribute to political campaigns and political parties (again, at this writing, $2,800 per person). Like foreigners, corporations and unions can't make hard-money donations at all.

To get around hard-money limits, *soft money* emerged. Soft money is money that people give to political *parties* instead of candidates (although that money ends up with the candidates anyway). Money can come from individuals or so-called *PACs*, but not directly from corporations or their treasury funds. However, corporations can siphon off little amounts of money for contribution through PACs. PACs are separate, segregated funds that are created mostly by corporations and unions. The funds come from union members or from corporate shareholders. PACs must register with the FEC and can only give up to $5,000 in hard money per candidate. The US Chamber of Commerce has a PAC, for example, as do Microsoft, the Teamsters union, and the National Rifle Association.[25]

PACs can also make unlimited "independent expenditures" that are related to campaigns—so long as the PACs don't coordinate with the campaign. Independent expenditures often translate into ads urging the election or defeat of a candidate. Tons of money pours into those efforts because there are no caps, provided again that the campaign or candidate are not directly consulted about the ad campaigns.

Outside money that's not coordinated with a candidate comes in two additional forms. One is by so-called *super PACs*. Super PACs can raise and spend unlimited amounts of money. Because they're regulated by the FEC, they must disclose their donors and how they're spending money. Super PACs are totally different things than PACs—even though they have "PAC" in the name. Unlike PACs, super PACs don't give money to campaigns. Like PACs, super PACs cannot coordinate with campaigns, but they've found a way to bypass the statutory contribution limits. Instead of giving $5,000 to a campaign through a PAC, a corporation can give, say, $50 million in unrestricted spending on the airwaves through a super PAC. Super PACs are independent entities that run ads on TV and can spend as much money as they want (although, again, they do have to disclose their donors to the FEC). So when ad money starts flooding into competitive districts from nowhere, it means a super PAC has gotten involved in a campaign.

Super PAC donors are mostly superrich individuals—not corporations—and they come from both sides of the political aisle.[26] The billionaire Koch brothers' donor network, for example, is "a conservative-leaning powerhouse," having spent in the neighborhood of $300 to $400 million on the 2018 midterm elections to shape conservative-leaning policy on a range of issues, including "education, philanthropy, immigration, health care, tax laws, courts, government regulation, prisons, and the economy." Former hedge fund founder and billionaire Tom Steyer spent around $110 million in 2018 "to shape and redefine the issues" associated with the Democratic Party, and former New York City mayor Michael Bloomberg dropped $80 million on House races.[27]

The second form of outside money is a section 501(c)(4) entity—a reference to the tax code's provisions for the creation of nonprofit organizations and social welfare groups. These entities can raise and spend an unlimited amount of money. And unlike a super PAC, a 501(c)(4) doesn't have to disclose where it gets the money—only its expenditures. Hence, money given to section 501(c)(4) entities is known as *dark money*. Because they are technically nonprofit entities, section 501(c)(4)s can only spend 49.9 percent of their time on politics. The rest of their time must be spent on other things—like holding annual meetings, for example. The NRA and Planned Parenthood are both section 501(c)(4) organizations. And they both spend a lot of time and money on campaigns and elections.

Dark money became possible in the wake of the Supreme Court's decision in *Citizens United*, which as you'll recall held that corporations have First Amendment rights that protect campaign "speech." Although section 501(c)(4) groups have long been exempt from disclosing funding sources, it wasn't until *Citizens United* that the statute was widely used to create "nonprofit" groups that engage in electoral politics.

The influx of dark money has affected how members of Congress do their jobs, forcing them "onto an endless fundraising hamster wheel in which they spend more and more time beating the bushes for campaign cash and less and less time actually legislating."[28] To the extent Congress does legislate, it is with an eye toward making big donors happy—many of whom are effectively anonymous. As a consequence, voters don't know who is influencing their congressional representatives, or in what way. Perhaps it's not surprising, then, that policy initiatives with widespread public support—like measured gun control—may nonetheless go nowhere in Congress. The painful truth is that the individual voter has been substantially cut out of the democratic process, and we don't even realize it.[29]

Voter Suppression

Most Americans believe they have a constitutional right to vote. But the original Constitution doesn't actually dictate *who* can vote. Voting rights in America are largely left to the states, with a few constitutional limitations. In 1870, the Fifteenth Amendment made it unconstitutional to deny or abridge voting on the basis of "race, color, or previous condition of servitude." The Nineteenth Amendment, ratified in 1920, banned discrimination in voting on the basis of sex.

The Constitution is vague when it comes to what kinds of

abridgements on voting rights are okay as well. In 1937, the Supreme Court upheld poll taxes—which mostly affected poor people and African Americans—on the rationale that the "privilege of voting is not derived from the United States, but is conferred by the state and, save as restrained by . . . the Federal Constitution, the state may condition suffrage as it deems appropriate." The Twenty-Fourth Amendment obliterated that decision in 1963 by providing that "[t]he right of citizens of the United States to vote . . . shall not be denied or abridged by the United States or any States by reason of failure to pay any poll tax or other tax."[30]

In 1965, Congress passed legislation aimed at disrupting other kinds of state efforts to discourage or prevent people from voting. In 2013, the Supreme Court struck down an important part of that statute, known as the Voting Rights Act. It required that certain states and local governments get a thumbs-up from the federal government before changing their voting practices. Congress had determined that racial discrimination was simply too entrenched in many states, known as covered jurisdictions. In an apparent effort to make voting harder, states (including most of the South) imposed various onerous conditions on voting or registering to vote. The statute contained a formula for determining which states and local governments needed "preclearance" by the federal government before they could impose new voting procedures.

In a Supreme Court case named *Shelby County v. Holder*, the court by a 5–4 vote struck down the statute's coverage formula for deciding which states were covered jurisdictions. Today, therefore, we don't know which states have to get preclearance anymore. The court reasoned that Congress's formula conflicted with the "equal sovereignty of the states," and was "based on 40-year-old facts having no logical relationship to the present day." Though admitting that the Fifteenth Amendment "commands that the right to vote shall not be abridged on account of race or color," the court decided that Congress must enact entirely new voting rights legislation to address the "serious and widespread intentional discrimination [that] persisted in covered jurisdictions."[31] But Congress hasn't done it.

In the five years since the *Shelby County* ruling, "nearly a thousand polling places have been shuttered across the country, many in Southern black communities."[32] Fewer polling places make it less convenient for people to vote—particularly if they don't own a car or cannot drive— and it means longer lines if they do manage to reach the polls. Many people might decide not to vote at all. There's thus a concern that state officials can affect the outcome of elections simply by tinkering with polling places and voting requirements. In Florida, for example, many young people registered to vote for the first time in the wake of the mass shooting at a high school in Parkland in February 2018, yet Florida blocked early voting on college and university campuses. (A judge struck the law down as unconstitutional.)[33]

States have passed all sorts of laws restricting access to voting in other ways, including making it hard for students to register and vote (in New Hampshire); eliminating early voting on the last Saturday before an election, restricting voter-registration drives, and eliminating election-day voter registration (in North Carolina); removing or "purging" massive numbers of voters from the rolls (in Ohio, under a law that the Supreme Court approved in a 5–4 decision in 2018); requiring that voters show documentary proof of citizenship (laws passed by Arizona and Kansas were blocked by courts); and banning "straight-ticket" voting (in Michigan, in a law which a federal court struck down as intending to discriminate against African Americans).[34]

Arguably, voting rights should be construed with kid gloves—much like the First or Second Amendments, which the court has taken great pains to protect. Yet for some reason, what is arguably the most fundamental right of American citizenship—the right to vote—is one that has captured relatively scant Supreme Court attention. When state governments take steps to tamper with voting access, the court is likely to let them get away with it.[35]

Redistricting

The practice of redistricting, or gerrymandering, began as an effort to carve up local maps to virtually guarantee that incumbent elected officials would be reelected. Because the new maps "pack and stack" one party's political supporters, they don't reflect a cross-section of the population—let alone a reasonable cartographic shape. The Supreme Court has refused to develop a standard for addressing political gerrymandering under the Constitution. Politicians from the majority party in each state game the system by picking and choosing their own voters, and drowning out others in the process.

The term *gerrymandering* comes from the name of a nineteenth-century governor of Massachusetts named Elbridge Gerry. In 1812, while he was in office, a new voting district was drawn in a shape that favored Gerry's party and resembled a salamander—hence the name gerrymandering.[36]

To understand the concept, imagine a tiny state that is perfectly square in shape. In that state live ninety people; sixty of them belong to the Purple Party, and thirty belong to the Green Party. Now imagine that the state is divided into three districts, each of which sends one person to the House of Representatives. Ideally, the three districts as a whole would reflect the sixty-to-thirty proportion of the state as a whole, such that two of the three representatives heading to Congress are from the Purple Party.

Now imagine that the Green Party happens to control the government at one point in time, and it decides how the lines are drawn. The

Green Party folks in power slice up the districts in contorted ways so that two of the three districts get a significant majority of Green Party voters. When it comes to sending representatives to Congress, therefore, the Greens will win—even if they are outnumbered by the Purples over-all. Once the Greens do this gerrymandering, they can stay in power for a long time by continuing to tinker with the districts to secure their "majority."

At the same time, representatives in the Green-heavy districts know they will get reelected time and again because their constituents are made up of a significant majority of knee-jerk Green Party voters. As a consequence, when they vote in the House of Representatives, they don't care a hoot about the Purple Party voters; the Purple Party voters don't make any difference to whether they get reelected in the solidly Green districts.[37]

Now keep in mind that, at the same time, the Constitution contains no limits on the number of times that a member of Congress can run for the same office; a person can have a lock on it for fifty years. After Franklin D. Roosevelt was elected to four terms, Republicans in Congress spearheaded the Twenty-Second Amendment, which limits presidents to two terms in office.[38] Congress is unhindered by a similar constitutional measure.[39] Thus, members of Congress can go to Washington without much concern about getting thrown out if they fail to duly represent their constituents. I'm not suggesting that term limits are the answer to gerrymandering—just that the lack of them may exacerbate the problem.

The issue with gerrymandering isn't that it's done—it's been done for a long time. The issue is that we don't know what to do about it. We lack a baseline for what a fair district would look like without gerrymandering. The way to resolve this problem is for the Supreme Court to give us a test. In 2004, in a case called *Vieth v. Jubelirer*, there was a redistricting done in Pennsylvania and Democrats lost two seats. Justice Antonin

Scalia wrote an opinion holding that redistricting is a "political question" that courts cannot address. Justice Anthony Kennedy, in his own opinion, concluded that gerrymandering is something the courts *can* get involved in but didn't offer a test. The four progressives on the court at that time came up with three different tests. And that's how things stand today. If the Supreme Court doesn't come up with a solution (most likely under the Equal Protection Clause), there is no other place for American voters to go for a fix.[40]

All told, the electoral means of holding members of Congress accountable to the people isn't really working. A combination of factors creates this perfect "power" storm, including tribalism in Congress, money in politics, gerrymandering, and the lack of congressional term limits. Two of the three branches of government—and decades of constitutional case law by the Supreme Court—are entirely premised on the assumption that voters can (and will) throw people out of office if they are not doing their jobs properly. If this core means of oversight isn't functioning well, it is a big problem for democratic governance in general.

CHAPTER 11

If the Constitution Stops Functioning, Why Should I Care?

We live in a constitutional democracy, and most of us are pretty sanguine about it. We walk around knowing that we have rights, and we assume that no matter what happens, the Constitution will protect those rights. But this view may be naive. The Constitution is just a piece of paper. If it is not enforced, it's meaningless. If we allow its provisions to be ignored, even "just this once"—e.g., because we happen to be ideologically aligned with the people in power at that point in time—we might as well take out a black Sharpie pen and start crossing things out. Damaging the Constitution under a particular president or a particular Congress means a damaged Constitution under the next set of leaders. It's like a banged-up car. If the side is smashed in, it doesn't matter who drives the car next. It will remain smashed unless and until it is fixed, which requires a body-shop expert and some money. Likewise, once we smash portions of the Constitution, there is no easy, cost-free fix.

Keep in mind that, once upon a time, way back in 1787, there was a diverse group of people who opposed ratification of the Constitution as we know it. They were called anti-federalists because they were against a system of government involving a central—i.e., federal—authority. They were worried that such a government would become corrupt and seize more and more power until it eventually became a tyrannical sovereign—precisely what the colonists rejected when they fled the

British monarchy. The anti-federalists wanted restraints on government power, and were especially concerned that the president could veto legislation even if it reflected the voters' will. They were also worried about Congress's power to create a standing national army and to levy taxes. George Mason, one of the primary anti-federalist voices during the constitutional convention, argued for including a bill of rights in the original Constitution to protect the gains to individual liberties made during the American Revolution. As one scholar explains, for the anti-federalists, "[t]he recurrent theme . . . is fear: fear that the national government would usurp the rights of the people; fear that without a Bill of Rights all liberty would be destroyed; fear that the presidency and Senate would lead to an aristocracy."[1]

It should still matter to every American whether the Constitution breaks down—because the alternative is a dictatorship. As Patrick Henry told the Virginia ratifying convention in 1788, "when I come to examine these features, sir, they appear to me horridly frightful: Among other deformities, it has an awful squinting; it squints toward monarchy. . . . Your President may easily become king."[2] The legislative branch was established to avoid a monarchy by checking the powers of the president, but the anti-federalists viewed the proposed Congress as a small cadre of quasi aristocracy that could not truly represent the people.

As we've seen, the scope of the president's powers under Article II is impossibly vague. Nobody wanted a king, but whether the president was supposed to be a "king lite"—or more like a prime minister, who under the British system happens to be chosen from the legislature—is an unanswerable question.[3] One thing is for certain: we have seen the steady expansion of executive power over the past century. As scholar Jeffrey Rosen explains, "Modern presidents rule by executive order rather than consulting with Congress. They direct a massive administrative state, with jurisdiction over everything from environmental policy to the regulation of the airwaves." Presidents have regularly waged undeclared wars without congressional authorization (including President Harry Truman in North Korea, President Richard Nixon in Cambodia, and President Bill Clinton in Bosnia, for example); President Franklin D. Roosevelt imprisoned nearly one hundred thousand Americans during World War II; President Trump separated thousands of parents from their children over misdemeanors at the border, some permanently; numerous presidents have called in federal troops to suppress working-class insurrections, which ended in American deaths; and President George W. Bush secretly authorized spying on Americans inside the United States without any review by the courts.[4]

I could go on, of course. This is not a Republican or a Democrat thing. It's a toolbox thing. In the words of Jack Goldsmith, a Harvard law professor who—under George W. Bush—headed the DOJ office that advises the White House on constitutional matters, "You can't be in that office with all its enormous responsibilities—when things don't happen, you get blamed for it—and not exercise all the powers that have accrued to it over time."[5] Powers that accrue over time remain with the office of the presidency, which is why people need to keep a careful watch on them. But that watch hasn't happened.

As a result, we are now at a crossroads in history where Congress is not functioning as a truly representative body or a measured check on the other two branches. Judges aren't the answer either, because federal courts' power is confined to resolving cases brought before them—and because giving too much power to an unelected branch of government with life tenure is itself a troubling prospect. There is a real chance of democracy failing in our lifetimes, with tyranny taking its place.

When thinking about the fragility of American democracy, it's worth keeping in mind why the framers of the Constitution opted for a republic in the first place—with representatives casting votes on behalf of constituents—rather than a direct democracy in which individual votes are simply counted up. The short of it is that they were worried about mob rule—or "factions," as James Madison put it. Factions form when public opinion spreads quickly, particularly on issues that evoke ideology or passion. People become polarized and look for opinions that mirror existing beliefs. Yet as Jeffrey Rosen notes, "Madison predicted that America's vast geography and large population would prevent passionate mobs from mobilizing. Their dangerous energy would burn out before it could inflame others."[6]

But the world was very different in 1787. There were partisan newspapers, to be sure, but compared with today's social media and other information technologies, Madison's concerns seem almost quaint. In eighteenth-century America, people barely traveled because roads were coarse. "With a good horse on the best of roads you can make 50 miles a day." There were only thirteen states and around four million people, most of whom were white and Protestant. Of the approximately seven hundred thousand black people in America at that time, about 90 percent were enslaved. Philadelphia was the largest city, with a population of fifty thousand consisting mostly of tradesmen or artisans, and a handful of wealthy merchants. Cities had open sewers, and people rarely bathed.

Most Americans lived on farms, where news was spread mostly by word of mouth or by "a battered three-week-old sheet that has seen many hands." People in rural areas grew their own food, made their own clothes, and built their own homes. Local stores traded goods for vegetables, as money was scarce. "Calling a doctor [was] regarded as a signal that death is near," and "the germ theory of disease [was] still 100 years in the future." White males lived an average of thirty-eight years, and children worked the farms. Only white male property owners could vote or hold office, and polling places were few and far between.

As a result, a portrait of government back then was one "by common consent largely left in the hands of a few wealthy folks who have the time and education to worry about such things. Citizens of the young nation defer to their 'betters' to make governmental decisions. These members of the community elite dominate the state and local power structure." And for their part, "[s]mall farmers jealously guard their right to be left alone by the central government."[7]

Today, smartphones and the Internet literally dictate our lives. We don't read maps anymore, because GPS technology lives in our hand-held computers, which we anachronistically call phones. A whopping 77 percent of Americans own a smartphone; another 13 percent have the old-fashioned "flip" kind. More than two-thirds of Americans are on Facebook, and three-quarters of them use the site every day. An even greater percentage are on the video-sharing platform YouTube.[8]

Technological advances continue at an alarming pace, with computers doubling their capacities every twelve to eighteen months, along with the information technologies that utilize them. Self-driving cars are being tested on the roads. Sophisticated recognition technologies represent the next frontier, with artificial intelligence (AI) "giving surveillance cameras digital brains to match their eyes, letting them analyze live video with no humans necessary." Already, the digital footprint left by Internet use can be harvested and searched to produce detailed dossiers of the intimate details of individuals' daily lives. Soon, the technological marriage of AI, closed-circuit televisions, and facial recognition technology will allow our movements to be tracked in real time by anyone who enrolls in a service—for a fee starting at about $7 per month.[9]

Suffice it to say that if James Madison was worried that politically divisive information would spread too easily in 1787, he'd be apoplectic today. Globally, we created 2.5 quintillion bytes of data each day in 2017—a pace that is only accelerating. More than 90 percent of the world's data was generated *in the last two years alone.* With more than 3.7 billion people using the Internet, Google processes more than 40,000 searches every second, and 5 billion every day. Every minute, we send 16 million text messages, swipe 990,000 times on Tinder, send 156 million emails, and make 154,200 calls on Skype. More than a trillion digital photos are taken every year, along with 45,788 Uber rides. With the right technology, this wealth of data will be accessible for mining so that businesses, individuals, and governments can find out virtually anything and everything about us in a matter of moments. The whole Fourth Amendment notion of "search" needs rethinking.[10]

What Looks Different About Democracy Versus Autocracy

Can it be, though, that all this worry about constitutionality is unnecessary? How realistic is it to think that America could actually become a tyrannical state—and what does that even mean? Consider the tragic case of University of Virginia student Otto Warmbier, who was arrested while on a budget tour of North Korea. The North Korean government charged him with a "hostile act" for allegedly stealing a propaganda poster from a floor in his hotel. After a one-hour trial, he was sentenced to fifteen years of hard labor. From a suburb of Cincinnati, his parents watched him confess on television "to undermining the regime at the behest of the unlikely triumvirate of an Ohio church, a university society, and the American government" by taking the poster. (Otto was Jewish.) Sobbing, he pleaded with his captors: "I have made the single worst decision of my life. But I am only human. . . . I beg you that you find it in your hearts to give me forgiveness and allow me to return home to my family." Seventeen months later, he was released in a comatose state and died shortly after his return to the United States. Doctors in the United States said he suffered traumatic brain injury after his conviction, but the North Koreans blamed his condition on botulism and sleeping pills. Others theorize that he attempted suicide.[11]

Would Otto's tale have gone differently if he had taken the poster from a hotel in the United States? You bet. Say he was a North Korean visiting Washington, DC, and pulled down a MAGA ("Make America Great Again") poster from behind the front desk at the Trump hotel, which is situated just blocks from the White House and the Capitol. He could be arrested for second-degree theft, which is a misdemeanor under DC law because the property is worth less than $1,000. The maximum penalty is a $1,000 fine and 180 days in prison.[12]

Before the government could take Otto's money or send him to jail, he would be entitled to a trial before a neutral fact finder while being represented by his own lawyer. At the trial, he would have a right to present evidence in the form of witnesses, documents, photographs, and other materials to undermine the government's case against him or to present his own—what's sometimes called affirmative—defense. If the government possessed evidence that helped Otto's case, it would have to turn that information over to Otto's attorneys. No evidence would be admitted during the trial unless it complied with a set of rules that are designed to ensure that information is reliable and fair. If he was convicted and errors were made during his trial, he would be able to appeal to a neutral, higher court.

Moreover, if the police roughed him up during the arrest or jail time, he could file a separate lawsuit for money damages on the grounds that his constitutional rights were violated. If the evidence showed that the police picked on him because of his political views— which appears to have been the case with the real Otto Warmbier—he would be able to sue the police under the First Amendment as well. He might get money and possibly an injunction ordering the government to change how it handles people in Otto's situation in the future. Although egregious things do happen in the American criminal justice system, therefore the process is structured so that arbitrary arrests, detention, imprisonment, and torture are not the norm—even if bad guys happen to be in charge from time to time.

Otto Warmbier was unspeakably unlucky to have committed his

petty theft in a country run by a tyrannical dictatorship. He is one of thousands of innocent people who vanish each year into the ruthlessness of the North Korean prison system. Other countries are bad too. In China today, "hundreds of ethnic Uighur Muslims spend their days in a high-pressure indoctrination program, where they are forced to listen to lectures, sing hymns praising the Chinese Communist Party and write 'self-criticism' essays," the goal being "to remove any devotion to Islam." Other ethnic Muslims in China are subject to "expanded police surveillance," which has involved "installing cameras in some people's homes." In the words of Michael Clarke, an expert on Xinjiang at Australian National University, "'Penetration of everyday life is almost really total now.'" Despite "overwhelming evidence, including official directives, studies, news reports," and eyewitness interviews of people who survived such reeducation camps, the Chinese government categorically denies that the policy exists.[13]

In Russia, "violent, premature or unexplained deaths of journalists" are so prevalent that "the country's own media monitors" have been keeping an online database since the early 1990s. For dissidents living abroad, "Russian intelligence officials have turned political poisonings into something of an art form." The grisly murder of dissident and *Washington Post* opinion writer Jamal Khashoggi in the Saudi Arabian consulate in Turkey shined a light on the widespread atrocities of the Saudi government against its citizens as well.[14] Factor in that President Trump seems to share some of these autocrats' values—and that he has been cozying up to them—and you can see the cause for concern.[15]

As Harvard professors Steven Levitsky and Daniel Ziblatt put it in their book *How Democracies Die*: "To better understand how elected autocrats subtly undermine institutions, it's helpful to imagine a soccer game. To consolidate power, would-be authoritarians must capture the referees, sideline at least some of the other side's star players and rewrite the rules of the game to lock in their advantage, in effect tilting the playing field against their opponents." They outline four elements to a democracy falling into a dictatorship: (1) control the referees, (2) attack opponents, (3) ignore the rules of the game, and (4) encourage violence.

Let's start with the referees, whose job it is to make sure people don't cheat. Under the Constitution, the referees of the president are Congress and the courts. In turn, the president and Congress referee the courts, and the courts and the president referee Congress. It's a three-legged stool, and all three are necessary for the stool to stand tall. If one referee refuses to do its job, the system goes out of balance. Think about a kids' soccer game. If Team A is paying the referee under the table, Team B will lose, even if it actually played a better game. Not only would that be unfair to Team B, but the entire game would lose its legitimacy. Unless corrected, parents of the Team B kids will pull out of the entire enterprise. It's simply no fun if the game is rigged. In government as well, if Congress is controlled by the president, or if judges and prosecutors make decisions based on political ideology rather than the facts and the law, the entire system of government loses its legitimacy—thus making way for totalitarianism.

The second thing dictators do to capture a democracy is sideline opponents, including politicians, leaders from the private sector who finance opponents, and media figures. An obvious way to do this is to buy them off with favors, with positions of power, with media access, or even with bribes. Under Peru's former president Alberto Fujimori, for example, "[b]y the late 1990s, every major television network, several daily newspapers, and popular tabloids were on the government's payroll." For opponents who cannot be bought, "old-school dictators often jailed, exiled, or even killed their rivals."[16] For his part, Trump has made a habit of calling the media "among the most dishonest groups of people I ever met," once promising supporters that "I'm going to open up our libel laws when they write purposely negative and horrible and false articles, [so] we can sue them and win lots of money."[17]

Third, to entrench power in what's nominally a democracy, would-be dictators distort the rule of law by reforming "the constitution, the electoral system, and other institutions in ways that disadvantage or weaken the opposition." They do this "under the guise of some public good, while in reality they are stacking the deck in favor of incumbents." In Hungary in 2010, the ruling party used its supermajority in parliament "to rewrite the constitution and electoral laws to lock in its advantage," including gerrymandering electoral districts to ensure it would retain control. It also banned campaign advertising in the private media, so only the public broadcast station—which it controlled—reached voters.

A final thread that can be found in authoritarian regimes is the toleration or encouragement of violence against opponents. This includes tacit forms—"[b]y refusing to unambiguously condemn it or punish" violence, for example, or by praising others for acts of political violence. President Trump is well-known for his violent rhetoric about "the old days" of political violence. In February 2016, he told a crowd in Nevada: "You know what they used to do to guys like that when they were in a place like this? They'd be carried out on a stretcher, folks. It's true. . . . I'd like to punch him in the face, I'll tell you."[18]

The Constitution itself does not spell out the unwritten norms that uphold democracies, which include "mutual tolerance and institutional forbearance." According to the authors of *How Democracies Die, mutual tolerance* means that a party in power treats the opposition "as legitimate contenders for power" and vice versa. If politicians aren't accustomed to demonizing rivals, they are less likely to break norms in order to maintain their own power. Think of your own life; if you're concerned that a nasty text will make its way around the neighborhood, you are less likely to send it. If you don't care what the neighbors think, any text goes.

Such institutional forbearance in politics means that government actors underutilize their broader constitutional powers—that they won't play hardball just for the sake of winning—"[i]n the spirit of fair play."

If a player comes to a poker match with a baseball bat, the rules of the card game don't matter. The only thing that matters is an impending swing. In everyday life as well, norms play a critical role in governing human behavior. If a person goes to the opera in his underwear, he won't go to jail. Most people don't do it because it's not socially acceptable. It will trigger stares, stink eyes, and judgment. Likewise, a functioning Congress depends on members caring what people on the other side of the aisle think. That's just not happening anymore. And too few people care about the consequences of how low they will go.

CHAPTER 12

Sustaining Democracy:
Some Takeaways

Article V.

The Congress, whenever two thirds of both Houses shall deem it necessary, shall propose Amendments to this Constitution, or, **on the Application of the Legislatures of two thirds of the several States, shall call a Convention for proposing Amendments**, which, in either Case, shall be valid to all Intents and Purposes, as Part of this Constitution, when ratified by the Legislatures of three fourths of the several States, or by Conventions in three fourths thereof, as the one or the other Mode of Ratification may be proposed by the Congress.

There is nothing in the Constitution on what this process would look like.

In April 2017, after his first one hundred days in office, Donald J. Trump considered the milestone in an interview with Fox News. He'd had a rough few months. Although he managed to get Neil Gorsuch confirmed to the Supreme Court, his immigration travel ban had been struck down, his effort to secure formal repeal of Obamacare had failed, and his approval rating was an abysmal 40 to 42 percent. For Trump, part of the blame was the Constitution itself. "It's a very rough system," he explained. "It's an archaic system. . . . It's really bad for the country."[1]

Trump's disdain for the Constitution is not just theoretical. He believes that how the Constitution works is fundamentally flawed—that no due process protections should attach to his zero-tolerance policy on immigration, for example. "When somebody comes in," he wrote on Twitter, "we must immediately, with no judges or Court Cases, bring them back from where they came."[2] Regular people have polarized views on immigration, to be sure, but unraveling *any* constitutional protection is dangerous business.

Perhaps most compelling is Trump's repeated insistence that the Constitution does not limit his power as president. To him, the appointment of Robert Mueller to investigate Russian interference with the 2016 presidential election is "totally UNCONSTITUTIONAL!"[3] Trump also takes the position that it's legally impossible for him to obstruct justice, and that he has an "absolute right" to pardon himself of criminal wrongdoing. That the Trump presidency has eroded parts of the Constitution isn't entirely Trump's fault. For his first two years in office, there was no cop on the block willing to police him right now. Republicans in Congress won't do it. But if the Constitution is allowed to lapse today, it will lose its authority as a set of rules to be followed tomorrow. For people in power, no accountability means more power for the taking.

A New Constitutional Convention?

The question for America today, therefore, is whether this is a Constitution worth keeping. History shows that there are many insidious ways that it can be thwarted if those in power get too much power. During the Reconstruction era following the Civil War, for example, white Southerners felt threatened by the enfranchisement of former slaves. The electorally dominant white male Democrats "changed the rules." "Between 1885 and 1908, all eleven post-Confederate states reformed their constitutions and electoral laws to disenfranchise African Americans" through "poll taxes, property requirements, literacy tests, and complex written ballots." Of course, most formerly enslaved people could not read or write. Georgia senator Robert Toombs declared at the time, "Give us a convention, and I will fix it so that . . . the Negro shall never be heard from."[4] (As I mentioned already, the Twenty-Fourth Amendment, passed in 1964, deemed poll taxes unconstitutional and made voting a right for all men and women over the age of twenty-one; seven years later, the Twenty-Sixth Amendment lowered the voting age to eighteen.)

Today, people across the nation are calling for another constitutional convention to fundamentally change the text of the Constitution itself. This little-known fact is extraordinary. Think about it. The last time a convention happened was 1787, and it produced the very document that we've spent the last umpteen pages talking about. The prospect of another one is real. At the annual convention of the American Legislative Exchange Council (ALEC) in August 2018, former Oklahoma senator Tom Coburn guessed that "we're three or four years away." (ALEC is an organization that links powerful lobbyists with lawmakers, so it's a force to be taken seriously.) Coburn is also a senior adviser to an organization called the Convention of States, which is one of several groups working to get two-thirds of state legislatures to request a constitutional convention. And under Article V of the Constitution, Congress "shall" convene a meeting under those circumstances.

To be sure, as we've seen, the Constitution is not self-executing— Congress might figure out ways around such a request. But to do so would be politically risky if the states are demanding it; and there's no telling what the outcome would be. For people like Coburn, a convention looks like the "only answer" for a "failing" republic that is "going to become a socialist, Marxist country like western Europe." "As far as me and my family and my guns," he explained, "I'm going to be free."

To date, twenty-eight of the required thirty-four state legislatures have "active bills calling for a convention." Two—Arizona and Wyoming—came on board since Trump was elected. Three others—Maryland, Nevada, and New Mexico—recently repealed laws that had previously called for a convention to consider a balanced budget amendment to the Constitution. In seven more states, the legislatures are completely controlled by Republicans: Idaho, Kentucky, Minnesota, Montana, South Carolina, Virginia, and Wisconsin. If those states seek a convention as well—particularly around a unified issue, which would give Congress less wiggle room to find a convention not mandatory—then we, as a country, will be in a full-scale constitutional meltdown.

Although Article V refers to states "calling a convention for proposing amendments," there would be nothing to stop a convention from becoming an effort to scrap the Constitution altogether and start all over again. After all, this is precisely what happened in 1787 with the Articles of Confederation. What began as an amendment process turned into a wholesale rewriting of the rules governing those in power in the United States. If that were to happen again, there's no telling what kind of government we'd end up with.

It's not hard to imagine an amendment to dictate that life begins at conception, or stating that immigrants are not protected by the Constitution at all, or making clear that the due process clause does not create any substantive rights—a provision that would open the door for government restrictions on population growth, child-rearing, the ability to travel from state to state without government interference, and personal medical choices other than abortion. Current backers of the convention idea want to repeal the federal income tax. Without money, of course, the federal government would shut down and cease to exist. It boggles the mind to contemplate how broadly this country's entrenched divisions would widen in that event.

The Convention of States reportedly already has 2.5 million supporters ready to mobilize—twice that of the NRA—along with high-profile people like Sarah Palin, Sean Hannity, Bobby Jindal, and Rand Paul who favor a constitutional convention. Other conservatives are against the idea because "a convention could 'rewrite our constitution and destroy its protection of our rights.'" Liberals are also mixed, with some supporting a convention to overturn the Supreme Court's green-lighting of corporate money in politics in the *Citizens United* decision.[5]

To be sure, for a new Constitution to be ratified, it would have to meet the existing document's requirement that three-fourths of the states agree. But in today's political climate, anything could happen. The Articles of Confederation itself required that the states unanimously consent to any changes. The framers of the Constitution simply ignored this, deciding that ratification by nine of the thirteen original states was just fine.

Moreover, there's no telling what the procedural rules and voting requirements of the convention might be. "There is absolutely no force that can override what the convention does," explained professor David Super at Georgetown Law School. "Congress can send them rules, state legislatures can send them rules, but they can do what they want. I'm not sure there'd even be one vote for blocking it on the Supreme Court. The precedent is that strong."[6]

Even Justice Scalia—a groundbreaker in the world of conservative constitutional thinking—believed that a new constitutional convention is a dangerous idea. In an April 2014 panel discussion with Justice Ruth Bader Ginsburg, he was asked about amending the Constitution and replied: "I certainly would not want a Constitutional Convention. I mean whoa. Who knows what would come out of that?" And in a speech he made to the conservative Federalist Society in 2015, he said, "A constitutional convention is a horrible idea. This is not a good century to write a constitution."[7]

Keep in mind that there are two pathways to a constitutional amendment: through Congress or through a state-initiated process. To date, thirty-three amendments have been proposed, and all came from Congress. The reason for also allowing states to trigger the process is a familiar one: checks and balances. If Congress were to amass too much power, the dual pathway theory goes, the states could step in and pull it back.

The fact that we haven't seen an amendment come from the states in the history of our nation—despite hundreds of attempts—only underscores that we should legitimately fear the unknown here. The earliest time that pro-convention activists could nab the seven additional states needed for a convention is 2019, when Montana's legislature is next in session. Observers on both sides of the political spectrum consider a constitutional convention a viable possibility at that point. As of 2017, Republicans control the entire legislatures in 33 of the 50 states. So momentum for a conservative-backed convention exists today like never before.[8]

"We the People" Must Be Our Own Constitution Cop

The question thus becomes: What can regular people do about this looming problem of the possible breakdown of our otherwise functioning constitutional system of government? How can we save our democracy from falling apart internally—let alone forestall a wholesale rewrite of the document itself? Some foundations:

- **Having a cop on the block matters.** The Constitution means something only if it's enforced.

- **There is a big difference between policy and politics.** Politics is about ideology. Policy is about using data and facts to reach a conclusion or argue for or against a particular outcome. Be careful not to confuse the two.
- **Once a precedent is in the government's "toolbox," it can be picked up for use at any time by any partisan.** When government actors push existing boundaries, they expand their power. Usually for keeps.
- **"Strict" reading of the Constitution is a myth.** There is no way to apply the Constitution without interpreting it, period.
- **American values are not in the Constitution.** But soft norms are critical to preserving individual liberties and ensuring an accountable government.
- **No constitutional power is absolute.** The Constitution should be viewed through a lens of accountability for all government actors, full stop.
- **With law, it all depends.** Constitutional questions are squishy, not black-and-white.

In answering the "what do we do now" question, we might want to supplement this list with a few additional concepts. One might be that, whether we happen to align ourselves individually with the Republican Party, the Democratic Party, or something else, we should all recognize that democracy is safer in a multi-party system. If people who push for more power get pushback from opponents, that power is necessarily contained, and containment of government power is necessary in order to avoid an autocracy. One plus zero equals, well, one.

Another concept might be that establishing fair procedures—and enforcing those procedures—matters in a functioning democracy. As we've seen with the breakdown of bipartisanship in Congress, if the team that's in the lead gets to change the rules in its favor halfway through the game, the integrity of the game itself suffers. And there's no buy-in from the fans of the losing team. People will get angry and seek out like-minded people. If those "people" are in fact Russian bots, everyone ends up scammed. Democracy loses. In thinking about fair procedures, let's also not forget those soft norms—like honesty, truthfulness, decency, mutual respect—the many things in everyday existence that give rise to meaningful, fruitful relationships and honorable lives. These things matter in government too.

As for what to do about our crumbling democracy, it's hard to ignore the bottom line: vote. Oh, and one more thing: vote. More people watch the Super Bowl than vote in presidential elections. That is due to many factors, including systemic disenfranchisement and the self-defeating belief that "my vote doesn't matter" anyway. As an educator, I also happen to think that this belief has to do with a dearth of constitutional literacy. People don't really understand the system, so they can't grasp what's at stake and prioritize accordingly. In addition, there's a ton of misinformation out there—including what amounts to manipulative lies designed to make people take positions that benefit the powerful, not themselves. Navigating through this quagmire can feel overwhelming, if not hopeless.

A preliminary step for voters is figuring out how to wade through information and identify what's worth believing and what is bunk. On this subject, soft norms come in handy. We know when we eat at a restaurant that if they serve dog food or have rats in the kitchen the health inspector will slap the operation with a fine or even close it down. For other vendors, it's their reputation that matters. We might choose a kitchen renovator based on referrals—we think about who we know that can be trusted to give the straight scoop about whether a contractor is honest, reliable, fair, and does good work. The notion is that, if the contractor gets enough horrible reviews on Yelp, he'll go out of business. His reputation is his livelihood, so he takes care to protect it.

These days, news outlets get away with lies and their reputations aren't affected. By the same token, traditionally trusted news sources are being hammered by the White House, so there's a steady distrust of the media across the board. This is a bit of a scam, folks. The media is actually an important means of protecting the public from a corrupt government. As the saying goes, sunshine is the best disinfectant. Prior to the Internet age, there were only a handful of news outlets, and they developed—and adhered to—a set of norms to ensure accurate and honest journalism. These included basic things like accuracy (double-checking sources) and objectivity (giving both sides of an issue). Despite the barrage of "fake news" today, some media outlets still try hard to abide by these norms. They self-police because their reputation matters to them. These are the ones that are worth reading, and they span the political spectrum. To find them, hop in a time machine and go back to, say, 1980. What did people read then? What did they watch? Sources like the *New York Times*, the *Chicago Tribune*, ABC, NBC, CBS, and PBS all come to mind. You get the point.

The other means of maximizing the quality of information you take in is to read original source documents. By this I mean that if a newspaper article discusses an indictment of a public figure, for example, it pays to read the actual indictment rather than just rely on reporters to tell you what it says. Back in the day, original documents meant going to a courthouse and pulling a case file or traveling to a public library and tediously rolling through microfiche. It was a total pain. The nice thing about the Internet is that all this stuff is now at your fingertips—a click of a mouse or a tap of a smartphone away, so to speak. Identifying websites or Twitter handles that will post original sources for you is also a nice feature of technology today. Don't trust what others tell you—read the thing for yourself.

In short, choosing whom to vote for is issue-based, and figuring out what to believe on a particular issue requires a new twenty-first-century skill: mining the Internet for good information. In recent years, we've learned something else about voting that wasn't a thing, say, thirty years ago. And that is that we can't assume that everyone will follow norms of decency and decorum if elected to office. So in choosing candidates, it's important to pick people whose values appear to align with our own, and with those of the current Constitution.

"We the People" and Government Accountability

A final note on a favorite soft norm of mine: government accountability. Although the word *accountability* isn't in the Constitution itself, it's pretty hard to refute that our structure of government is premised on accountability for all who hold power. Nobody is above the law. Under the Constitution, the people are the sole source of governing power—elected and appointed officials are not *entitled* to it.[9] Every exercise of their power flows through—not from—the Constitution. And every person exercising that power remains ultimately and exclusively accountable to the people.

Having fled a tyrannical monarchy, the founders of this country understandably wanted a government that not only granted its people more freedoms but also responded to them. The Declaration of Independence thus provides that "to secure these rights, Governments are instituted among Men, deriving their just powers from the consent of the governed." It adds that "whenever any Form of Government becomes destructive of these ends, it is the Right of the People to alter or abolish it."[10] In Federalist No. 49, Alexander Hamilton likewise stated that the people should be consulted whenever the structure of government is altered "[a]s the people are the only legitimate fountain of power."[11]

The framers' decision to opt for a republic instead of a direct democracy did not mean that the white male aristocracy—who were assumed to ascend to the upper echelons of the federal government—would somehow become mini-kings, however. Instead, it's the Constitution's opening salvo that "*We the People* of the United States . . . do ordain and establish this Constitution for the United States of America" (emphasis mine).[12] The Supreme Court has also repeatedly reinforced the notion that government exercises only delegated powers that are channeled from the people through the Constitution.[13] "To hold otherwise is to overthrow the basis of our constitutional law."[14]

The founders' idea that power flows from the people is necessarily linked to the understanding that those who exercise power in the people's name *must be accountable to them*.[15] As we've seen, the Constitution's very structure reflects a number of safeguards that foster accountability.[16] Among other things, the framers established the federal government as one of limited and enumerated powers.[17] Before the government can act, it must be able to trace its authority for its actions directly back to some provision in the Constitution, which was "ordain[ed] and establish[ed]" by the people.[18] So, in order for there to be accountability under our Constitution, the source of federal power—the people—must have some say in how it is exercised.

Now, one might respond to my little speech with the retort that, if the people choose to have a single-party government—indeed, even an autocracy—then so be it. If the government's power traces back to the people, and the people want a king, then "We the People" can have a king, right? Well, wrong. The Constitution assumes that the populace is safer if government adheres to principles of constitutional structure even if it is cumbersome to do so and even if occasional lapses seem innocuous.[19] We're back to the cop-on-the-block phenomenon. It's hard to reasonably debate that self-interest and corruption in government aren't destabilizing. Autocracy might mean the lesser of two evils in some circumstances—think Russia after the fall of the Soviet Union or Iraq after the defeat of Saddam Hussein. Many people in both countries have pined for the good old days when their lives were easier under a dictatorship. Democracy is messy. Consensus is messy. Compromise is messy. Which is all to say that our Constitution has served us pretty well. It has stood the test of 230 years' time, and it is worth preserving.

Don't you think?

Acknowledgments

The author would like to acknowledge with appreciation the feedback and insights received on drafts of this book from colleagues, research assistants, and friends, including Julie Coan, Gilda Daniels, Garrett Epps, Jeff Feinstein, Lauren Fleming, Raquel Flynn, Michele Gilman, Simone Glinberg, Steve Grossman, Colleen James, Dave Jaros, Clarissa Lindsey, Gene Mazo, Mike Meyerson, Adeen Postar, Calvin Riorda, Becky Saltzman, Max Stearns, Christine Stutz, Charles Tiefer, Ben Weinberger, and the students in Carrie Hamlett's fall 2018 high school history class.

Glossary

AFFIRMATIVE ACTION: A series of tools utilized to remedy previous race discrimination with the goal of increasing minority presence and diversity in areas such as higher education, admissions, and employment.

APPELLATE COURT: A court that has the power to review the decisions made by a trial court or intermediate appellate court.

BEYOND A REASONABLE DOUBT: The standard of proof that is required for a criminal conviction. This standard is the highest possible standard and requires that there be *absolutely no doubt*. If a percentage were to be assigned, this standard of proof would require more than 99.99 percent certainty.

BICAMERAL: Legislatures that have two chambers are bicameral. The federal legislative branch is bicameral and consists of the Senate and the House of Representatives. States also have bicameral legislatures, though the names of each chamber can vary. In all bicameral bodies, legislation must pass successfully through each chamber.

BIPARTISAN: A piece of legislation or policy that is supported by two political parties.

CLEAR AND CONVINCING: The intermediate level standard of proof. If a percentage were to be assigned, this standard of proof would be about a 70 percent certainty.

CLOTURE: A legislative procedure that can be implemented under certain circumstances to kill a filibuster by placing a time restriction on debate and forcing a vote on a bill.

CONSTITUENT: An individual who has the ability to cast a vote in order to elect a particular representative in that individual's respective district.

DARK MONEY: Money given to a section 501(c)(4) entity, which is a reference to the federal tax code's provisions for the creation of nonprofit organizations and social-welfare groups. These entities can raise and spend an unlimited amount of money. And unlike a super PAC, a 501(c)(4) doesn't have to disclose where it gets the money—only its expenditures. Hence, money given to section 501(c)(4) entities is known as *dark money*.

DEFAMATION: The making of a false claim about someone publicly.

DEMOCRACY: A form of government whereby the people elect their represented officials.

DISENFRANCHISEMENT: The denial of an individual's or group's right or privilege; most commonly arises in the form of voter disenfranchisement (e.g., taking away a convicted felon's right to vote).

FEDERALISM: The division of power between federal and state governments. This is often referred to as a power struggle between the sovereigns.

FEDERALIST: Someone who believes in strong power for the federal government and relatively weaker power for the states.

FELONY: A crime that carries the possibility of incarceration of one year or more.

FILIBUSTER: The purposeful delay of a bill by prolonged debate in an effort to curtail the passing of the bill.

FRAMERS OF THE CONSTITUTION: Delegates at the Constitutional Convention in 1787.

GERRYMANDERING: The legislative act of changing district lines to dilute or concentrate members of a constituency group and gain a political advantage for one political party.

GRAND JURY: A group of individuals empaneled by a prosecutor to perform an investigative function by considering testimony and other types of evidence; it also approves criminal charges in an indictment against a party. *See* INDICTMENT.

HABEAS CORPUS: Latin: "that you have the body." The legal process whereby a petitioner asserts that he or she is being unlawfully and illegally detained or imprisoned and seeks relief in a civil court of law.

HARD MONEY: Donations made directly to a campaign or a candidate.

IMMUNITY: In the civil arena, immunity is a defense that protects a person from liability for money damages. In the criminal arena, immunity can be granted to a witness by the government. Criminal immunity can be either transactional or use and derivative use. Transactional immunity protects a person from being charged with an offense completely. Use and derivative immunity only protects a person's testimony from being used against them.

IMPEACHMENT: The legislative equivalent of bringing a criminal-type charge against a high government official.

INCUMBENT: Someone who presently holds a position in office or a specific title. (Often discussed in reference to political candidates and their nonincumbent challengers.)

INDICTMENT: A document containing criminal charges against a party that is issued by a grand jury.

INFORMATION: A document containing criminal charges against a party that is issued by a prosecutor's office versus a grand jury.

INJUNCTION: A court order that directs a person to stop doing something or forces a person to take action.

JUDICIAL PRECEDENT: (Also referred to as stare decisis.) Law created by past cases that judges apply to present cases bearing similar facts and issues.

JURISDICTION OF A COURT: The power of a court to hear a case on a particular subject or involving a particular defendant.

LIBEL: Written defamation. See DEFAMATION.

MISDEMEANOR: A crime that involves a small fine and/or the possibility of incarceration for less than one year.

MONARCHY: Form of government where there is one person in charge who often inherits the position by blood.

ORIGINALISM: The belief or theory that the Constitution should be interpreted with the same intent that the framers had at the time of ratification.

PACs: Separate, segregated campaign funds that are created mostly by corporations and unions. The funds often come from union members or from corporate shareholders. PACs must register with the FEC and can only give up to $5,000 in hard money per candidate.

PAROLE: Early release from prison after a person is determined eligible by a designated parole board.

PETIT JURY: A group of individuals empaneled by a court to decide factual questions in dispute at trial.

POLICY: The rationale behind a rule; the reasons behind a statute or regulation that governs private conduct. It is distinct from politics, which is often ideological.

POLITICAL QUESTION: An issue that is deemed appropriate for only the legislature to decide, thus the judiciary will refuse to intervene.

PROBABLE CAUSE: There are two types of probable cause: (1) probable cause to arrest, and (2) probable cause to search. In order for probable cause to arrest to be present, it must be established that there was a crime committed and this particular person being arrested is suspected of having committed the crime. Probable cause to search requires sufficient evidence that a crime has been committed but includes the requisite likelihood that evidence of the crime is located in the specific area to be searched. For both, the probable cause standards in their simplest forms can be viewed as more likely than possible.

REGULATION: A law created by an agency instead of Congress.

RETRIBUTION: A theory of punishment in criminal law that people should be punished equally in accordance with the severity of the crime committed.

SLANDER: Spoken defamation. *See* DEFAMATION.

SOFT MONEY: Money that people give to political parties instead of candidates.

SPECIAL OR INDEPENDENT COUNSEL: A prosecutor who is specially assigned to investigate a particular incident or person in response to a determination by the Department of Justice that a conflict of interest exists.

STANDING: A requirement whereby a party must demonstrate a connection between a legal harm and their injury in order to bring suit.

SUPER PACs: Entities that can raise and spend unlimited amounts of money in a campaign. Because they're regulated by the FEC, they must disclose their donors and how they are spending money.

WARRANT: A document signed by a judicial magistrate that authorizes law enforcement to either make an arrest of a person or search a specific location. The warrant must be supported by probable cause.

WRIT OF CERTIORARI: Process whereby a party seeks review from the Supreme Court.

WRIT OF MANDAMUS: Court order to a government official that directs the official to perform a duty of the office.

The Constitution of the United States of America

CONSTITUTION OF THE UNITED STATES

We the People of the United States, in Order to form a more perfect Union, establish Justice, insure domestic Tranquillity, provide for the common defence, promote the general Welfare, and secure the Blessings of Liberty to ourselves and our Posterity, do ordain and establish this Constitution for the United States of America.

Article. I.

Section. 1. All legislative Powers herein granted shall be vested in a Congress of the United States, which shall consist of a Senate and House of Representatives.

Section. 2. The House of Representatives shall be composed of Members chosen every second Year by the People of the several States, and the Electors in each State shall have the Qualifications requisite for Electors of the most numerous Branch of the State Legislature.

No Person shall be a Representative who shall not have attained to the age of twenty five Years, and been seven Years a Citizen of the United States, and who shall not, when elected, be an Inhabitant of that State in which he shall be chosen.

Representatives and direct Taxes shall be apportioned among the several States which may be included within this Union, according to their respective Numbers, which shall be determined by adding to the whole Number of free Persons, including those bound to Service for a Term of Years, and excluding Indians not taxed, three fifths of all other Persons. The actual Enumeration shall be made within three Years after the first Meeting of the Congress of the United States, and within every subsequent Term of ten Years, in such Manner as they shall by Law direct. The Number of Representatives shall not exceed one for every thirty Thousand, but each State shall have at Least one Representative; and until such enumeration shall be made, the State of New Hampshire shall be entitled to chuse three, Massachusetts eight, Rhode-Island and Providence Plantations one, Connecticut five, New-York six, New Jersey four, Pennsylvania eight, Delaware one, Maryland six, Virginia ten, North Carolina five, South Carolina five, and Georgia three.

When vacancies happen in the Representation from any State, the Executive Authority thereof shall issue Writs of Election to fill such Vacancies.

The House of Representatives shall chuse their Speaker and other Officers; and shall have the sole Power of Impeachment.

Section. 3. The Senate of the United States shall be composed of two Senators from each State, chosen by the Legislature thereof, for six Years; and each Senator shall have one Vote.

Immediately after they shall be assembled in Consequence of the first Election, they shall be divided as equally as may be into three Classes. The Seats of the Senators of the first Class shall be vacated at the Expiration of the second Year, of the second Class at the Expiration of the fourth Year, and of the third Class at the Expiration of the sixth Year, so that one third may be chosen every second Year; and if Vacancies happen by Resignation, or otherwise, during the Recess of the Legislature of any State, the Executive thereof may make temporary Appointments until the next Meeting of the Legislature, which shall then fill such Vacancies.

No Person shall be a Senator who shall not have attained to the Age of thirty Years, and been nine Years a Citizen of the United States, and who shall not, when elected, be an Inhabitant of that State for which he shall be chosen.

The Vice President of the United States shall be President of the Senate but shall have no Vote, unless they be equally divided.

The Senate shall chuse their other Officers, and also a President pro tempore, in the Absence of the Vice President, or when he shall exercise the Office of President of the United States.

The Senate shall have the sole Power to try all Impeachments. When sitting for that Purpose, they shall be on Oath or Affirmation. When the President of the United States is tried the Chief Justice shall preside: And no Person shall be convicted without the Concurrence of two thirds of the Members present.

Judgment in Cases of Impeachment shall not extend further than to removal from Office, and disqualification to hold and enjoy any Office of honor, Trust or Profit under the United States: but the Party convicted shall nevertheless be liable and subject to Indictment, Trial, Judgment and Punishment, according to Law.

Section. 4. The Times, Places and Manner of holding Elections for Senators and Representatives, shall be prescribed in each State by the Legislature thereof; but the Congress may at any time by Law make or alter such Regulations, except as to the Places of chusing Senators.

The Congress shall assemble at least once in every Year, and such Meeting shall be on the first Monday in December, unless they shall by Law appoint a different Day.

Section. 5. Each House shall be the Judge of the Elections, Returns and Qualifications of its own Members, and a Majority of each shall constitute a Quorum to do Business; but a smaller Number may adjourn from day to day, and may be authorized to compel the Attendance of absent Members, in such Manner, and under such Penalties as each House may provide.

Each House may determine the Rules of its Proceedings, punish its Members for disorderly Behaviour, and, with the Concurrence of two thirds, expel a Member.

Each House shall keep a Journal of its Proceedings, and from time to time publish the same, excepting such Parts as may in their Judgment require Secrecy; and the Yeas and Nays of the Members of either House on any question shall, at the Desire of one fifth of those Present, be entered on the Journal.

Neither House, during the Session of Congress, shall, without the Consent of the other, adjourn for more than three days, nor to any other Place than that in which the two Houses shall be sitting.

Section. 6. The Senators and Representatives shall receive a Compensation for their Services, to be ascertained by Law, and paid out of the Treasury of the United States. They shall in all Cases, except Treason, Felony and Breach of the Peace, be privileged from Arrest during their Attendance at the Session of their respective Houses, and in going to and returning from the same; and for any Speech or Debate in either House, they shall not be questioned in any other Place.

No Senator or Representative shall, during the Time for which he was elected, be appointed to any civil Office under the Authority of the United States, which shall have been created, or the Emoluments whereof shall have been encreased during such time; and no Person holding any Office under the United States, shall be a Member of either House during his Continuance in Office.

Section. 7. All Bills for raising Revenue shall originate in the House of Representatives; but the Senate may propose or concur with amendments as on other Bills.

Every Bill which shall have passed the House of Representatives and the Senate, shall, before it become a law, be presented to the President of the United States: If he approve he shall sign it, but if not he shall return it, with his Objections to that House in which it shall have originated, who shall enter the Objections at large on their Journal, and proceed to reconsider it. If after such Reconsideration two thirds of that House shall agree to pass the Bill, it shall be sent, together with the Objections, to the other House, by which it shall likewise be reconsidered, and if approved by two thirds of that House, it shall become a Law. But in all such Cases the Votes of both Houses shall be determined by Yeas and Nays, and the Names of the Persons voting for and against the Bill shall be entered on the Journal of each House respectively. If any Bill shall not be returned by the President within ten Days (Sundays excepted) after it shall have been presented to him, the Same shall be a Law, in like Manner as if he had signed it, unless the Congress by their Adjournment prevent its Return, in which Case it shall not be a Law

Every Order, Resolution, or Vote to which the Concurrence of the Senate and House of Representatives may be necessary (except on a question of Adjournment) shall be presented to the President of the United States; and before the Same shall take Effect, shall be approved by him, or being disapproved by him, shall be repassed by two thirds of the Senate and House of Representatives, according to the Rules and Limitations prescribed in the Case of a Bill.

Section. 8. The Congress shall have Power To lay and collect Taxes, Duties, Imposts and Excises, to pay the Debts and provide for the common Defence and general Welfare of the United States; but all Duties, Imposts and Excises shall be uniform throughout the United States;

To borrow Money on the credit of the United States;

To regulate Commerce with foreign Nations, and among the several States, and with the Indian Tribes;

To establish an uniform Rule of Naturalization, and uniform Laws on the subject of Bankruptcies throughout the United States;

To coin Money, regulate the Value thereof, and of foreign Coin, and fix the Standard of Weights and Measures;

To provide for the Punishment of counterfeiting the Securities and current Coin of the United States;

To establish Post Offices and post Roads;

To promote the Progress of Science and useful Arts, by securing for limited Times to Authors and Inventors the exclusive Right to their respective Writings and Discoveries;

To constitute Tribunals inferior to the supreme Court;

To define and punish Piracies and Felonies committed on the high Seas, and Offences against the Law of Nations;

To declare War, grant Letters of Marque and Reprisal, and make Rules concerning Captures on Land and Water;

To raise and support Armies, but no Appropriation of Money to that Use shall be for a longer Term than two Years;

To provide and maintain a Navy;

To make Rules for the Government and Regulation of the land and naval Forces;

To provide for calling forth the Militia to execute the Laws of the Union, suppress Insurrections and repeal Invasions;

To provide for organizing, arming, and disciplining, the Militia, and for governing such Part of them as may be employed in the Service of the United States, reserving to the States respectively, the Appointment of the Officers, and the Authority of training the Militia according to the discipline prescribed by Congress;

To exercise exclusive Legislation in all Cases whatsoever, over such District (not exceeding ten Miles square) as may, by Cession of Particular States, and the Acceptance of Congress, become the Seat of the Government of the United States, and to exercise like Authority over all Places purchased by the Consent of the Legislature of the State in which the Same shall be, for the Erection of Forts, Magazines, Arsenals, dock-Yards and other needful Buildings;—And

To make all Laws which shall be necessary and proper for carrying into Execution the foregoing Powers and all other Powers vested by this Constitution in the Government of the United States, or in any Department or Officer thereof.

Section. 9. The Migration or Importation of such Persons as any of the States now existing shall think proper to admit, shall not be prohibited by the Congress prior to the Year one thousand eight hundred and eight, but a Tax or duty may be imposed on such Importation, not exceeding ten dollars for each Person.

The Privilege of the Writ of Habeas Corpus shall not be suspended, unless when in Cases or Rebellion or Invasion the public Safety may require it.

No Bill of Attainder or ex post facto Law shall be passed.

No Capitation, or other direct, Tax shall be laid, unless in Proportion to the Census of Enumeration herein before directed to be taken.

No Tax or Duty shall be laid on Articles exported from any State.

No Preference shall be given by any Regulation of Commerce or Revenue to the Ports of one State over those of another: nor shall Vessels bound to, or from, one State, be obliged to enter, clear or pay Duties in another.

No Money shall be drawn from the Treasury, but in Consequence of Appropriations made by Law; and a regular Statement and Account of the Receipts and Expenditures of all public Money shall be published from time to time.

No Title of Nobility shall be granted by the United States: And no Person holding any Office of Profit or Trust under them, shall, without the Consent of the Congress, accept of any present, Emolument, Office, or Title, of any kind whatever, from any King, Prince or foreign State.

Section. 10. No State shall enter into any Treaty, Alliance, or Confederation; grant Letters of Marque and Reprisal; coin Money; emit Bills of Credit; make any Thing but gold and silver Coin a Tender in Payment of Debts; pass any Bill of Attainder, ex post facto Law, or Law impairing the Obligation of Contracts, or grant any Title of Nobility.

No State shall, without the Consent of the Congress, lay any Imposts or Duties on Imports or Exports, except what may be absolutely necessary for executing it's inspection Laws: and the net Produce of all Duties and Imposts, laid by any State on Imports or Exports, shall be for the Use of the Treasury of the United States; and all such Laws shall be subject to the Revision and Controul of the Congress.

No State shall, without the Consent of Congress, lay any Duty of Tonnage, keep Troops, or Ships of War in time of Peace, enter into any Agreement or Compact with another State, or with a foreign Power, or engage in War, unless actually invaded, or in such imminent Danger as will not admit of delay.

Article. II.

Section. 1. The executive Power shall be vested in a President of the United States of America. He shall hold his Office during the Term of four Years, and, together with the Vice President, chosen for the same Term, be elected, as follows:

Each State shall appoint, in such Manner as the Legislature thereof may direct, a Number of Electors, equal to the whole Number of Senators and Representatives to which the State may be entitled in the Congress: but no Senator or Representative, or Person holding an Office of Trust or Profit under the United States, shall be appointed an Elector.

The Electors shall meet in their respective States, and vote by Ballot for two Persons, of whom one at least shall not be an Inhabitant of the same State with themselves. And they shall make a List of all the Persons voted for, and of the Number of Votes for each; which List they shall sign and certify, and transmit sealed to the Seat of the Government of the United States, directed to the President of the Senate. The President of the Senate shall, in the Presence of the Senate and House of Representatives, open all the Certificates, and the Votes shall then be counted. The Person having the greatest Number of Votes shall be the President, if such Number be a Majority of the whole Number of Electors appointed; and if there be more than one who have such Majority, and have an equal Number of Votes, then the House of Representatives shall immediately chuse by Ballot one of them for President; and if no Person have a Majority, then from the five highest on the List the said House shall in like Manner chuse the President. But in chusing the President, the Votes shall be taken by States, the Representatives from each State having one Vote; a quorum for this Purpose shall consist of a Member or Members from two thirds of the States, and a Majority of all the States shall be necessary to a Choice. In every Case, after the Choice of the President, the Person having the greatest Number of Votes of the Electors shall be the Vice President. But if there should remain two or more who have equal Votes, the Senate shall chuse from them by Ballot the Vice President.

The Congress may determine the Time of chusing the Electors, and the Day on which they shall give their Votes; which Day shall be the same throughout the United States.

No Person except a natural born Citizen, or a Citizen of the United States, at the time of the Adoption of this Constitution, shall be eligible to the Office of President; neither shall any person be eligible to that Office who shall not have attained to the Age of thirty five Years, and been fourteen Years a Resident within the United States.

In Case of the Removal of the President from Office, or of his Death, Resignation, or Inability to discharge the Powers and Duties of the said Office, the Same shall devolve on the Vice President, and the Congress may by Law provide for the Case of Removal, Death, Resignation or Inability, both of the President and Vice President, declaring what Officer shall then act as President, and such Officer shall act accordingly, until the Disability be removed, or a President shall be elected.

The President shall, at stated Times, receive for his Services, a Compensation, which shall neither be increased nor diminished during the Period for which he shall have been elected, and he shall not receive within that Period any other Emolument from the United States, or any of them.

Before he enter on the Execution of his Office, he shall take the following Oath or Affirmation:—"I do solemnly swear (or affirm) that I will faithfully execute the Office of President of the United States, and will to the best of my Ability, preserve, protect and defend the Constitution of the United States."

Section. 2. The President shall be Commander in Chief of the Army and Navy of the United States, and of the Militia of the several States, when called into the actual Service of the United States; he may require the Opinion, in writing, of the principal Officer in each of the executive Departments, upon any Subject relating to the Duties of their respective Offices, and he shall have Power to Grant Reprieves and Pardons for Offences against the United States, except in Cases of Impeachment.

He shall have Power, by and with the Advice and Consent of the Senate, to make Treaties, provided two thirds of the Senators present concur; and he shall nominate, and by and with the Advice and Consent of the Senate, shall appoint Ambassadors, other public Ministers and Consuls, Judges of the supreme Court, and all other Officers of the United States, whose Appointments are not herein otherwise provided for, and which shall be established by Law: but the Congress may by Law vest the Appointment of such inferior Officers, as they think proper, in the President alone, in the Courts of Law, or in the Heads of Departments.

The President shall have Power to fill up all Vacancies that may happen during the Recess of the Senate, by granting Commissions which shall expire at the End of their next Session.

Section. 3. He shall from time to time give to the Congress Information on the State of the Union, and recommend to their Consideration such Measures as he shall judge necessary and expedient; he may, on extraordinary Occasions, convene both Houses, or either of them, and in Case of Disagreement between them, with Respect to the Time of Adjournment, he may adjourn them to such Time as he shall think proper; he shall receive Ambassadors and other public Ministers; he shall take Care that the Laws be faithfully executed, and shall Commission all the Officers of the United States.

Section. 4. The President, Vice President and all Civil Officers of the United States, shall be removed from Office on Impeachment for and Conviction of, Treason, Bribery, or other high Crimes and Misdemeanors.

Article. III.

Section. 1. The judicial Power of the United States, shall be vested in one supreme Court, and in such inferior Courts as the Congress may from time to time ordain and establish. The Judges, both of the supreme and inferior Courts, shall hold their Offices during good Behaviour, and shall, at stated Times, receive for their Services, a Compensation, which shall not be diminished during their Continuance in Office.

Section. 2. The judicial Power shall extend to all Cases, in Law and Equity, arising under this Constitution, the Laws of the United States, and Treaties made, or which shall be made, under their Authority;—to all Cases affecting Ambassadors, other public ministers and Consuls;—to all Cases of admiralty and maritime Jurisdiction;—to Controversies to which the United States shall be a Party;—to Controversies between two or more States;—between a State and Citizens of another State;—between Citizens of different States;—between Citizens of the same State claiming Lands under Grants of different States, and between a State, or the Citizens thereof, and foreign States, Citizens or Subjects.

In all Cases affecting Ambassadors, other public Ministers and Consuls, and those in which a State shall be Party, the supreme Court shall have original Jurisdiction. In all the other Cases before mentioned, the supreme Court shall have appellate Jurisdiction, both as to Law and Fact, with such Exceptions, and under such Regulations as the Congress shall make.

The Trial of all Crimes, except in Cases of Impeachment, shall be by Jury; and such Trial shall be held in the State where the said Crimes shall have been committed; but when not committed within any State, the Trial shall be at such Place or Places as the Congress may by Law have directed.

Section. 3. Treason against the United States, shall consist only in levying War against them, or in adhering to their Enemies, giving them Aid and Comfort. No Person shall be convicted of Treason unless on the Testimony of two Witnesses to the same overt Act, or on Confession in open Court.

The Congress shall have Power to declare the Punishment of Treason, but no Attainder of Treason shall work Corruption of Blood, or Forfeiture except during the Life of the Person attainted.

Article. IV.

Section. 1. Full Faith and Credit shall be given in each State to the public Acts, Records, and judicial Proceedings of every other State. And the Congress may by general Laws prescribe the Manner in which such Acts, Records and Proceedings shall be proved, and the Effect thereof.

Section. 2. The Citizens of each State shall be entitled to all Privileges and Immunities of Citizens in the several States.

A Person charged in any State with Treason, Felony, or other Crime, who shall flee from Justice, and be found in another State, shall on Demand of the executive Authority of the State from which he fled, be delivered up, to be removed to the State having Jurisdiction of the Crime.

No Person held to Service or Labour in one State, under the Laws thereof, escaping into another, shall, in Consequence of any Law or Regulation therein, be discharged from such Service or Labour, but shall be delivered up on Claim of the Party to whom such Service or Labour may be due.

Section. 3. New States may be admitted by the Congress into this Union; but no new State shall be formed or erected within the Jurisdiction of any other State; nor any State be formed by the Junction of two or more States, or Parts of States, without the Consent of the Legislatures of the States concerned as well as of the Congress.

The Congress shall have Power to dispose of and make all needful Rules and Regulations respecting the Territory or other Property belonging to the United States; and nothing in this Constitution shall be so construed as to Prejudice any Claims of the United States, or of any particular State.

Section. 4. The United States shall guarantee to every State in this Union a Republican Form of Government, and shall protect each of them against Invasion; and on Application of the Legislature, or of the Executive (when the Legislature cannot be convened) against domestic Violence.

Article. V.

The Congress, whenever two thirds of both Houses shall deem it necessary, shall propose Amendments to this Constitution, or, on the Application of the Legislatures of two thirds of the several States, shall call a Convention for proposing Amendments, which, in either Case, shall be valid to all Intents and Purposes, as Part of this Constitution, when ratified by the Legislatures of three fourths of the several States, or by

Conventions in three fourths thereof, as the one or the other Mode of Ratification may be proposed by the Congress; Provided that no Amendment which may be made prior to the Year One thousand eight hundred and eight shall in any Manner affect the first and fourth Clauses in the Ninth Section of the first Article; and that no State, without its Consent, shall be deprived of its equal Suffrage in the Senate.

Article. VI.

All Debts contracted and Engagements entered into, before the Adoption of this Constitution, shall be as valid against the United States under this Constitution, as under the Confederation.

This Constitution, and the Laws of the United States which shall be made in Pursuance thereof; and all Treaties made, or which shall be made, under the Authority of the United States, shall be the supreme Law of the Land; and the Judges in every State shall be bound thereby, any Thing in the Constitution or Laws of any state to the Contrary notwithstanding.

The Senators and Representatives before mentioned, and the Members of the several State Legislatures, and all executive and judicial Officers, both of the United States and of the several States, shall be bound by Oath or Affirmation, to support this Constitution; but no religious Test shall ever be required as a Qualification to any Office or public Trust under the United States.

Article. VII.

The Ratification of the Conventions of nine States, shall be sufficient for the Establishment of this Constitution between the States so ratifying the same.

The Word, "the," being interlined between the seventh and eighth Lines of the first Page, The Word "Thirty" being partly written on an Erazure in the fifteenth Line of the first Page, The Words "is tried" being interlined between the thirty second and thirty third Lines of the first Page and the Word "the" being interlined between the forty third and forty fourth Lines of the second Page.

done in Convention by the Unanimous Consent of the States present the Seventeenth Day of September in the Year of our Lord one thousand seven hundred and Eighty seven and of the Independence of the United States of America the Twelfth. In witness whereof We have hereunto subscribed our Names,

Attest WILLIAM JACKSON
Secretary

Gᵒ. WASHINGTON—Presidᵗ.
and deputy from Virginia

New Hampshire	JOHN LANGDON NICHOLAS GILMAN
Massachusetts	NATHANIEL GORHAM RUFUS KING
Connecticut	Wᴹ SAMᴸ JOHNSON ROGER SHERMAN
New York	ALEXANDER HAMILTON
New Jersey	WIL: LIVINGSTON DAVID BREARLEY. Wᴹ PATTERSON. JONA: DAYTON
Pennsylvania	B FRANKLIN THOMAS MIFFLIN ROBᵀ MORRIS GEO. CLYMER THOˢ FITZSIMONS JARED INGERSOL JAMES WILSON GOUV MORRIS

Delaware	Geo: Read
	Gunning Bedford jun
	John Dickinson
	Richard Bassett
	Jaco: Broom
Maryland	James McHenry
	Dan of St Thos Jenifer
	Danl Carroll
Virginia	John Blair—
	James Madison Jr.
North Carolina	Wm Blount
	Richd Dobbs Spaight
	Hu Williamson
	J. Rutledge
South Carolina	Charles Cotesworth Pinckney
	Charles Pinckney
	Pierce Butler
Georgia	William Few
	Abr Baldwin

In Convention Monday, September 17th 1787.

Present

The States of

New Hampshire, Massachusetts, Connecticut, MR Hamilton from New York, New Jersey, Pennsylvania, Delaware, Maryland, Virginia, North Carolina, South Carolina and Georgia.

Resolved,

That the preceeding Constitution be laid before the United States in Congress assembled, and that it is the Opinion of this Convention, that it should afterwards be submitted to a Convention of Delegates, chosen in each State by the People thereof, under the Recommendation of its Legislature, for their Assent and Ratification; and that each Convention assenting to, and ratifying the Same, should give Notice thereof to the United States in Congress assembled. Resolved, That it is the Opinion of this Convention, that as soon as the Conventions of nine States shall have ratified this Constitution, the United States in Congress assembled should fix a Day on which Electors should be appointed by the States which shall have ratified the same, and a Day on which the Electors should assemble to vote for the President, and the Time and Place for commencing Proceedings under this Constitution. That after such Publication the Electors should be appointed, and the Senators and Representatives elected: That the Electors should meet on the Day fixed for the Election of the President, and should transmit their Votes certified, signed, sealed and directed, as the Constitution requires, to the Secretary of the United States in Congress assembled, that the Senators and Representatives should convene at the Time and Place assigned; that the Senators should appoint a President of the Senate, for the sole Purpose of receiving, opening and counting the Votes for President; and, that after he shall be chosen, the Congress, together with the President, should, without Delay, proceed to execute this Constitution.

By the Unanimous Order of the Convention

Go: WASHINGTON—Presid^t.

W. JACKSON Secretary.

Notes

Introduction

1. In re: Bruce Lindsey, 148 F.3d 1100, 1106 (D.C. Cir. 1998), cert. denied, 525 U.S. 996 (1998).
2. Andrew Cohen, "The Torture Memos, 10 Years Later," *The Atlantic*, February 6, 2012, https://www.theatlantic.com/national/archive/2012/02/the-torture-memos-10-years-later/252439/; John Yoo and Robert J. Delahunty, Office of the Deputy Assistant Attorney General, "Application of Treaties and Laws to al Qaeda and Taliban Detainees," Op. O.L.C., January 9, 2002, https://nsarchive2.gwu.edu//NSAEBB/NSAEBB127/02.01.09.pdf.
3. Jeffrey Rosen, "Conscience of a Conservative," *New York Times*, September 9, 2007, https://www.nytimes.com/2007/09/09/magazine/09rosen.html.
4. *See* Kyllo v. United States, 533 U.S. 27, 40 (2001) (holding that using a device that is not in general public use constitutes a search).
5. *See* United States v. Jones, 565 U.S. 400, 403–04 (2012) (holding that attaching a GPS device to a vehicle constitutes a search under the Fourth Amendment).
6. Montesquieu, *The Spirit of the Laws, Volume 1*, trans. Thomas Nugent (London: J. Nourse, 1777), 221–37, https://sourcebooks.fordham.edu/mod/montesquieu-spirit.asp.

CHAPTER 1: The Basics: Each Branch Has a Job Description—and Two Bosses

1. Miranda v. Arizona, 384 U.S. 436, 457–58 (1966).
2. *See* Bivens v. Six Unknown Named Agents of Federal Bureau of Narcotics, 403 U.S. 388, 390 (1971).
3. *See, e.g.*, Monell v. Dep't of Soc. Servs. of City of New York, 436 U.S. 658, 690 (1978) (explaining that a local government may be sued under the Civil Rights Act).
4. Bourree Lam, "Why Are So Many Zappos Employees Leaving?," *The Atlantic*, January 15, 2016, https://www.theatlantic.com/business/archive/2016/01/zappos-holacracy-hierarchy/424173/.

5. U.S. Const. art. 1, § 8, cl. 18.

6. Chrysler Corp. v. Brown, 441 U.S. 281, 286 n.4 (1979).

7. Robert A. Dahl, *Modern Political Analysis*, 2nd ed. (Prentice Hall, 1970), 41.

8. Newdow v. Rio Linda Union School Dist., 597 F.3d 1007, 1028 (9th Cir. 2010) ("In the monarchies of Europe, it was believed that God gave the King his power, and the people had only such limited rights as the King graciously bestowed upon them.").

9. U.S. Const. Pmbl.

10. *See* Lichter v. United States, 334 U.S. 742, 755 n.3 (1948) (highlighting the importance of the phrase "We the People"); *see also* Hess v. Port Auth. Trans-Hudson Corp., 513 U.S. 30, 55 n.3 (1994) (stating the founders' purpose to provide justice to the people).

11. The Declaration of Independence, para. 2 (U.S. 1776).

12. James Madison, "The Federalist No. 49: Method of Guarding Against the Encroachments of Any One Department of Government by Appealing to the People Through a Convention," *New York Packet*, February 2, 1788.

13. Alexander Hamilton, "The Federalist No. 78: The Judiciary Department," *New York Packet*, May 28, 1788.

14. James Madison, "The Federalist No. 10: The Union as a Safeguard Against Domestic Faction and Insurrection," *New York Packet*, November 22, 1787.

15. James Madison, "The Federalist No. 37: Concerning the Difficulties of the Convention in Devising a Proper Form of Government," *New York Packet*, January 11, 1788.

16. Downes v. Bidwell, 182 U.S. 244, 359 (1901) ("[N]o utterance of this court has intimated a doubt that in its operation on the people, by whom and for whom it was established, the national government is a government of enumerated powers.") *See also* McCulloch v. Maryland, 17 U.S. 316, 403 (1819) ("The government proceeds directly from the people.").

17. John Rawls, *Political Liberalism* (New York: Columbia University Press, 1993), 217.

CHAPTER 2: Congress: Lots of Power to a Herd of Cats

1. James Madison, "The Federalist No. 48: These Departments Should Not Be So Far Separated as to Have No Constitutional Control over Each Other," *New York Packet*, February 1, 1788.

2. Under the Trump administration, there's been discussion of Congress's power to hold uncooperative witnesses in contempt—or to hold the DOJ

in contempt for refusing to turn over documents relating to ongoing criminal investigations. The congressional-contempt power is hard to enforce. Congress can order its sergeant at arms to physically force a witness to appear, but that's hardly realistic. Barring that, it needs the executive branch to bring a case against a witness, which it might refuse to do. As for DOJ investigations, there is a separation-of-powers problem with politicizing criminal investigations via congressional oversight, although it is not banned by the Constitution's text. *See* 2 U.S.C. § 192.

3. *See generally* Tom Goldstein, "Justice Thomas and Constitutional 'Stare Indecisis,'" *SCOTUSblog*, October 8, 2007, https://www.scotusblog.com/2007/10/justice-thomas-and-constitutional-stare-indecisis/.

4. Youngstown Sheet & Tube Co. v. Sawyer, 343 U.S. 579–87 (1952). (Note that the court stepped in here where Congress did not—which branch should be the one checking a particular action of another branch is not addressed in the Constitution.)

5. *See generally* Erwin Chemerinsky, *Constitutional Law: Principles and Policies*, 5th ed. (New York: Wolters Kluwer, 2015), § 4.1.

6. Trump v. Hawaii, 138 S. Ct. 2392, 2410 (2018).

7. U.S. Const. art. I, § 8, cl. 1.

8. United States v. Butler, 297 U.S. 1, 68–69 (1936).

9. Helvering v. Davis, 301 U.S. 619, 640–41 (1937).

10. National Federation of Independent Business v. Sebelius, 567 U.S. 519, 563, 587 (2012).

11. *See* Sonzinsky v. United States, 300 U.S. 506, 514 (1937).

12. South Dakota v. Dole, 483 U.S. 203, 207 (1987).

13. *Id.* 208.

14. *See* Richard Lieb, "Federal Supremacy and State Sovereignty: The Supreme Court's Early Jurisprudence," *American Bankruptcy Institute Law Review* 15, no. 1 (Spring 2007): 3.

15. McCulloch v. Maryland, 17 U.S. (4 Wheat.) 316, 407 (1819).

16. *See generally* Chemerinsky, *Constitutional Law*.

17. McCulloch, 17 U.S. at 415.

18. 42 U.S.C. §§ 300gg; 45 C.F.R. § 147.126; *see also* Robert I. Field, "Government as the Crucible for Free Market Health Care: Regulation, Reimbursement, and Reform," *University of Pennsylvania Law Review* 159, no. 6 (June 2011): 1669.

19. Michael Lee, "Unilateralism, Defunding, and the Shrapnel of Health Reform," *Yale Law & Policy Review* (2011): 41–43, *inter alia*.

20. Ilya Somin, "The Individual Mandate and the Meaning of 'Proper,'" (George Mason Law & Economics Research Paper No. 12–73, May 3, 2013), https://papers.ssrn.com/sol3/papers.cfm?abstract_id=2167381.
21. Gibbons v. Ogden, 22 U.S. 1 (1824).
22. Carter v. Carter Coal Co., 298 U.S. 238, 303–04 (1936).
23. *See* United States v. Gray, 260 F.3d 1267, 1274 (11th Cir. 2001) (stating that "[t]he relationship between robbery and commerce is clear" as it "deprives the victim of its ability to use money or property in commerce, while enabling the perpetrator to use money or property that he otherwise would not possess.")
24. Heart of Atlanta Motel, Inc. v. United States, 379 U.S. 241, 253 (1964).
25. United States v. Lopez, 514 U.S. 549 (1995); *see generally* Chemerinsky, *Constitutional Law*, § 3.4.
26. National Federation of Independent Business v. Sebelius, 567 U.S. 519, 547 (2012).
27. U.S. Const. art. I, § 9, cl. 8.
28. Noel King, "How Ben Franklin and King Louis XVI Inspired the Emoluments Clause," National Public Radio, March 10, 2017, https://www.npr.org/2017/03/10/519593268/how-ben-franklin-and-king-louis-xvi-inspired-emoluments-clause.
29. *See generally* D.C. v. Trump, 291 F. Supp. 3d 725 (D. Md. 2018).
30. 5 U.S.C. § 7342; 41 C.F.R. §§ 102–42.
31. *See* Trump, 291 F. Supp. 3d at 725.
32. *See* Eric M. Freedman, "The Law as King and the King as Law: Is a President Immune from Criminal Prosecution Before Impeachment?," *Hastings Constitutional Law Quarterly* 20, no. 1 (Fall 1992): 7.
33. *See* Lawrence Lessig, "What an Originalist Would Understand 'Corruption' to Mean," *California Law Review* 102, no. 1 (February 2014): 1.
34. U.S. Const. art. II, § 4; Under Article I, Section 5, clause 2 of the U.S. Constitution, a senator or representative may be expelled if there is a formal vote on a resolution agreed to by two-thirds of the members of the Senate or House body who are present—not by impeachment. *See* U.S. Const. art. I, § 5, cl. 2.
35. *See* Fred H. Altshuler, "Comparing the Nixon and Clinton Impeachments," *Hastings Law Journal* 51, no. 4 (April 2000): 745.
36. *See generally* U.S. Const. art. II, § 4.
37. Chemerinsky, *Constitutional Law*, § 4.7.
38. Nixon v. United States, 506 U.S. 224, 234 (1993).

CHAPTER 3: The (Real) Powers of the President: No More Kings

1. Bureau of Justice Statistics, *Data Collection: Census of Federal Law Enforcement Officers*, 2008, https://www.bjs.gov/index.cfm?ty=dcdetail&iid=250.
2. US. Const. art. II, § 2.
3. 18 U.S.C. § 175(a).
4. Niki Kuckes, "The Democratic Prosecutor: Explaining the Constitutional Function of the Federal Grand Jury," *Georgetown Law Journal* 94, no. 5 (June 2006): 1265.
5. Note, however, that in the United States, many prisons—particularly at the state and local levels—are actually run by private corporations, which to a large degree are not bound by the Constitution at all.
6. U.S. Const. art. I, § 9, cl. 3 ("No Bill of Attainder or ex post facto Law will be passed."); Morrison v. Olson, 487 U.S. 654, 726 (1988) (Scalia, J., dissenting); United States v. Armstrong, 517 U.S. 456, 464 (1996) [quoting Bordenkircher v. Hayes, 434 U.S. 357, 364 (1978)].
7. *See* Lauren Carroll, "How the War on Drugs Affected Incarceration Rates," *PolitiFact,* July 10, 2016, http://www.politifact.com/truth-o-meter/statements/2016/jul/10/cory-booker/how-war-drugs-affected-incarceration-rates/ (noting that the current incarcerated population of 2.2 million reflects a 500 percent growth over the past four decades).
8. John Walters, "How the Clinton Administration Is Abandoning the War Against Drugs" (Washington, DC: Heritage Foundation, June 16, 1994), https://www.heritage.org/crime-and-justice/report/how-the-clinton-administration-abandoning-the-war-against-drugs.
9. Robert J. Delahunty and John C. Yoo, "Dream On: The Obama Administration's Nonenforcement of Immigration Laws, the DREAM Act, and the Take Care Clause," *Texas Law Review* 91, no. 4 (March 2013): 781–856.
10. Edward G. Carmines and Matthew Fowler, "The Temptation of Executive Authority: How Increased Polarization and the Decline in Legislative Capacity Have Contributed to the Expansion of Presidential Power," *Indiana Journal of Global Legal Studies* 24, no. 2 (2017): 369–94.
11. Janet Napolitano, "Exercising Prosecutorial Discretion with Respect to Individuals Who Came to the United States as Children" (Washington, DC: U.S. Department of Homeland Security, June 15, 2012), https://www.dhs.gov/xlibrary/assets/s1-exercising-prosecutorial-discretion-individuals-who-came-to-us-as-children.pdf.

12. Delahunty and Yoo, 800.

13. *See* Mistretta v. United States, 488 U.S. 361, 416 (1989) (Scalia, J., dissenting); *see id.* 373; Whitman v. American Trucking Associations, 531 U.S. 457, 474–75 (2001).

14. *See* Cary Coglianese, "The Rhetoric and Reality of Regulatory Reform," *Yale Journal on Regulation* 25, no. 1 (2008): 85 (noting the idea that procedural controls impose "paralysis by analysis" on regulatory agencies).

15. John C. Duncan Jr., "A Critical Consideration of Executive Orders: Glimmerings of Autopoiesis in the Executive Role," *Vermont Law Review* 35, no. 2 (Winter 2010): 333.

16. Executive Order No. 9-2 (January 28, 1873).

17. Executive Order No. 11063 (November 20, 1962); Executive Order No. 11375 (October 13, 1967).

18. *See* Louis Fisher, "The Unitary Executive and Inherent Executive Power," *University of Pennsylvania Journal of Constitutional Law* 12, no. 2 (February 2010): 569.

19. Douglas E. Kneeland, "Nixon Discharges Cox for Defiance; Abolishes Watergate Task Force; Richardson and Ruckelshaus Out," *New York Times*, October 22, 1973, http://www.nytimes.com/learning/general/onthisday/big/1020.html.

20. Federal Election Commission v. NRA Political Victory Fund, 513 U.S. 88, 102 (1994); Jill Lepore, *These Truths: A History of the United States* (New York: W. W. Norton, 2018), 644, 688.

21. Tom Huddleston Jr., "LeBron James' New Lakers Contract Will Make Him the Best-Paid NBA Player—Ever," CNBC, July 3, 2018, https://www.cnbc.com/2018/07/02/lakers-deal-will-make-lebron-james-highest-career-earning-nba-player.html.

22. U.S. Const. art. I, § 2, cl. 2.

23. Professors Lawrence Lessig and Cass Sunstein suggest that, without the Opinion Clause, it is not evident that the president would have had the power to direct the departments to report to him as a matter of constitutional necessity. The Opinion Clause thus prevents Congress from creating agencies completely severed from presidential control. *See* Lawrence Lessig and Cass R. Sunstein, "The President and the Administration," *Columbia Law Review* 94, no. 1 (1994): 34.

24. *See* Richard J. Pierce Jr., Sidney A. Shapiro, and Paul R. Verkuil, *Administrative Law and Process*, 3rd ed. (New York Foundation Press, 1999), 80–81.

25. *See* Myers v. United States, 272 U.S. 52, 163–64 (1926) ("Article II grants

to the President . . . the power of appointment and removal of executive officers—a conclusion confirmed by his obligation to take care that the laws be faithfully executed."); *see also* Humphrey's Executor v. United States, 295 U.S. 602, 631–32 (1935) (upholding statute that curtailed the removal power).

26. Morrison v. Olson, 487 U.S. 654, 696–97 (1988).

27. 28 C.F.R. § 600 (1999).

28. *See* Mark Strasser, "The Limits of the Clemency Power on Pardons, Retributivists, and the United States Constitution," *Brandeis Law Journal* 41, no. 1 (2002): 148.

29. Schick v. Reed, 419 U.S. 256, 266 (1974).

30. *See* Erwin Chemerinsky, *Constitutional Law: Principles and Policies*, 5th ed. (New York: Wolters Kluwer, 2015), § 3.6 (for a broader discussion of the war powers).

31. *See* Baker v. Carr, 369 U.S. 186, 210–11 (1962) (defining the leading test for political questions).

32. *See* 50 U.S.C. § 1541, *et seq.*

33. *See generally* Julia L. Chen, "Restoring Constitutional Balance: Accommodating the Evolution of War," *Boston College Law Review* 53, no. 5 (November 2012): 1767.

34. Whitney v. Robertson, 124 U.S. 190, 194 (1988).

35. Chemerinsky, *Constitutional Law*, § 4.6.2.

CHAPTER 4: The Courts: What Was That About Kings?

1. Marbury v. Madison, 5 U.S. 137 (1 Cranch) (1803).

2. Paul Taylor, "Congress's Power to Regulate the Federal Judiciary: What the First Congress and the First Federal Courts Can Teach Today's Congress and Courts," *Pepperdine Law Review* 37, no. 3 (2010): 861.

3. *See* Andrew Coan and Toni Massaro, "Matthew Whitaker's Supreme Court Positions Are Incoherent, May Cause Constitutional Crisis," *USA Today*, November 14, 2018, https://www.usatoday.com/story/opinion/2018/11/14/matthew-whitaker-acting-attorney-general-supreme-court-constitutional-crisis-column/1977742002/.

4. There are a number of additional threshold hurdles to bringing a case in federal court and some state courts, such as personal jurisdiction and venue. *See generally* Steven S. Gensler, *Federal Rules of Civil Procedure, Rules and Commentary*, 2019 ed. (Thompson Reuters, 2019).

5. Article III lists a number of other types of controversies, such as those between two or more states, that can be heard in federal court, but they are

less important for purposes of understanding the basics about the federal court system. There is also something called *supplemental jurisdiction*—where a state law dispute can essentially piggyback on a federal question or diversity jurisdiction. U.S. Const. art. III, § 2, cl. 1; 28 U.S.C. §§ 1331, 1367.

6. Sup. Ct. R. 10.
7. Merriam-Webster, "habeas corpus," accessed February 2, 2019, https://www.merriam-webster.com/dictionary/habeas%20corpus.
8. Ira C. Lupu, Peter J. Smith, and Robert W. Tuttle, "The Imperatives of Structure: The Travel Ban, the Establishment Clause, and Standing to Sue," *Take Care* (blog), accessed January 2019, https://takecareblog.com/blog/the-imperatives-of-structure-the-travel-ban-the-establishment-clause-and-standing-to-sue.
9. Plessy v. Ferguson, 163 U.S. 537, 541 (1896) (overruled in 1954 by Brown v. Board of Education).
10. Plessy v. Ferguson, 163 U.S. at 544.
11. Brown v. Board of Education of Topeka, Shawnee County, Kansas, 347 U.S. 483, 494 (1954).
12. Jason Mazzone, "The Commandeerer in Chief," *Notre Dame Law Review* 83 (November 2007): 320 n. 363.
13. Loving v. Virginia, 388 U.S. 1, 4 n.3 (1967).
14. *Id*. 3.
15. *Id*. 12, 11.
16. Merriam-Webster, "equal," accessed February 2, 2019, https://www.merriam-webster.com/dictionary/equal.
17. Railway Mail Association v. Corsi, 326 U.S. 88, 89–90 (1945); *see generally* *SCOTUS Now* (blog), "The Right to Discriminate in Historical Perspective," Chicago-Kent College of Law, April 9, 2014, http://blogs.kentlaw.iit.edu/iscotus/the-right-to-discriminate-in-historical-perspective.
18. Katzenbach v. McClung, 379 U.S. 294, 304–05 (1964).
19. Roberts v. United States Jaycees, 468 U.S. 609, 612 (1984).
20. Boy Scouts of America v. Dale, 530 U.S. 640, 644 (2000).
21. *See generally* Ian Millhiser, "When 'Religious Liberty' Was Used to Justify Racism Instead of Homophobia," *ThinkProgress*, February 27, 2014, https://thinkprogress.org/when-religious-liberty-was-used-to-justify-racism-instead-of-homophobia-67bc973c4042#.n0zt81r31.

CHAPTER 5: Speech, Religion, and the First Amendment

1. Merriam-Webster, "abridge," accessed February 28, 2019, https://www.merriam-webster.com/dictionary/abridge.
2. Erwin Chemerinsky, *Constitutional Law: Principles and Policies*, 5th ed. (New York: Wolters Kluwer, 2015), § 11.6.1.
3. Lynch v. Donnelly, 465 U.S. 668, 672 (1984).
4. *See* Malnak v. Yogi, 592 F.2d 197, 199 (3rd Cir. 1979).
5. *See* Alden v. Maine, 527 U.S. 706, 763 (1999) (Souter, J., dissenting) (describing natural law as "a universally applicable proposition discoverable by reason").
6. *See* Fitts v. Kolb, 779 F. Supp. 1502, 1506 (D.S.C. 1991) ("The most notorious example of the use of the criminal law to punish seditious libel occurred in the royal Court of Star Chamber. There, truth was not a defense, and a defendant was not entitled to a jury trial on the issue of whether the alleged statement was defamatory."); Chemerinsky, *Constitutional Law*, § 11.1.1.
7. Patterson v. People of Colorado, 205 U.S. 454, 462 (1907) [quoting Commonweath v. Blanding, 20 Mass (3 Pick.) 304, 313–14 (1825)].
8. *Id.* 458–59, 462, 464 (1907); *see generally* Chemerinsky, *Constitutional Law*, § 11.1.1.
9. Derigan Silver and Dan V. Kozlowski, "The First Amendment Originalism of Justices Brennan, Scalia and Thomas," *Communication Law & Policy* 17, no. 4 (Autumn 2012): 385.
10. Whitney v. California, 274 U.S. 357, 375 (1927) (Brandeis, J., concurring); *see generally* Chemerinsky, *Constitutional Law*, § 11.1.2.
11. New York Times Co. v. Sullivan, 376 U.S. 254, 273 (1964).
12. Kent Greenawalt, "Free Speech Justifications," *Columbia Law Review* 89, no. 1 (January 1989): 120.
13. *See* Gitlow v. New York, 268 U.S. 652, 666 (1925) (holding that the First Amendment applies to the states through its incorporation under the Fourteenth Amendment's due process clause).
14. Schenck v. United States, 249 U.S. 47, 52 (1919); *see generally* Chemerinsky, *Constitutional Law*, § 11.3.2.1 (noting that the First Amendment does not allow a person to yell "fire" in a crowded theater).
15. *See* City Council of Los Angeles v. Taxpayers for Vincent, 466 U.S. 789, 816–17 (1984) (upholding law prohibiting posting of signs on public utility poles).
16. Renton v. Playtime Theatres, Inc., 475 U.S. 41, 47–48 (1986).

17. Massachusetts Board of Retirement v. Murgia, 427 U.S. 307, 312–13 (1976).

18. Linda J. Wharton, Susan Frietsche, and Kathryn Kolbert, "Preserving the Core of Roe: Reflections of Planned Parenthood v. Casey," *Yale Journal of Law & Feminism* 18, no. 2 (2006): 328.

19. New York Times Co. v. United States, 403 U.S. 713, 714 (1971).

20. Madsen v. Women's Health Center, Inc., 512 U.S. 753, 776 (1994) (holding that an authority has the right to consider, without unfair discrimination, appropriate uses of public places).

21. *See* Cox v. New Hampshire, 312 U.S. 569, 575–76 (1941).

22. *See* Rust v. Sullivan, 500 U.S. 173 (1991); FCC v. League of Women Voters of California, 468 U.S. 364 (1984).

23. Chemerinsky, *Constitutional Law*, § 11.2.4.4.

24. *See* City of Chicago v. Morales, 527 U.S. 41, 64 (1999) (holding unconstitutional a law vaguely prohibiting loitering).

25. *See* United States v. Stevens, 559 U.S. 460, 481 (2010); Schad v. Borough of Mt. Ephraim, 452 U.S. 61, 68 (1981).

26. *See* Osborne v. Ohio, 495 U.S. 103, 112–13 (1990).

27. Janus v. American Federation of State, County, and Municipal Employees, Council 31, 138 S. Ct. 2448 (2018), *overruling* Abood v. Detroit Board of Education, 431 U.S. 209 (1977); Miami Herald Publishing Co. v. Tornillo, 418 U.S. 241 (1974); Talley v. California, 362 U.S. 60 (1960); West Virginia State Board of Education v. Barnette, 319 U.S. 624 (1943).

28. *See generally* Marc Rohr, "Grand Illusion?," *Willamette Law Review* 38, no. 1 (Winter 2002): 1 ("Advocacy of the commission of a particular criminal act does, after all, tend to heighten the risk that the criminal act will be committed").

29. Brandenburg v. Ohio, 395 U.S. 444, 447 (1969); Chemerinsky, *Constitutional Law*, §§ 11.3.2.1–5.

30. Virginia v. Black, 538 U.S. 343, 366–67 (2003).

31. *Id.* (finding that the act of cross burning itself is insufficient to justify banning speech under the First Amendment); Cohen v. California, 403 U.S. 15, 20–22 (1971) (setting forth violent response test); Terminello v. Chicago, 337 U.S. 1, 6 (1949) (holding that the jury instructions in a case involving disturbing the peace were insufficiently protective of speech); Chaplinsky v. New Hampshire, 315 U.S. 568, 573–74 (1942) (upholding criminal conviction based on defendant's speech); *see generally* Chemerinsky, *Constitutional Law*, §§ 11.3.3.2–3.4.

32. Reno v. ACLU, 521 U.S. 844 (1997) (Internet); Denver Area Educational

Communications Consortium, Inc. v. FCC, 518 U.S. 727 (1996) (cable); Sable Communications v. FCC, 492 U.S. 115 (1989) (telephone); FCC v. Pacifica Foundation, 438 U.S. 726 (1978) (broadcast media); Miller v. California, 413 U.S. 15 (1973) (setting forth test for obscenity); Cohen v. California, 403 U.S. 15 (1971) (holding that profane and indecent language is protected, with exceptions); Roth v. United States, 354 U.S. 476 (1957) (holding that obscenity is not protected under the First Amendment).

33. Tim Wu, "The Right to Evade Regulation: How Corporations Hijacked the First Amendment," *New Republic*, June 3, 2013, https://newrepub lic.com/article/113294/how-corporations-hijacked-first-amendment -evade-regulation.

34. Maggie Astor, "Roy Moore Sues 4 Women, Claiming Defamation and Conspiracy," *New York Times*, April 30, 2018, https://www.nytimes .com/2018/04/30/us/politics/roy-moore-lawsuit.html; John Bowden, "Trump Suggests Changes to Libel Laws over Woodward Book," *The Hill*, September 5, 2018, https://thehill.com/homenews/administra tion/405102-trump-suggests-changes-to-libel-laws-over-woodward -book; Jonathan Stempel, "Roy Moore Files $95M Defamation Suit Against CBS, Comedian Cohen," *Insurance Journal*, September 6, 2018, https://www.insurancejournal.com/news/southeast/2018/09/06/500270 .htm.

35. Dun & Bradstreet, Inc. v. Greenmoss Builders, Inc., 472 U.S. 749, 754–55 (1985) (holding that defamation of a private figure requires a showing of falsity); New York Times Co. v. Sullivan, 376 U.S. 254, 267–68 (1964) (holding that defamation of a public official requires proof of actual malice, i.e., knowledge of falsity or reckless disregard of whether it was false); Chemerinsky, *Constitutional Law*, § 11.3.5.2.

36. 5 U.S.C. § 7323; Matt Zaprotsky, "FBI Agent Peter Strzok Fired Over Anti-Trump Texts," *Washington Post*, August 13, 2018, https://www .washingtonpost.com/world/national-security/fbi-agent-peter-strzok -fired-over-anti-trump-texts/2018/08/13/be98f84c-8e8b-11e8-b769 -e3fff17f0689_story.html?utm_term=.b504a1e6ecf2.

37. Pickering v. Board of Education, 391 U.S. 563, 574–75 (1968); United Public Workers v. Mitchell, 330 U.S. 75, 93–94 (1947) (discussing 5 U.S.C. § 7324, parts of which have since been repealed).

38. Davis v. Federal Election Commission, 554 U.S. 724, 738 (2008) (finding impermissible burden on First Amendment right to spend money for campaign speech); Texas v. Johnson, 491 U.S. 397, 420 (1989) (noting

that flag-burning is expressive conduct within the protection of the First Amendment).

39. Citizens United v. Federal Election Commission, 558 U.S. 310, 354, 372 (2010).

40. 44 Liquormart, Inc. v. Rhode Island, 517 U.S. 484, 516 (1996).

41. Lorillard Tobacco Co. v. Reilly, 533 U.S. 525, 556, 566 (2001).

42. Chemerinsky, *Constitutional Law*, § 12.1.1.

43. Lemon v. Kurtzman, 403 U.S. 602 (1971).

44. Abington School District v. Schempp, 374 U.S. 203, 240 (1963) (Brennan, J., concurring).

45. United States v. Ballard, 322 U.S. 78, 86 (1944).

46. Thomas v. Review Board of the Indiana Employment Security Division, 450 U.S. 707, 708 (1981).

47. Everson v. Board of Education, 330 U.S. 1, 18 (1947).

48. Capitol Square Review and Advisory Board v. Pinette, 515 U.S. 753, 777 (1995).

49. *See* Christopher B. Harwood, "Evaluating the Supreme Court's Establishment Clause Jurisprudence in the Wake of *Van Orden v. Perry* and *McCreary County v. ACLU*," *Missouri Law Review* 71, no. 2 (Spring 2006): 317–53. "Those who adhere to the accommodation approach cite historical evidence, specifically, the Founders' writings and practices, to support their view that the Framers understood the scope of the establishment ban to be sufficiently narrow to allow significant government involvement in the religious sphere." *Id.* 353.

50. County of Allegheny v. ACLU, Greater Pittsburgh, 492 U.S. 573, 621 (1989).

51. Edwards v. Aguillard, 482 U.S. 578 (1987); Wallace v. Jaffree, 472 U.S. 38 (1985); Stone v. Graham, 449 U.S. 39 (1980).

52. *See* Trinity Lutheran Church of Columbia, Inc. v. Comer, 137 S. Ct. 2012, 2024–25 (2017) (holding that the denial of church's grant application violated free exercise rights because policy expressly discriminated against otherwise eligible recipients solely because of religious character).

53. Eric Lichtblau, "Hate Crimes Against American Muslims Most Since Post-9/11 Era," *New York Times*, September 18, 2016, https://www.nytimes.com/2016/09/18/us/politics/hate-crimes-american-muslims-rise.html.

54. Reynolds v. United States, 98 U.S. 145, 145–46 (1978).

55. United States v. Lee, 455 U.S. 252, 258–59 (1982).

56. *See, e.g.,* Thomas v. Review Board of the Indiana Employment Security

Division, 450 U.S. 707 (1981) (holding that denial of unemployment benefits for claimant's termination due to religious opposition to the production of ornaments violated the First Amendment); Sherbert v. Verner, 374 U.S. 398 (1963) (finding that the denial of unemployment benefits for not working on Saturdays was unconstitutional).

57. 42 U.S.C. § 2000bb; (struck down by City of Boerne v. Flores, 521 U.S. 507 (1997)); Burwell v. Hobby Lobby Stores, Inc., 134 S. Ct. 2751 (2014); National Institute of Family and Live Advocates v. Becerra, 138 S. Ct. 2361, 2385 (2018) (Breyer, J. dissenting).

CHAPTER 6: Guns and the Second Amendment

1. *See* Carol Berkin, "To 'Counteract the Impulses of Interest and Passion': James Madison's Insistence on a Bill of Rights," *Georgetown Journal of Law & Public Policy* 15, no. 15 (Summer 2017): 529–30 (describing ratification debates over limiting federal power); Eugene Volokh, "The Amazing Vanishing Second Amendment," *New York University Law Review* 73, no. 3 (June 1998): 835 (describing history of "well-regulated militia" language);

   Paul Finkelman, "The Living Constitution and the Second Amendment: Poor History, False Originalism, and a Very Confused Court," *Cardozo Law Review* 37 (December 2015): 631. ("The Second Amendment . . . was a response to Antifederalists who feared the national government would abolish the state militias or not provide them with arms as required by the Constitution.")

2. David Kopel, "Firearms Technology and the Original Meaning of the Second Amendment," *Washington Post*, April 3, 2017, https://www.washingtonpost.com/news/volokh-conspiracy/wp/2017/04/03/firearms-technology-and-the-original-meaning-of-the-second-amendment/?utm_term=.01f6d1127406.

3. District of Columbia v. Heller, 554 U.S. 570, 582 (2008).

4. Alexander Hamilton, "The Federalist No. 29: Concerning the Militia," *Daily Advertiser*, January 10, 1788.

5. *See generally* David C. Williams, "The Unitary Second Amendment," *New York University Law Review* 73, no. 3 (June 1988): 825–26.

6. United States v. Miller, 307 U.S. 174, 178 (1939).

7. Heller, 554 U.S. at 577, 584.

8. Plessy v. Ferguson, 163 U.S. 537 (1896); Brown v. Board of Education of Topeka, 347 U.S. 483 (1954).

9. Heller, 554 U.S. at 705 (Breyer, J. dissenting); *see* Erwin Chemerinsky,

Constitutional Law: Principles and Policies, 5th ed. (New York: Wolters Kluwer, 2015), § 10.10. Two years later, in McDonald v. City of Chicago, 561 U.S. 742 (2010), the Supreme Court held that the DC handgun decision holding that the Second Amendment right to keep and bear arms for purpose of self-defense applied to the states—here, Illinois—as well as to the federal government and the District of Columbia (which is not technically a state).

10. Heller, 554 U.S. at 627.
11. *See* Kumar v. Patel, 227 So.3d 557, 559 (Fla. 2017); Evelyn Reyes, "Florida's Stand Your Ground Law; How to Get Away with Murder," *Intercultural Human Rights Law Review* 12 (2017): 157 (citing 200 percent increase in justifiable homicide in Florida in the two years after the law passed).
12. Heller, 554 U.S. 626.
13. David T. Hardy, "*District of Columbia v. Heller* and *McDonald v. City of Chicago*: The Present as Interface of Past and Future," *Northeastern University Law Review* 3, no. 1 (Spring 2011): 219.

CHAPTER 7: Crime and the Fourth, Fifth, Sixth, and Eighth Amendments

1. Riley v. California, 573 U.S. 373, 401–02 (2014).
2. *See* Harlow v. Fitzgerald, 457 U.S. 800, 819 (1982).
3. Rodriguez v. Swartz, 899 F.3d 719, 717–28 (9th Cir. 2018).
4. Payton v. New York, 445 U.S. 573, 583–84 (1980); U.S. Const. amend. XIV (The Fourth Amendment provides that "[t]he right of the people to be secure in their persons, houses, papers, and effects, against unreasonable searches and seizures, shall not be violated, and no Warrants shall issue, but upon probable cause, supported by Oath or affirmation, and particularly describing the place to be searched, and the persons or things to be seized.").
5. *See* Maryland v. Pringle, 540 U.S. 366, 370 (2003) (explaining that "the substance of all the definitions of probable cause is a reasonable ground for belief of guilt") (quotations omitted); *but see* Arizona v. Gant, 556 U.S. 332, 343 (2009) (noting that searches incident to arrest are an exception to the warrant requirement).
6. The latest word on this came in 2018, when the Supreme Court held that a warrant is usually required for police to get cell-site location information from a cell phone provider—the "pings" that occur when cell phones communicate with cell phone towers; the pings can be pieced together

to show the phone holder's location at a given time. Carpenter v. United States, 138 S. Ct. 2206, 2221 (2018).

7. Kyllo v. United States, 533 U.S. 27, 33 (2001).

8. Katz v. United States, 389 U.S. 347, 361 (1967) (phone booths); Stoner v. California, 376 U.S. 483, 490 (1964) (hotel rooms).

9. *See* Caldwell v. Lewis, 417 U.S. 583, 590 (1974).

10. Katz, 389 U.S. at 351 (1967).

11. Kyllo, 533 U.S. at 31–33 (2001). *See* Olmstead v. United States, 277 U.S. 438, 466 (1928), *overruled in part by* Katz, 389 U.S. 347 (1967); Florida v. Jardines, 569 U.S. 1 (2013); California v. Greenwood, 486 U.S. 35, 37 (1988); United States v. Knotts, 460 U.S. 276, 281 (1983); Berger v. New York, 388 U.S. 41 (1967).

12. United States v. Warshak, 631 F.3d 266, 288 (6th Cir. 2010) (emails), *cert denied*, 135 U.S 500 (2014); Smith v. Maryland, 442 U.S. 735, 744 (1979) (phone numbers dialed); United States v. Miller, 425 U.S. 435, 443 (1976) (bank records) [citing United States v. White, 401 U.S. 745, 751–52 (1971)]; Couch v. United States, 409 U.S. 322, 335–36 (1973) (tax documents); White, 401 U.S. at 748–49 (government informants).

13. Frida Ghitis, "Google Knows Too Much About You," CNN, February 9, 2012, https://www.cnn.com/2012/02/09/opinion/ghitis-google-privacy/index.html.

14. Carpenter v. United States, 138 S. Ct. 2206, 2221 (2018).

15. Schmerber v. California, 384 U.S. 757, 767 (1966).

16. Mapp v. Ohio, 367 U.S. 643, 656 (1961).

17. Miranda v. Arizona, 384 U.S. 436, 478–79 (1966); Terry v. Ohio, 392 U.S. 1 (1968) (stop and frisk); Carroll v. United States, 267 U.S. 132, 149 (1925).

18. 50 U.S.C. ch. 36.

19. *See* Martin-Trigona v. Gouletas, 634 F.2d 354, 360 (7th Cir. 1980).

20. *See generally* Colin Starger and Michael Bullock, "Legitimacy, Authority, and the Right to Affordable Bail," *William & Mary Bill of Rights Journal* 26, no. 3 (March 2018): 589.

21. Duckworth v. Eagan, 492 U.S. 195, 204 (1989) (explaining that if counsel cannot be immediately provided, police may not question a suspect unless the right is waived or counsel is present).

22. Murray v. Giarratano, 492 U.S. 1, 3–4 (1989).

23. Brewer v. Williams, 430 U.S. 387 (1977); Gideon v. Wainwright, 372 U.S. 335 (1963); Kirby v. Illinois, 406 U.S. 682, 688–89 (1972).

24. *See* Kelly v. Robinson, 479 U.S. 36, 49 (1986).

25. *See generally* Arthur H. Garrison, "The Bush Administration and the Office of Legal Counsel (OLC) Torture Memos: A Content Analysis of the Response of the Academic Legal Community," *Cardozo Public Law Policy & Ethics Journal* 11 (Fall 2012): 1.

26. Hudson v. McMillian, 503 U.S. 1, 6 (1992).

27. Farmer v. Brennan, 511 U.S. 825, 837 (1994); Estelle v. Gamble, 429 U.S. 97, 104–6 (1976).

28. Preiser v. Rodriguez, 411 U.S. 475, 494 (1973).

29. Death Penalty Information Center, "Facts About the Death Penalty," accessed January 19, 2019, https://deathpenaltyinfo.org/documents/Fact Sheet.pdf.

30. Furman v. Georgia, 408 U.S. 238, 309–10 (1972) (Stewart, J., concurring).

31. *See* Gregg v. Georgia, 428 U.S. 153, 179–81 (1976).

32. Death Penalty Information Center, "Facts About the Death Penalty."

33. Kelly Phillips Erb, "Considering the Death Penalty: Your Tax Dollars at Work," *Forbes*, May 1, 2014, https://www.forbes.com/sites/kellyphil lipserb/2014/05/01/considering-the-death-penalty-your-tax-dollars-at -work/#5c361441664b.

34. *See* McClesky v. Kemp, 481 U.S. 279, 297 (1987) (rejecting defendant's allegations that a discretionary Georgia death penalty statute was implemented on a racially disproportionate basis even though statistical evidence demonstrated that decision makers did not act with discriminatory purposes).

35. Death Penalty Information Center, "Facts About the Death Penalty."

CHAPTER 8: Liberty and Equality: Fifth and Fourteenth Amendments

1. *See generally* Alexander Tsesis, "Self-Governance and the Declaration of Independence," *Cornell Law Review* 97, no. 4 (May 2012): 693.

2. Greene v. McElroy, 360 U.S. 474, 492 (1959).

3. Goldberg v. Kelly, 397 U.S. 254, 264–65 (1970) (holding that there is a right to an "evidentiary hearing" prior to termination of welfare benefits).

4. Mathews v. Eldridge, 424 U.S. 319 (1976).

5. Slaughter-House Cases, 83 U.S. 36 (1872); *see generally* Erwin Chemerinksy, *Constitutional Law: Principles and Policies*, 5th ed. (New York: Wolters Kluwer, 2015), § 6.3.2, 9.1.2.

6. *See* Chemerinsky, *Constitutional Law,* § 6.5.

7. Skinner v. Oklahoma, 316 U.S. 535, 541 (1942).

8. Lindsley v. Natural Carbonic Gas Co., 220 U.S. 61 (1911); McGowan v. Maryland, 366 U.S. 420 (1961).

9. Prigg v. Pennsylvania, 41 U.S. 539, 611 (1842).

10. Dred Scott v. Sandford, 60 U.S. 393, 404–05 (1857).

11. Michael J. Nolan, "Defendant, Lynch Thyself: A California Appellate Court Goes from the Sublime to the Ridiculous in *People v. Anthony J.*," *Howard Scroll* 4 (Spring 2001): 53–60.

12. Civil Rights Cases, 109 U.S. 3 (1883).

13. Jones v. Alfred H. Mayer Co., 392 U.S. 409, 413 (1968).

14. *See* Plessy v. Ferguson, 163 U.S. 537 (1896); Chemerinsky, *Constitutional Law*, § 3.7.1.

15. *See* Brown v. Board of Education, 347 U.S. 483 (1954); William O. Douglas, *The Court Years: 1939 to 1975* (New York: Random House, 1980), 113.

16. *See generally* Richard Kluger, *Simple Justice: The History of* Brown v. Board of Education *and Black America's Struggle for Equality* (New York: Knopf, 1975), 257.

17. Charles Fairman, "Foreward: The Attack on the Segregation Cases," *Harvard Law Review* 70, no. 1 (November 1956): 83, 84–85.

18. "Text of 96 Congressmen's Declaration on Integration; 1868 Conditions Noted," *New York Times*, March 12, 1956.

19. Cooper v. Aaron, 358 U.S. 1, 16 (1958).

20. Griffin v. County School Bd. of Prince Edward County, 377 U.S. 218, 225 (1964).

21. *See* Derek W. Black, "Abandoning the Federal Role in Education: The Every Student Succeeds Act," *California Law Review* 105, no. 5 (October 2017): 1309.

22. Gregory v. Ashcroft, 501 U.S. 452, 468 (1991) (discussing Age Discrimination in Employment Act and Commerce Clause); *see generally* Jack M. Balkin, "What *Brown* Teaches Us About Constitutional Theory," *Virginia Law Review* 90, no. 6 (October 2004): 1537, 1543–50.

23. Alvin Chang, "The Data Proves That School Segregation Is Getting Worse," *Vox*, March 5, 2018, https://www.vox.com/2018/3/5/17080218/school-segregation-getting-worse-data.

24. *See* Green v. County School Board, 391 U.S. 430 (1968); Griffin, 377 U.S. 218 (1964); Rogers v. Paul, 382 U.S. 198 (1965); Chemerinsky, *Constitutional Law*, § 9.3.4.

25. Ricci v. DeStefano, 557 U.S. 557, 577 (2009) (requiring a plaintiff to establish that a defendant had discriminatory intent or motive when claiming a disparate-treatment violation under Title VII).

26. *See* Trump v. Hawaii, 138 S. Ct. 2392 (2018); Korematsu v. United States, 323 U.S. 214, 218 (1944); Hirabayashi v. United States, 320 U.S. 81, 94–95 (1943).

27. Regents of the University of California v. Bakke, 438 U.S. 265 (1978); Grutter v. Bollinger, 539 U.S. 306 (2003); Fisher v. University of Texas at Austin, 570 U.S. 297 (2013). *See* Glenn Ellison and Parag A. Pathak, "The Efficiency of Race-Neutral Alternatives to Race-Based Affirmative Action: Evidence from Chicago's Exam Schools," National Bureau of Economic Research Working Paper 22589 (September 2016), http://www.nber.org/papers/w22589.pdf.

28. Hoyt v. Florida, 368 U.S. 57, 62 (1961); Goesaert v. Clearly, 335 U.S. 464 (1948) (finding no equal protection question based on gender distinctions).

29. *See* Bradwell v. State of Illinois, 83 U.S. 130 (1872); *see also* Hoyt, 368 U.S. 57 (1961) (jury service); Goesaert, 335 U.S. 464 (1948) (bartending); Radice v. New York, 264 U.S. 292 (1924) (working from 10:00 p.m. to 6:00 a.m.); Minor v. Happersett, 88 U.S. 162 (1874) (voting).

30. U.S. Const. amend. XIX; U.S. Const. amend. XV; Leser v. Garnett, 258 U.S. 130 (1922) (upholding the constitutionality of the Nineteenth Amendment); Chemerinsky, *Constitutional Law*, § 9.4.

31. Reed v. Reed, 404 U.S. 71, 77 (1971).

32. Craig v. Boren, 429 U.S. 190, 197 (1976).

33. United States v. Virginia, 518 U.S. 515 (1996).

34. Personnel Administrator of Massachusetts v. Feeney, 442 U.S. 256, 270 (1979); Roe v. Wade, 410 U.S. 113, 164–66 (1973).

35. 262 U.S. 390, 397–98 (1923).

36. *Id.* at 400.

37. *See* Erwin Chemerinsky, "Substantive Due Process," *Touro Law Review* 15, no. 4 (1999): 1501.

38. Planned Parenthood of Southeastern Pennsylvania v. Casey, 505 U.S. 833, 877–78, 893 (1992).

39. Garrett Epps, "How the 'Fundamental Right' to Abortion Faded Away," *The Atlantic*, October 16, 2014, https://www.theatlantic.com/politics/archive/2014/10/the-disappearing-right-to-abortion/381510/.

40. Obergefell v. Hodges, 135 S. Ct. 2584 (2015) (holding that same-sex couples have a constitutional right to marry); United States v. Windsor, 570 U.S. 744 (2013) (striking down federal laws that interpreted the word *marriage* as only applying to opposite-sex couples); Romer v. Evans, 517

U.S. 620 (1996) (declaring a Colorado voter initiative that would have repealed all laws protecting homosexuals from discrimination).

41. Masterpiece Cakeshop, Ltd. v. Colorado Civil Rights Commission, 138 S. Ct. 1719 (2018).
42. *See* Plyler v. Doe, 457 U.S. 202 (1982); Graham v. Richardson, 403 U.S. 365, 372 (1971).
43. Knauff v. Shaughnessy, 338 U.S. 537, 542–43 (1950).
44. Truax v. Raich, 239 U.S. 33, 40 (1915).
45. Ambach v. Norwick, 441 U.S. 68 (1979); *compare* Graham v. Richardson, 403 U.S. 365 (1971), *with* Mathews v. Diaz, 426 U.S. 67 (1976); Chemerinsky, *Constitutional Law*, §§ 9.5.3, 9.5.4.
46. *See* Plyler v. Doe, 457 U.S. 202 (1982).

CHAPTER 9: What Does the Constitution Say About the States?

1. *See* Slaughter-House Cases, 83 U.S. 36, 115 (1872) ("The privileges and immunities of Englishmen were established and secured by long usage and by various acts of Parliament. But it may be said that the Parliament of England has unlimited authority and might repeal the laws which have from time to time been enacted.").
2. "Federalism," US History, http://www.ushistory.org/gov/3.asp, accessed February 2, 2019.
3. Bank of Augusta v. Earle, 38 U.S. 519, 597 (1839) (holding that "[t]he only rights [a corporation] can claim are the rights which are given to it in that character, and not the rights which belong to its members as citizens of a state").
4. Paul v. Virginia, 75 U.S. (8 Wall.) 168 (1868) (holding that a trust is not a citizen); Corfield v. Coryell, Fed. Case. No. 3230, 4 Wash. C.C. 371 (1823) [discussed in United States v. Guest, 383 U.S. 745 (1966)]; Crandall v. State of Nevada, 73 U.S. 35 (1867) (striking down Nevada law).
5. Doe v. Bolton, 410 U.S. 179 (1973) (abortions); McBurney v. Young, 569 U.S. 221 (2013) (public records); Hicklin v. Orbeck, 437 U.S. 518 (1978) (job preference for residents in-state); Baldwin v. Fish and Game Commission of Montana, 436 U.S. 371 (1978) (hunting).
6. Luther v. Bordon, 48 U.S. (7 How.) 1 (1849); Erwin Chemerinsky, *Constitutional Law: Principles and Policies*, 5th ed. (New York: Wolters Kluwer, 2015), § 2.8.3.
7. McCulloch v. Maryland, 17 U.S. (4 Wheat.) 316, 402, 407–8 (1819).
8. *See generally* Chemerinsky, *Constitutional Law*, § 3.10.

9. New York v. United States, 505 U.S. 144, 188 (1992).

10. Printz v. United States, 521 U.S. 898, 899–901 (1997).

11. National Federation of Independent Business v. Sebelius, 567 U.S. 519, 581 (2012).

CHAPTER 10: Why It Matters How Politicians Get Hired and Fired

1. For a discussion of the Electoral College and related case law, *see* Elizabeth D. Lauzon, "Challenges to President Electoral College and Electors," *American Law Reports Fed.* 20, no. 2 (2007): 183.

2. National Archives and Records Administration: U.S. Electoral College, "About the Electors," accessed February 2, 2019, https://www.archives .gov/federal-register/electoral-college/electors.html#restrictions.

3. Alexander Hamilton, "The Federalist No. 68: The Mode of Electing the President," *New York Packet*, March 14, 1788.

4. Ray v. Blair, 343 U.S. 214, 224–25 (1952) (discussing the Twelfth Amendment).

5. Alvin Chang, "Trump Will Be the 4th President to Win the Electoral College After Getting Fewer Votes Than His Opponent," *Vox*, December 19, 2016, https://www.vox.com/policy-and-politics/2016/11/9/13572112 /trump-popular-vote-loss.

6. World Population Review, "US States—Ranked by Population 2019," accessed February 2, 2019, http://worldpopulationreview.com/states/.

7. Apportionment Act of 1911, ch. 5, 37 Stat. 13 (1911).

8. Charles Tiefer, *The Polarized Congress: The Post-Traditional Procedure of Its Current Struggles* (Lanham, MD: University Press of America, 2016): 9–16.

9. For a current list, *see* "Committees of the U.S. Congress," accessed January 19, 2019.

10. *See* Christopher S. Yoo, "Presidential Signing Statements: A New Perspective," *University of Pennsylvania Law Review* 164, no. 7 (June 2016): 1801.

11. Sheldon Goldman, "Judicial Confirmation Wars: Ideology and the Battle for the Federal Courts," *University of Richmond Law Review* 38 (March 2005): 871, 878; Nina Totenberg, "A Timeline of Clarence Thomas–Anita Hill Controversy as Kavanaugh to Face Accuser," NPR, September 23, 2018, https://www.npr.org/2018/09/23/650138049/a-timeline-of-clarence -thomas-anita-hill-controversy-as-kavanaugh-to-face-accuser.

12. Abigail Abrams, "Here Are All the People We Know the FBI Talked

to for the Kavanaugh Report," *Time*, October 4, 2018, http://time.com/5415845/kavanaugh-fbi-investigation-witnesses/.

13. Tiefer, *The Polarized Congress*, 34.

14. *Id.* at 26.

15. Congressional Budget and Impoundment Control Act of 1974, Pub. L. No. 93-344, 88 Stat. 297 (1974).

16. Tonja Jacobi and Jeff VanDam, "The Filibuster and Reconciliation: The Future of Majoritarian Lawmaking in the U.S. Senate," *University of California Davis Law Review* 47, no. 1 (November 2013): 261.

17. Jake Lestock, "How the Congressional Reconciliation Process Works," National Conference of State Legislatures, January 13, 2017, http://www.ncsl.org/blog/2017/01/13/how-the-congressional-reconciliation-process-works.aspx; John Patrick Pullen, "The House Has to Revote on the Tax Bill Because It Broke the Byrd Rule. What Is the Byrd Rule?," *Time*, December 20, 2017, http://time.com/5072689/gop-tax-bill-2017-what-is-the-byrd-rule/?iid=sr-link1.

18. Tiefer, *Polarized Congress*, 146–50.

19. *See* Rollcall Staff, "Have House-Senate Conferences Gone the Way of the Dodo?," *Roll Call*, April 25, 2008, http://www.rollcall.com/issues/53_127/-23250-1.html.

20. *See generally* Tiefer, *Polarized Congress*.

21. "The Government's Sentencing Memorandum," https://www.politico.com/f/?id=00000167-a496-df35-adef-fdf76fa30001;QuintForgey,"Trump: 'I Did Not Commit a Campaign Violation,'" *Politico*, January 5, 2019, https://www.politico.com/story/2019/01/05/trump-campaign-violation-cohen-sdny-prosecutors-fec-1082569.

22. *See* Citizens United v. Federal Election Commission, 558 U.S. 310, 343–44 (2010).

23. Tillman Act of 1907, 34 Stat. 864; Federal Election Campaign Act of 1971, 52 U.S.C. § 30101 et seq. (as amended); Bipartisan Campaign Reform Act of 2002, 2 U.S.C. § 441b (as amended); Citizens United, 558 U.S. at 365-66 (declaring parts of BCRA unconstitutional). George F. Will, "Sham Concern for Corruption," *Washington Post*, May 16, 2002, https://www.washingtonpost.com/archive/opinions/2002/05/16/sham-concern-for-corruption/e2e1b7aa-40ba-43b8-af8b-58e23c42dcba/?utm_term=.6c3e1d565ade (discussing sham issue ads). *See also* McConnell v. Federal Election Commission, 540 U.S. 93, 94 (2003) (discussing BCRA's approach to sham issue ads and soft money; overruled in part by *Citizens United*).

24. Sam Power, "What Are the Benefits of Campaign Finance Reform?,"

Washington Post, November 17, 2015, https://www.washingtonpost.com
/news/monkey-cage/wp/2015/11/17/what-are-the-benefits-of-campaign
-finance-reform/?utm_term=.f807ca9b4fa6.

25. Open Secrets, "Top PACs," Center for Responsive Politics, accessed February 2, 2019, https://www.opensecrets.org/pacs/toppacs.php.

26. *See* "Super PAC Spending," *Los Angeles Times*, November 20, 2012,
http://graphics.latimes.com/2012-election-superpac-spending/; Idrees
Kahloon, "Does Money Matter?," *Harvard Magazine*, July/August 2016,
https://www.harvardmagazine.com/2016/07/does-money-matter.

27. Steve Peoples, "'Koch Brothers' Rebrand Underway as They Continue to
Pump Money into Politics," *Chicago Tribune*, July 28, 2018, http://www
.chicagotribune.com/news/nationworld/politics/ct-koch-brothers-rebrand
-20180728-story.html; Edward-Isaac Dovere, "Tom Steyer's $110 Million
Plan to Redefine the Democrats," *Politico*, July 31, 2018, https://www.politico
.com/story/2018/07/31/steyer-democrats-millions-midterms-751245.

28. Alan Ehrenhalt, "'Dark Money' by Jane Mayer," *New York Times* (January 19, 2016), https://nytimes.com/2016/01/24/books/review/dark-money
-by-jane-mayer.html; Andy Kroll, "Follow the Dark Money," *Mother
Jones*, July/August 2012, https://www.motherjones.com/politics/2012/06/
history-money-american-elections/; *see generally* Jane Mayer, *Dark Money:
The Hidden History of the Billionaires Behind the Rise of the Radical Right*
(New York: Doubleday, 2016).

29. *See* Yascha Mounk, "America Is Not a Democracy," *The Atlantic,* March
2018, https://www.theatlantic.com/magazine/archive/2018/03/america-is
-not-a-democracy/550931/.

30. Breedlove v. Suttles, 302 U.S. 277, 293 (1937); U.S. Const. amends. XV,
XIX, XXVI, § 1; *see generally* Garrett Epps, "What Does the Constitution Actually Say About Voting Rights?," *The Atlantic*, August 19, 2013,
https://www.theatlantic.com/national/archive/2013/08/what-does-the
-constitution-actually-say-about-voting-rights/278782/. Voting is also mentioned in Section 2 of the Fourteenth Amendment, but that "can't mean
that everyone must be allowed to vote," *Id.*

31. Shelby County v. Holder, 570 U.S. 529, 553–54, 558, 565 (2013); *see gen-
erally* Stephanie N. Kang, "Restoring the Fifteenth Amendment: The
Constitutional Right to an Undiluted Vote," *University of California Los
Angeles Law Review* 62, no. 5 (2015): 1392 (observing that the Supreme
Court has not "honor[ed] the Fifteenth Amendment's robust protections
of minority voting rights").

32. Matt Vasilogambros, "Polling Places Remain a Target Ahead of Novem-

ber Elections," *Pew*, September 4, 2018, https://www.Pcwtrusts.org/en /research-and-analysis/blogs/stateline/2018/09/04/polling-places-remain -a-target-ahead-of-november-elections.

33. League of Women Voters of Florida, Inc. v. Detzner, 314 F. Supp. 3d 1205, 1215–20 (N.D. Fla. 2018); Alex Daugherty, "Youth Voter Registration Went Up 41 percent in Florida after Parkland," *Miami Herald*, July 20, 2018, https://www.miamiherald.com/news/politics-government .article215169905.html.

34. Husted v. A. Phillip Randolph Institute, 138 S. Ct. 1833 (2018) (upholding Ohio law).

35. Matt Vasilogombros, "Polling Places Remain a Target Ahead of November Elections," Max Feldman and Wendy R. Weiser, "The State of Voting 2018—Updated," Brennan Center for Justice, August 3, 2018, http:// www.brennancenter.org/blog/state-voting-2018-updated.

36. Laughlin McDonald, "The Looming 2010 Census: A Proposed Judicially Manageable Standard and Other Reform Options for Partisan Gerrymandering," *Harvard Journal on Legislation* 46, no. 1 (Winter 2009): 243–44.

37. Dave Daley, "New Poll: Everybody Hates Gerrymandering," FairVote, September 12, 2017, https://www.fairvote.org/new_poll_everybody_hates _gerrymandering.

38. Bruce G. Peabody and Scott E. Gant, "The Twice and Future President: Constitutional Injustices and the Twenty-Second Amendment," *Minnesota Law Review* 83, no. 3 (February 1999): 565–67.

39. Tiffanie Kovacevich, "Constitutionality of Term Limitations: Can States Limit the Terms of Members of Congress?," *Pacific Law Journal* 23, no. 4 (July 1992): 1677–79 (discussing state efforts to impose term limits).

40. Vieth v. Jubelirer, 541 U.S. 267, 290–91, 307, 320–21, 346–48, 357 (2004).

CHAPTER 11: If the Constitution Stops Functioning, Why Should I Care?

1. U.S. History, "Antifederalists," accessed February 2, 2019, http://www .ushistory.org/us/16b.asp; Paul Finkelman, "Complete Anti-Federalist," *Cornell Law Review* 70 no. 1 (November 1984): 183.

2. David Josiah Brewer, *The World's Best Orations*, Vol. II (Chicago: Ferd P. Kaiser Publishing, 1928): 35.

3. *See* Jeremi Suri, "The Presidency Is Too Big to Succeed," *The Atlantic*, May 9, 2018, https://www.theatlantic.com/ideas/archive/2018/05/the -real-reason-the-presidency-is-impossible/559877/.

4. Finkelman, "Complete Anti-Federalist," 183; Zachary Rind, "10

Tragic Times the US Government Massacred Striking Workers," List-verse, September 14, 2017, http://listverse.com/2017/09/14/10-tragic-times-the-us-government-massacred-striking-workers/; James Risen and Eric Lichtblau, "Bush Lets U.S. Spy on Callers Without Courts," *New York Times*, December 16, 2005, https://www.nytimes.com/2005/12/16/politics/bush-lets-us-spy-on-callers-without-courts.html; Jeffrey Rosen, "America Is Living James Madison's Nightmare," *The Atlantic*, October 2018, https://www.theatlantic.com/magazine/archive/2018/10/james-madison-mob-rule/568351/.

5. Charlie Savage, "Shift on Executive Power Lets Obama Bypass Rivals," *New York Times*, April 23, 2012, https://www.nytimes.com/2012/04/23/us/politics/shift-on-executive-powers-lets-obama-bypass-congress.html.

6. Rosen, "America Is Living James Madison's Nightmare."

7. Frank Whelan, "In the America of 1787, Big Families Are the Norm and Life Expectancy Is 38," *Morning Call*, June 28, 1987, http://articles.mcall.com/1987-06-28/features/2569915_1_horse-farming-rural-america/2.

8. Mark Abadi, "11 Dramatic Ways the World Has Changed in the Last 20 Years Alone," *Business Insider*, March 29, 2018, https://www.businessinsider.com/progress-innovation-since-1998-2018-3; Aaron Smith and Monica Anderson, "Social Media Use in 2018," Pew Research Center, March 1, 2018, http://www.pewinternet.org/2018/03/01/social-media-use-in-2018/.

9. Emerging Future, "Human Intuitive Perspective of Technological Advancement in Five Years," accessed February 2, 2019, http://theemergingfuture.com/speed-technological-advancement.htm; Martin Bryant, "20 Years Ago Today, the World Wide Web Opened to the Public," Next Web, August 6, 2011, https://thenextweb.com/insider/2011/08/06/20-years-ago-today-the-world-wide-web-opened-to-the-public/; Alyson Shontell, "The First Ever Email, the First Tweet, and 10 Other Famous Internet Firsts," *Yahoo! Finance*, April 23, 2013, https://finance.yahoo.com/news/the-first-ever-email--the-first-tweet--and-12-other-famous-internet-firsts-181209886.html; James Vincent, "Artificial Intelligence Is Going to Supercharge Surveillance," *The Verge*, January 23, 2018, https://www.theverge.com/2018/1/23/16907238/artificial-intelligence-surveillance-cameras-security.

10. *See generally* Andrew Guthrie Ferguson, "Big Data and Predictive Reasonable Suspicion," *University of Pennsylvania Law Review* 163 no. 2 (January 2015): 354, 364.

11. Doug Bock Clark, "The Untold Story of Otto Warmbier, American

Hostage," *GQ*, July 23, 2018, https://www.gq.com/story/otto-warm bier-north-korea-american-hostage-true-story; Doug Bock Clark, "Otto Warmbier: What Happened in the North Korean Jail That Led to American's Death?," *Post Magazine*, October 19, 2018, https://www.scmp.com/magazines/post-magazine/long-reads/article/2169308/otto-warm bier-what-happened-north-korean-jail-led.

12. D.C. Code § 22-2312 (2018).

13. Charles Buckley, "China Is Detaining Muslims in Vast Numbers. The Goal: 'Transformation,'" *New York Times*, September 8, 2018, https://www.nytimes.com/2018/09/08/world/asia/china-uighur-muslim-deten tion-camp.html.

14. "Deaths of Journalists in Russia," Internet Archive: Wayback Machine, 2011, https://web.archive.org/web/20110819032825/http://journal ists-in-russia.org/journalists/index/federaldistrictplus%3AChechnya; Amanda Erickson, "Analysis: The Long, Terrifying History of Russian Dissidents Being Poisoned Abroad," *Chicago Tribune*, March 6, 2018, http://www.chicagotribune.com/news/nationworld/ct-russian-dissidents -poisoned-20180306-story.html.

15. Josh Smith and Phil Stewart, "Trump Surprises with Pledge to End Military Exercises in South Korea," Reuters, June 12, 2018, https://www .reuters.com/article/us-northkorea-usa-military/trump-surprises-with -pledge-to-end-military-exercises-in-south-korea-idUSKBN1J812W; Aaron David Miller and Richard Sokolsky, "Donald Trump in Helsinki Was Terrifying. Cancel the Washington Sequel," *USA Today,* July 24, 2018, https://www.usatoday.com/story/opinion/2018/07/24/cancel-donald -trump-vladimir-putin-helsinki-sequel-column/816245002/; Editorial Board, "Will Donald Trump Stand Up to China?," *New York Times*, September 18, 2018, https://www.nytimes.com/2018/09/18/opinion/uighurs -china-human-rights.html.

16. Steven Levitsky and Daniel Ziblatt, *How Democracies Die* (New York: Crown, 2018), 62–66, 78–90, 126.

17. Hadas Gold, "Donald Trump: We're Going to 'Open Up' Libel Laws," *Politico*, February 26, 2016, https://www.politico.com/blogs/on-media /2016/02/donald-trump-libel-laws-219866.

18. Jeremy Diamond, "Donald Trump on Protester: 'I'd Like to Punch Him in the Face,'" CNN, February 23, 2016, https://www.cnn.com/2016/02/23 /politics/donald-trump-nevada-rally-punch/index.html.

CHAPTER 12: Sustaining Democracy: Some Takeaways

1. Benjamin Kentish, "Donald Trump Slams 'Archaic' US Constitution That Is 'Really Bad' for the Country," *The Independent*, April 30, 2017, https://www.independent.co.uk/news/world/americas/us-politics/don ald-trump-us-constitution-archaic-really-bad-fox-news-100-days-trump -popularity-ratings-barack-a7710781.html.

2. Abigail Tracy, "Donald Trump Is Growing Frustrated with the Constitution," *Vanity Fair*, June 25, 2018, https://www.vanityfair.com/news /2018/06/donald-trump-immigration-border-constitution.

3. Donald J. Trump (@realDonaldTrump), Twitter, June 4, 2018, 7:01 AM, https://twitter.com/realdonaldtrump/status/1003637916919320577? lang=en.

4. Steven Levitsky and Daniel Ziblatt, *How Democracies Die* (New York: Crown, 2018), 62–66, 78–90, 126.

5. Lartey, "Conservatives Call for Constitutional Intervention Last Seen 230 Years Ago"; *The Guardian*, August 11, 2018, https://www.theguardian .com/us-news/2018/aug/11/conservatives-call-for-constitutional-conven tion-alec; Convention of States Action, "COS Simulation," accessed February 2, 2019, https://conventionofstates.com/cos-simulation; U.S. Const. amend. XVI.

6. "America Might See a New Constitutional Convention in a Few Years," *The Economist*, September 30, 2017, https://www.economist.com/briefing /2017/09/30/america-might-see-a-new-constitutional-convention-in-a -few-years.

7. Christian Gomez, "Justice Scalia's Warning of a Constitutional Convention," *New American*, February 24, 2016, https://www.thenewamer ican.com/usnews/constitution/item/22625-justice-scalia-s-warning-of-a -constitutional-convention.

8. "America Might See a New Constitutional Convention in a Few Years."

9. *See* Martin S. Flaherty, "Relearning Founding Lessons: The Removal Power and Joint Accountability," *Case Western Reserve Law Review* 47, no. 3 (1997): 1563, 1586, citing Gordon S. Wood, *The Creation of the American Republic, 1776–1787* (Williamsburg, VA: University of North Carolina, 1998), 550 ("Because the Federalists regarded the people as 'the only legitimate fountain of power,' no department was theoretically more popular and hence more authoritative than any other.").

10. The Declaration of Independence, para. 2 (U.S. 1776).

11. Alexander Hamilton, "The Federalist No. 49: Method of Guarding Against

the Encroachment of Any One Department of Government by Appealing to the People Through a Convention," *New York Packet*, February 5, 1788.

12. U.S. Const. pmbl.; *see also* Vieth v. Jubelirer, 541 U.S. 267, 356 (2004) (Breyer, J., dissenting) (observing that the preamble's "We the People" language reflects a "fundamental principle" of American government that anchors a constitutional design that is "basically democratic"); United States v. International Union United Automobile, Aircraft & Agricultural Implement Workers, 352 U.S. 567, 593 (1957) (Douglas, J., dissenting) ("Under our Constitution it is We The People who are sovereign. The people have the final say. The legislators are their spokesmen.").

13. *See* U.S. Term Limits, Inc. v. Thornton, 514 U.S. 779, 821 (1995) ("[T]he Framers, in perhaps their most important contribution, conceived of a Federal Government directly responsible to the people, possessed of direct power over the people, and chosen directly, not by States, but by the people."); Youngstown Sheet & Tube Co. v. Sawyer, 343 U.S. 579, 640 (1952) ("[T]he Federal Government[,] as a whole, possesses only delegated powers. The purpose of the Constitution was not only to grant power, but to keep it from getting out of hand.") (Jackson, J., concurring.); Hawke v. Smith, 253 U.S. 221, 226–27 (1920) (noting that "[t]he Constitution of the United States was ordained by the people," who "grant" authority to Congress, and "[i]t is not the function of courts or legislative bodies, national or state, to alter the method which the Constitution has fixed"); Downes v. Bidwell, 182 U.S. 244, 359 (1901) (Fuller, Harlan, Brewer, and Peckham, J. J., dissenting) ("[N]o utterance of this court has intimated a doubt that in its operation on the people, by whom and for whom it was established, the national government is a government of enumerated powers, the exercise of which is restricted to the use of means appropriate and plainly adapted to constitutional ends, and which are 'not prohibited, but consist with the letter and spirit of the Constitution.'"); McCulloch v. Maryland, 17 U.S. (4 Wheat.) 316, 403 (1819) ("The government proceeds directly from the people; is 'ordained and established' in the name of the people.").

14. Downes, 182 U.S. 359.

15. As Harold Bruff has observed, "*The Federalist Papers* are replete with emphasis on the need to ensure public knowledge of accountability for particular actions." Harold H. Bruff, "On the Constitutional Status of the Administrative Agencies," *American University Law Review* 36 (1987): 491, 507–8 (citing Alexander Hamilton, "The Federalist No. 70," 456).

16. *See* Rebecca L. Brown, "Liberty, the New Equality," *New York University*

Law Review 77, no. 6 (2002): 1491, 1518 (citing U.S. Const. article I, § 7, cl. 2, (requiring concurrence of two differently constituted legislative houses to pass legislation)); U.S. Const. art. IV, § 2, cl. 1 (ensuring that states do not discriminate against citizens of other states); U.S. Const. Amends. I–VIII (limiting power of Congress to legislate in areas affecting certain individual rights).

17. *See* National Federation of Independent Business v. Sebelius, 567 U.S. 519, 529–35 (2012).

18. U.S. Const. pmbl.; *see also* Lillian BeVier and John Harrison, "The State Action Principle and Its Critics," *Virginia Law Review* 96, no. 8 (2010): 1767, 1793 ("The structural provisions of the Constitution embody the delegation of power from the people to their rulers and provide convincing evidence that the power to govern flows from the people—who, as principals, 'ordain[ed] and establish[ed]' the Constitution—to the government actors to whom they delegated it" (alterations in original) (emphasis omitted).

19. Harold J. Krent, "Fragmenting the Unitary Executive: Congressional Delegations of Administrative Authority Outside the Federal Government," *Northwestern University Law Review* 85, no. 11 (1990): 62, 65.

Index

About the Author

Kim Wehle is a Constitution demystifier, tenured professor of law, lawyer, and on-air and off-air legal expert, analyst, and commentator for CBS News, as well as a contributor for BBC World News and BBC World News America on PBS, an op-ed contributor for *The Bulwark* and an opinion contributor for *The Hill*. A graduate of Cornell University and the University of Michigan Law School, she was formerly an assistant United States attorney and an associate counsel in the Whitewater investigation.

Wehle has also appeared as a guest legal analyst regarding Special Counsel Robert Mueller's probe into Russian influence in the 2016 presidential election and other legal issues, including on CNN, MSNBC, NPR's *Morning Edition*, *PBS NewsHour*, and Fox News. Her articles have appeared in the *Baltimore Sun*, the *Los Angeles Times*, and on NBC News *THINK*. She is regularly interviewed and cited by prominent print journalists on a range of legal issues.

She lives in Chevy Chase, Maryland, with her children and her cavapoo, Charlie.